THE MAKING OF THE
COLD WAR ENEMY

THE MAKING OF THE

COLD WAR ENEMY

Culture and Politics in the Military-Intellectual Complex

RON ROBIN

PRINCETON UNIVERSITY PRESS
PRINCETON AND OXFORD

Second printing, and first paperback printing, 2003
Paperback ISBN 0-691-11455-2

The Library of Congress has cataloged the cloth edition of this book as follows

Robin, Ron Theodore.
The making of the Cold War enemy : culture and politics in the
military-intellectual complex / Ron Robin.
p.   cm.
Includes bibliographical references and index.
ISBN 0-691-01171-0
1. United States—Foreign relations—1945–1989. 2. United States—Intellectual life—
20th century. 3. Cold War—Social aspects—United States. 4. Research institutes—
United States—History—20th century. 5. Intellectuals—United States—Political
activity—History—20th century. 6. United States—Foreign relations—Asia.
7. Asia—Foreign relations—United States. I. Title.
E744.R63   2001
973.92′01′9—dc21   00-060623

British Library Cataloging-in-Publication Data is available

This book has been composed in Electra LH

Designed by C. Alvarez

Printed on acid-free paper. ∞

www.pupress.princeton.edu

Printed in the United States of America

10 9 8 7 6 5 4 3 2

To Shani Shaltiel Robin and Eli Robin

Contents

Illustrations

Abbreviations

CCF Communist Chinese Forces

CIA Central Intelligence Agency

CIE Civilian Information and Education Division

CRESS Center for Research in the Social Sciences

DDE Dwight D. Eisenhower Presidential Library

FEC Far East Command

FCRC Federal Contract Research Center

FOD Field Operation Division

FRUS *Foreign Relations of the United States*

HBP Haydon Boatner Papers, Hoover Institute of War, Revolution, and Peace, Stanford University

HRRC Human Resources Research Center

HRRI Human Resources Research Institute

HRRL Human Resources Research Laboratory

HST Harry S. Truman Presidential Library

HumRRO Human Relations Research Office

IDA   Institute for Defense Analysis

IPOR   International Public Opinion Research

JCS   Joint Chiefs of Staff

KAC   *The Korean Armistice Conference*

LSRM   Laura Spelman Rockefeller Memorial Foundation

MAC   Douglas MacArthur Archives, Norfolk, Va.

MIT   Massachusetts Institute of Technology

M&M   Vietcong Motivation and Morale Project

NK   North Korea

NLF   National Liberation Front

OCB   Operations Coordinating Board

OCPW   Office of the Chief of Psychological Warfare

ONR   Office of Naval Research

ORO   Operations Research Office

OWI   Office of War Information

PLA   People's Liberation Army

POW   Prisoner of War

PSB   Psychological Strategy Board

PSICK   "A Preliminary Study of the Impact of Communism on Korea"

PTRC   Personnel and Training Research Center, United States Air Force

RAC   Research Analysis Corporation

RG 319   National Archives, Record Group 319, Records of the Army Staff, G-3

RG 333   National Archives, Record Group 333, Records of Headquarters, United Nations Command, Korea

RG 338   National Archives, Record Group 338, Records of US Army Commands Headquarters, 22nd Army, POW-Internee Information Center

RG 389   National Archives, Record Group 389, Records of the Provost Marshal General, 22nd Army, POW-Civilian Information Center

ROK Republic of Korea

SORO Special Operations Research Office

SSRC Social Sciences Research Council

TAS *The American Soldier*

UN COM United Nations Command, Korea

VC Vietcong

VOA Voice of America

Acknowledgments

I wrote this book from the heights of a gloomy tower overlooking the University of Haifa, Israel. The tower, known locally as the Temple of Doom, shudders every now and again from the blasts of a nearby quarry. Occasionally the tremors are caused by more ominous events within its bowels.

The campus community reflects the rifts of contemporary Israeli society. Students of every conceivable persuasion and ethnic group stalk the classrooms, sometimes in uneasy peace, sometimes bent on confrontation. The student body can expect little guidance from the faculty, the product of many different educational systems and the bearers of irreconcilable political and intellectual worldviews. It is a challenging, even disheartening place. It is also the most fascinating academic setting I have ever witnessed.

In many ways my university has supplied the inspiration for this study of a group of intellectuals who, for a brief illusory moment, endorsed a common cultural code, shared a consensual political worldview, and believed fervently, almost innocently, in the existence of a universal academic culture. My story has a touch of irony because from the very beginning I was aware of the disappointing ending.

Many friends and colleagues have coaxed me through this difficult task of navigating events past without being stranded on the shoals of the present. Marilyn Young patiently read innumerable drafts of this manuscript. I am the fortunate recipient of her advice, knowledge, and generosity. My editor and friend, Brigitta van Rheinberg, was, as always, an exacting and sympathetic critic. Gently, but firmly, she pushed me toward writing a more ambitious book than I had originally planned. Over the course of many a Berkeley summer, David Hollinger, Paul Flemer, and Richard Hill have read and commented on various portions of this manuscript. A skeptical Stanley Waterman continuously called me to order whenever my prose or thoughts began to wander.

Michael Sherry read the penultimate draft and supplied indispensable finetuning. Bruce Cumings and Everett Rogers offered important advice, and supplied unknown sources for two parts of my story. I am grateful for the kindness of these three strangers. Faith Gleicher Boninger and Jonathan (Yoni) Cohen, my colleagues at Haifa's department of communication studies scoured patiently through early drafts. Michael Shafer, Allan Millett, Ilan Pappe, Maoz Azaryahu, Gabriel Weimann, Ron Spector, and David Engerman were all kind enough to help me iron out many a rough edge. Maria denBoer caught more errors in the final text than I care to remember. James Curtis captured the spirit of my work in his compilation of the index. Special thanks to Anne Reifsnyder for guiding this book through a complicated transatlantic production process. Carmina Alvarez designed the layout of the book and produced its eye-catching cover.

Bo Stråth, of the European University Institute in Florence, offered me numerous opportunities to air my thoughts at workshops and seminars. Edgar Schein and Charles Wolf, two central players in the events related in this book, reconstructed their understanding of some of the episodes. John Arps supplied me with fascinating leaflets from the Gulf War.

I am grateful for the financial support received from the Harry S. Truman Presidential Library and the Douglas MacArthur Memorial Archives. A professional staff of archivists at these two sites, the Dwight D. Eisenhower Presidential Library, and the National Archives were instrumental in producing this book. Mini grants from the University of Haifa's research authority and the faculty of the humanities offset some of the costs involved in this project. Victor Rothenberg, my Berkeley impresario: thank you for organizing my summer junkets.

To my family: my partner-in-life Livi Wolff Robin, our children Gal, Sivan, Noa, and Matan—you deserve a medal for your endurance. I dedicate this book to my parents, Shani Shaltiel Robin and Eli Robin.

THE MAKING OF THE
COLD WAR ENEMY

Rumors of an Enemy

Throughout most of the Cold War rumors of an enemy plagued the United States. The nation's policy makers and military strategists stalked and feared an elusive predator based on suggestion and autosuggestion, the blurring of fact and fiction, and the projection of collective fears and desires. Much like everyday rumors, the enemy-as-rumor represented an attempt to resolve uncertainty, compensate for crucial information voids, and reframe a chaotic world in familiar forms. Rumor—an amalgam of opaque knowledge and cultural codes—transformed a distant adversary into a clear and present danger. Plausible, yet unauthenticated explanations replaced an uncomfortably ambiguous reality.[1]

This powerful rumor induced periodic harsh twists and sudden turns in the nation's global and domestic policies. The mutant enemy appeared everywhere—in foreign lands and at home. Exorcising his presence became a national obsession. Occasionally the rumored enemy unleashed dangerous forms of escapism. The "cult of the superweapon"—the dependency on superior American technology as a substitute for a painstaking assessment of enemy strengths and weaknesses—was the most prominent example of the impulse to circumvent rather than confront the enemy.[2] These and other reactions to the presence of the Cold War enemy shared a crucial common denominator: the image of the enemy was derived from an uneven mixture of fragmented information and unauthenticated presumptions. It was a rumor.

The concept of a rumor does not deny the presence of existential threats facing the United States during the course of the Cold War. In fact, the predominant image of the enemy was, at times, quite realistic. Nevertheless, veracity had little to do with the rumor's reception. The rumor spread because it provided a culturally compelling explanation for an uncertain predicament; fact and accuracy played a supporting role only. The sinister face of the enemy emerged primarily from a common "universe of discourse" and a pool of "shared assumptions" permeating American society at mid-century.[3] Its resonance was derived from, and coincided with, the collective codes and values of the time.

Much like other forms of contagion, this rumor would not have spread without the presence of powerful vectors. The rumor colonized the innermost fiber of the American body politic and confronted negligible resistance due to the privileged status of its agents. A variety of public opinion leaders participated in the transformation of assumptions, fears, and selective information into a plausible, widely accepted construction of the enemy. And, as is often the case with everyday rumors, the clients and consumers of this imaginary enemy were swayed by the credentials of its agents rather than the accuracy of their testimony.

Few of the many groups of opinion leaders responsible for the spread of the rumor could match the resonance of its academic agents. Most Americans at mid-century still regarded science as being fundamentally more reliable than other forms of discourse. The idea that scientific theory may be "accepted for reasons other than evidence—for simplicity, agreement with common sense," or political prudence—was rarely entertained.[4] The academic community still basked in the triumphs of World War II accomplishments. Its lingering prestige obviated any critical analysis of academia's observations on the significance of the Cold War in general and the face of the enemy in particular. Thus, it comes as no surprise that absorption of the rumor into contemporary scientific discourse was of particular importance. It transformed a speculative version of the enemy into a powerful working hypothesis. It is with these thoughts in mind that I offer this study of the academic alchemists responsible for transforming a welter of ambiguous data into an authoritative portrait of the enemy.

The following pages move beyond the familiar tale of mercenary science and the brutalization of knowledge-seeking in the national security state. Cold War academia did, indeed, labor in "the shadow of war." However, I do not accept the conventional analysis of a one-way conduit of influence, in which academia developed a pathological dependency on government, the military, and attendant foundations. There is, of course, little doubt that the underwriters of the warfare state affected the evolution of disciplinary knowledge, influenced academia's social structure, and imperiled the notion of academic freedom. Nevertheless, Michael Sherry reminds us, "militarization, like industrialization, was complex and multifaceted: individuals and interests could grasp one aspect of it and resist another."[5]

The academic co-production of this critical rumor was informed by numerous intellectual developments that were not directly or exclusively related to the military-industrial complex. The national security state was far from being a seamless, monolithic operation, and there was never a unitary militarization of academia. The academic construction of the enemy was powered as much by internal intellectual developments as by the impingement of external political forces. "The way in which universities, other institutions, and the larger culture responded to the cold war," Rebecca Lowen observes, "was determined not simply by the tensions between the United States and the Soviet Union but also by concerns that preceded" or developed contemporaneously with, or independently of, the Cold War.[6] The transformation of the university from a "community of scholars" to a "loose collection of academic entrepreneurs," the rise of new disciplinary frameworks, generational shifts within the universities, and the burgeoning of interdisciplinary paradigms are just some of the factors affecting the construction of the enemy that were not the exclusive products of national security imperatives.

Most of the academic warriors involved in the making of the Cold War enemy were behavioral scientists, a new, multidisciplinary academic coalition for addressing the nation's social and political concerns. I have not approached these behavioralists as the compliant prisoners of institutional benefactors. Moreover, I intend to demonstrate that the much-maligned government-supported behavioral research was often ingenious and intellectually stimulating. I argue that the major fault of Cold War behavioralism was not its mercenary nature, but, rather, its pervasive contempt for complexity, the uncritical acceptance of contemporary cultural mores, and the denial of its intellectual limitations. Behavioralists and their intellectual kin failed to acknowledge that the creation of theoretical knowledge and the formation of practical policy were fundamentally disparate activities. The criteria for success in the theoretical domains of academic inquiry—innovation, originality, speculation—were of little relevance in the domain of policy, where applicability, tangible results, and cost-effectiveness—economic and political—were the overriding criteria. The conflating of theory and policy in the Cold War military-intellectual complex caused havoc and eventually ruined the credibility of the nation's academic establishment.[7]

My analysis of the behavioral sciences parts company with Ellen Herman's important study of twentieth-century social research. Herman dismisses the behavioral sciences as a label for a loose institutional coalition, a conduit for facilitating the flow of funds from government to privileged projects. She prefers to focus on one discipline—psychology—as the core of most crucial intellectual and solcial developments. By contrast, I have approached the behavioral sciences as a quintessential paradigm and major disseminator of fundamental intellectual and institutional shifts in American academia at mid-century. No one discipline, however broadly defined, could have accomplished such a mission.[8] Born in the immediate post–World War II years, the behavioral sciences challenged the traditional intellectual and social arrangements in the so-called soft sciences. The behavioralist creed rejected, in particular, the social sciences' division of the spheres of human experience—politics, society, and biology—into discrete units. Believing that disciplinary divisions weakened the validity of scientific findings, behavioralists espoused a unified theory of human action; all social knowledge was one and indivisible.

Freed from the checks and balances of conventional knowledge creation, with its rigid departmental divisions and its respect for disciplinary enclosures, behavioralists produced provocative, multidisciplinary, yet often whimsical intellectual concepts for government consumption. In contrast to traditional modes of university research, cognizant of divisional limitations and wrapped in a protective cover of disciplinary qualifications, behavioralists offered a cosmic cogency, clarity, and resolution. Gone was the world in which human conduct was obscure, the product of undiscovered motives and unpredictability. Reality, according to the Cold War behavioralist, could be deciphered by a unified theory of human action. The quest for an inclusive supertheory assumed that human conduct adhered to a series of behavioral "laws"; even accidents appeared to follow a predictable path.

Quantification was the chosen method for routinizing peculiarities and standardizing different behavioral phenomena. The quest for precision, the discovery of regularities, and demands for verification and testability were the ostensible reasons offered for this "trust in numbers." In actual fact, a distinct, sometimes covert, and, often, unacknowledged social conservatism underscored such declarations of detachment and objectivity. As a rule, behavioralists were suspicious of diversity and social change, and avoided the role of social critic. They discounted the power of ideas and values as motivating forces in the human experience, preferring, instead, to treat ideology and belief systems as mere rationalizations of behavioral modes. Thus, behavioralists argued that individuals, rather than formal groups or institutions, were the proper units of analysis. Groups, whatever their size, shape, or social origins, were approached as collections of autonomous, self-seeking individuals.

This focus on measuring rather than critiquing, as well as the preoccupation with conduct rather than ideas, relieved behavioralists of the need to probe and question existing political, economic, and social arrangements. Quantification reflected as well an insistent denial of ambiguity in human affairs. Given their suspicion of nonmeasurable observations, behavioralists ignored fuzzy cultural circumstance and historical happenstance, preferring to approach the human experience as the sum of a crisp, quantifiable, and predictable combination of sociological, psychological, and biological reactions.

In the field of defense research, the subject of this book, this behavioralist impulse produced a shrinking agenda of complexity. Issues that could not be measured were either ignored or trivialized in order to fit the paradigm. In fact, the more distant and inscrutable the subject matter, the more relevant and intimate it appeared to be. Culturally distant people and events were translated into measurable ideal types, mostly by fostering a series of primitive pictures of the Other. Complex cultural phenomena were reduced to basic human instincts of violence, greed, or sexual drives. In defense-related research such concepts offered little autonomy for the enemy. "It was never necessary to inquire what the enemy *wants* to do, but only what the enemy *can* do," a critical Anatol Rapoport recalled. "If he can blackmail us, he will. If he can do us in, he will."[9] The remote and the strange had to appear ruthlessly simple. Essentially different behavioral phenomena were given an underlying structural similarity; peculiarities were routinized.

Portrayals of the enemy as primitive, brutal, and unchanging were not solely the result of methodological bias. These constructs drew upon deep institutional and cultural sources and, presumably, compounded and reflected widespread contemporary insecurities as well. Behavioralists were both spectators in, and creators of, what sociologist Gabriel Weimann has called in another context the "theater of terror," a repertoire of scenarios aimed more at reducing ambiguous or unknown phenomena to a familiar, brutal, and dramatic format, rather than deciphering its complexity.[10] The behavioralists' image of the enemy dramatized, simplified, and accepted uncritically the clear and present dangers that seemed to lurk around every corner. Such brutal choreographies were, of course, related to methodological bias. However, they were nurtured first and foremost by common cultural and political codes.

Using the rise and fall of the behavioral sciences as point of departure and final destination, this study traces the role of academia in producing an authoritative version of the enemy during the course of the Cold War. I have not attempted to provide an exhaustive chronology of behavioralism in action. Instead, I have exhumed and examined several exemplary projects prepared at the behest of government and military clients during a crucial period of the Cold War, from the late 1940s to the mid-1960s. The research projects analyzed here resonated far beyond the confines of specific problems or strictly military affairs. These projects were generated by, or contributed to, the creation of new paradigms, were part and parcel of the founding of new academic fields, such as mass communication studies, and nurtured a potent coalition of disciplines claiming affinity with the behavioral sciences.

Contrary to the majority of studies on academic advisors in the Cold War, I have paid particular attention to the masters of conventional warfare. Most historical inquiries of the military-intellectual complex in the Cold War are concerned with weapons development or academia's nuclear strategists.[11] In the conventional analysis of the Cold War as a series of strategical threats and nuclear gambits, the period's numerous hot wars appear as distracting sideshows of the main event. Invariably, these studies ignore those defense intellectuals who were not among the creators or theorists of weapons of mass destruction. Here, I move beyond the "Wizards of Armageddon" and focus, instead, on a less visible group of scholar-warriors who were preoccupied with defining strategies for addressing limited, conventional warfare in the thermonuclear age. It is the contention of this study that crucial observations on the nature of the enemy—observations informing both nuclear theorists and prominent "national security managers"—were produced by the analysts of conventional warfare.[12]

The vast majority of the academic agents of the rumored enemy were behavioral scientists, a self-proclaimed coalition of psychologists, sociologists, and political scientists, seeking to produce multidisciplinary solutions for their government clients. Throughout the 1950s, behavioralists were not privy to the inner sanctum of nuclear strategy. At the Rand Corporation, the major center for defense-related behavioral research, they were patronized by their peers in the physics and economic divisions for their lack of scientific rigor. Paradoxically, such marginalization had unforeseen benefits. Denial of access to the inner sanctum of nuclear strategy pushed behavioral scientists toward the very practical and immediate issues of conventional warfare. Instead of theoretical scenarios, these academic warriors produced working documents for the management of problems related to conventional warfare. Their greatest triumph was, by default, in the early 1950s, when their theories and assumptions were present in the map rooms, prison camps, and battlefields of Korea, Vietnam, and turbulent Third World trouble spots. Their working documents contained authoritative interpretations of the enemy's culture and the significance of conventional warfare in an atomic age.

For obvious reasons my study pays special attention to the developing image of the enemy during the Korean War. As the first major overt clash between East and West, the Korean conflict contributed directly to the establishment of an American-dominated international order and affected quite dramatically both domestic and foreign policy.[13] Whether this Asian conflict was the defining event of the Cold War or a reinforcement of existing trends is a matter of contention. There is, however, little doubt that the Korean War hastened the creation of the national security state, strengthened existing images of the enemy, and preordained future American entanglements in Asia. The presence of academic advisors at crucial nodes of the Korean conflict serves as the focal point of this study. Whether hovering in the background, or actively participating in the creation of policy, behavioral scientists were influential participants in this important event in the annals of the Cold War.

Some of the chapters in this study move beyond the real to the virtual. Working under the assumption that debates surrounding events that never happened are often as revealing as the autopsies of actual occurrences, I have included brief glances at an abortive project and an imaginary one. Project Camelot, an ambitious attempt by prominent behavioralists to formulate a model of Third World insurgency, was hastily discontinued during its planning stages following a series of indiscretions. While never producing a critical mass of research material, Project Camelot generated an animated exchange on the merits of government-ordained science in general and the accuracy of its predictions in particular.

Contrary to the real, albeit brief existence of Project Camelot, the Iron Mountain Project was a hoax. *Report from Iron Mountain*, supposedly the final report of a committee on the dangers of world peace, achieved notoriety due to its successful mimesis of the culture of defense intellectuals. The debate surrounding the hoax provided an opportunity to expose, critique, and, ultimately, discredit the metanarrative of military-academic science and its attendant image of the enemy. Both the Camelot controversy and the Iron Mountain parody signaled the declining authority of behavioralists within the military-intellectual complex, and were indicators, in general, of a troubled relationship between academia and the nation-state.

The Projects

The initial fusion of academic and military interests in the post–World War II period occurred in Korea. Several teams of academic advisors were intimately involved in decisive episodes of this early foray into the conventional battlefields of the Cold War. The air force's Human Resources Research Institute (HRRI) initiated the first large Korean study. During the Christmas season of 1950–51, a team of prominent academic advisors conducted fieldwork in Korea in an effort to pry open the secrets of "Bolshevik" communication theory. In what would become standard procedure, these researchers applied American theories of mass communication and social control to this very foreign context. The point of this exercise was to prove that behavioral laws, as developed in the United States in the immediate aftermath of World War II, had strong universal qualities.

The most influential of the many air force-funded projects in Korea was the Rand Corporation's advisory role at the Korean armistice talks. In addition to providing blow-by-blow commentaries on the enemy's every gesture at the bargaining table, Rand's experts furnished psychological analyses of enemy counterparts and "how to negotiate" tactics to guide the ill-prepared military delegates at the talks. The Rand analysis of enemy behavior at the Korean bargaining table was based upon the concept of an operational code, a concordance of beliefs, values, and perceptions that determined the enemy's political decisions. The operational code assumed that the enemy did not address the external world, but an image of the external world. The enemy's distortion of contemporary events was said to result from the displacement of private and formative early childhood experiences that were common or rampant in Russian society and its authoritarian clones.

The operational code implied that the ideological differences between the two warring sides were of little significance. This guiding theory rejected the possibility of cognition among those who held extreme political positions on either side of the political spectrum. Ideological positions were, according to the operational code, manifestations of emotional dysfunction that one could unmask by means of Freudian apparati, such as repression, displacement, and projection. Rand's advisors did not imply that intimate childhood events exclusively determined adult behavior. Projection of childhood traumas was usually invoked when observed political behavior appeared to be "irrational," by which was meant different from the American norm.

The presence of over 170,000 prisoners of war (POWs) in UN compounds served as the main database for Korea's other major military-funded behavioral analyses of the enemy. The common objective of the POW studies was to discount the importance of ideology as a motivating force in modernizing nations, and to discover, instead, behavioral strategies for winning over converts in enemy societies. These imaginative attempts to circumvent ideology clashed with General Douglas MacArthur's ambitious reeducation program for enemy POWs in Korea. MacArthur's educational experts working out of the Tokyo headquarters of the Far East Command's Civilian Information and Education Division (CIE) set about deprogramming enemy POWs from the supposedly mesmerizing trance of communism. Unwilling to accept the behavioralist discounting of ideas, these reeducation officials approached internal turmoil within the prison stockades as a critical ideological struggle between democratically oriented prisoners and communist adversaries. Their attempts to sway the fortunes of this struggle contributed to a mass refusal of repatriation, thereby transforming the relatively simple issue of the exchange of prisoners into the major stumbling block of the final phases of the war. The signing of an armistice agreement was delayed for over a year as negotiators wrestled with the deceivingly simple issue of POW repatriation.

The repatriation of American POWs from Chinese-administered camps offered additional signs of the fusion of images of the enemy with other political and cultural issues. When confronted by rumors of POW collaboration and communist brainwashing capabilities, behavioralists offered a series of imaginative and mostly counterintuitive explanations. Their studies of repatriated American POWs dismissed the brainwashing thesis and disproved rumors of mass collaboration. In perhaps the most provocative of all claims, behavioralists argued that the ideal American POW was not the aggressive resister, whose frequent clashes with authorities they described as dysfunctional rather than patriotic. Instead, they argued that the ideologically innocent, those who were impervious to ideas in general, were the most resistant to the enemy's proselytizing.

Despite overwhelming evidence to the contrary, the behavioralists charged with debriefing American POWs argued that race had not been an issue within the prison camps. In part, such color-blindness reflected efforts to counteract public fears of enemy infiltration into domestic American domains. These behavioralists feared, as well, that revelations of racial tensions would play into the hands of opponents of integration in the armed forces. Korea was the first integrated war in modern American history, and the critics of this bold gesture were many. To the degree that African American soldiers exhibited deviant behavior, behavioralists argued that the source was pathologies common to all poor and undereducated prisoners.

The multiple and contradictory narratives of the POW experience suggest that representations of the enemy—the ultimate other—were hopelessly intertwined with a series of domestic debates on race, class, and even gender. Skeptical public reactions to scientific assessments of the POW crisis revealed the waning authority of science to adjudicate contested issues in American society in general and the domain of military policy in particular.

A particularly visible indication of the pending crisis occurred in the Vietnamese theater. At Rand Corporation, the most prominent locus of defense-related behavioral inquiry, researchers abandoned psychocultural strategies for deciphering the enemy's behavior in Vietnam, and embraced, instead, a doctrine of rational choice. Espousal of rational choice was ostensibly in response to the rapidly growing climate of insurgency in Indo-China. Rand's counterinsurgency experts proposed defeating insurgents by modifying the behavior of peasant supporters through a harsh coercive campaign of counterterror. Rand advisors argued that forceful, suppressive measures would lead Vietnamese peasants to a rational calculation of the costs and benefits of continuing support of insurgency. According to this theory, the embattled, yet calculating peasant would ultimately choose to abandon, if not actively resist, rebel forces. Despite the controversial nature of this model, and even though the Rand reports did not offer solid historical examples or empirical evidence to sustain this refurbished image of the enemy, the military accepted these recommendations with breathtaking alacrity.

The sudden endorsement of rational choice and, conversely, the abrupt jettisoning of traditional psychocultural explanations of behavior, did little to salvage the declining fortunes of the behavioral sciences. Indeed, by the mid-

1960s the behavioral enterprise was subject to numerous critiques of its underlying ideology and intellectual underpinnings, including the speculative construction of images of the enemy. The most conspicuous attack on the behavioral enterprise occurred during the course of Project Camelot, the ambitious
army attempt to develop a global counterinsurgency strategy. Funded and
supported by the army's Special Operations Research Office (SORO), Camelot brought together interdisciplinary teams of behavioral scientists whose
task was to produce tools for predicting and controlling Third World insurgency. This large-scale effort dedicated to translating behavioral expertise into
the language of foreign policy and military action was dominated by rational-
choicers, many of whom had previously espoused conflicting psychocultural-
oriented theories of enemy motivation. Ostensibly, public furor over military
involvement in the civilian domain of foreign policy led to the project's cancellation in 1965. In actual fact, Camelot and its clones—some of which
continued discreetly after the passing of the Camelot debate—faltered and
eventually faded due to self-doubt rather than external criticism. During the
course of congressional Camelot hearings, and in a series of retrospective
articles, prominent members of the Camelot team questioned the relationship
between "science"—as a specific intellectual enterprise associated with experimental, quantitative, and value-free inquiry—and the production of knowledge within the behavioral and social sciences.

The Camelot debate was followed by the ultimate indignity: a parody of
the defense intellectual. Despite its obvious imaginary origins, *Report from
Iron Mountain* was an uncomfortable facsimile of the logic of defense-related
science. It exposed the uncritical belief in a "national interest" espoused by a
powerful cohort of ostensibly nonpartisan behavioral and social scientists. Iron
Mountain revealed, as well, the specious and flimsy construction of the enemy
permeating most, if not all major policy decisions during the course of the
Cold War. The Iron Mountain debate exposed, in particular, the dependency
of the American nation-state on the presence—real or imaginary—of a powerful enemy. Diminishing fears of the Soviet Other as an existential threat
introduced doubts in, and instability of, well-entrenched concepts of the
American self.

Both the Camelot affair and the Iron Mountain debate dwelt on the problematic scientific logic informing the image of the nation's adversaries. These
debates questioned, in particular, the behavioralists' cavalier dismissal of specific cultural, ideological, or historical context. The Rand Corporation's political scientists at the Korean armistice talks had approached ideology—all ideologies—as a displacement of childhood traumas, rather than a cognitive,
culturally saturated reaction to contemporary events. As for the sociologists
and psychologists of the enemy POWs in Korea, they had contended that
techniques of behavior modification developed in the United States could
transform ideologically motivated foreign enemies into useful, pragmatic al-

lies. The experts charged with analyzing the experiences of returning American POWs swiftly transformed their research from mere observations of deviant and disloyal behavior among prisoner-collaborators into a riveting debate on social control in modern societies. The counterinsurgency experts in Vietnam espoused a universal concept of rational choice that dismissed the impact of culture on behavior.

All of these academic studies, irrespective of their differences, rejected the notion of informed intuition or complexity. The military intellectuals of conventional warfare damned humanists as prisoners of the mystique of culture. They claimed for themselves distinct advantages, for they were not held in awe by the lack of familiarity with seemingly esoteric cultures. They argued that all human phenomena could be deciphered by implementing rigorous scientific methodology.

Critics responded that these bold declarations on science and objectivity were pretentious at best. They argued that behavioralism in general and defense-related projects in particular were immersed in hypotheses that were too speculative to be refuted by conventional scientific logic. The psychoanalysis of the enemy could not be falsified because it was pure conjecture; it had no meaningful empirical reference points. Rational choice theory, as the basis for deciphering enemy actions, was equally speculative. Both psychoculture and rational choice were unassailable, because they were theories rather than empirical constructs.

The Paradigm

Given the speculative nature of their theories, how did behavioral scientists come to monopolize the function of interpreters and decipherers of foreign cultures? In addition, what accounts for the swift rise and sharp disappearance of psychocultural explanations of the enemy, and the equally sudden rise of rational choice?

Here, I offer an explanation based on the "paradigm," Thomas Kuhn's concept of the dynamics of scientific inquiry.[14] Although Kuhn's monumental study of the production of knowledge is derived from the history of physics, his theory offers a conduit for understanding the privileging of those academic fields seeking to emulate the physical and natural sciences.[15]

My study focuses, in particular, on Kuhn's questioning of scientific activity as a cumulative process, and his qualifications regarding the scientist as an intrepid discoverer. In a counterintuitive fashion, Kuhn argued that scientific advancements are not built solely on the achievements of predecessors; theories are not discarded merely because new knowledge or sharper forms of analysis have disproved them. Moreover, the development of scientific theories is as much a sociological as an intellectual process. Scientific activity is governed by paradigms, which Kuhn defined as "universally recognized scientific achievements that for a time provide model problems and solutions to a community of practitioners."[16] In the pre-paradigm stage numerous theories compete for acceptance. The eventual codification of one particular theory as a paradigm, and the subsequent dismissal of competing constructs, has little to do with which theory is closer to some stable truth but, rather, which theory can be enforced by its disciples. In other words, the paradigm is a sociological construct, and not necessarily the result of some innovative scientific breakthrough.

The dominant paradigm, according to Kuhn, is the product of a community of scientists who produce and enforce "normal science," a codex of rules governing the dimensions and direction of inquiry. Paradigms are, by definition, axiomatic. They are never questioned, and the activities of their adherents are limited to puzzle-solving, the unremitting effort to resolve all pertinent problems within the boundaries of preconceived and rigid intellectual parameters. According to Kuhn, one of "the most striking features" of "normal" scientific activity is "how little" it aims "to produce novelties, conceptual or phenomenal." Normal science, far from seeking new horizons, requires an enforcement of orthodoxy and the suppression of competing views. Members of the scientific community are expected to conform to the norms of inquiry defined by the paradigm. Nonconformance, or any questioning of the paradigm per se, is usually met by sanctions. Those who espouse older or novel views are "simply read out of the profession," or, even worse, denied funding.[17]

Paradigm revolutions, always infrequent and quite complex, occur in times of crisis. Confronted with repeated failures to solve problems within the established scientific framework, the ruling paradigm loses its authority to regulate and curtail dissent, thereby providing space for a new paradigm to emerge. However, Kuhn stressed that crisis is not due to the discovery of new facts. The new paradigm offers new cognitive standards, not new information. The new paradigm offers a new way of looking at familiar phenomena, rather than the discovery of hitherto inaccessible facts. Its ultimate success hinges upon the ability of its advocates to produce a critical mass of believers. The paradigm is, then, a unified body of cognitive strategies shared by a cohesive community of researchers.

In a striking manner the fluctuations within the behavioral sciences movement follow the path marked by Kuhn. Having adopted variations of psychoculture as their paradigm, behavioral scientists focused on what Kuhn called "puzzle-solving" — attempts to prove that seemingly deviant phenomena did, in fact, fit the dominant paradigm. Such puzzle-solving activities account for the fact that, during the Korean War, the manifest ineffectiveness of theories for understanding the enemy's collective character and motivation did not affect immediately the fortunes of the behavioral sciences community. It was only during the protracted Vietnam conflict that the paradigm reached what

Kuhn called the crisis state. The inability to explain away the ineffectiveness of psychocultural strategies as merely a technical issue that could be rectified by puzzle-solving upset existing intramural intellectual arrangements. Fundamental challenges to the paradigm's validity led to its swift abandonment rather than modification, and the adaptation of a new cognitive framework for understanding the enemy. Even though the new paradigm of rational choice was espoused by many of the partisans of its psychocultural predecessor, there was no linkage between the two strategies. In fact, they were incompatible.

Viewing these developments through the lens offered by Kuhn suggests that the rise and fall of the behavioral sciences cannot be assigned exclusively to politics or funding. Rigid strategies, the stubborn quest for a unified code of human behavior, and an intolerant attitude toward ambiguity were, in large part, the result of the juggernaut of paradigm. The endorsement of psychocultural strategies, their ultimate abandonment, and their replacement by a conversely harsh theory of rational choice offer a particularly vivid example of the dynamics of scientific paradigms.

This battle of paradigms resonated far beyond the academic estate. Behavioral scientists were observers of, and active participants in, defining the meaning of the Cold War. They contributed to a portrait of the enemy that both reflected and fueled predominant ideological strains within the American body politic. As scholarly partners in the national security state, they were instrumental in defining and disseminating a Cold War culture. Whether their assumptions and theories were scientifically valid is beside the point. The importance of the canon lay in its epistemological authority, its power to fashion a set of working assumptions for understanding the Cold War. The presentation of this intellectual context, its fluctuations and variations, in Korea, Vietnam, and Washington, D.C., is the primary concern of this study.

PART ONE
DEFINING THE PARADIGM

1.
Inventing the Behavioral Sciences

Statistical Soldiers

The American Soldier (TAS) was a misleadingly modest title for a very ambitious project. Published in 1949, TAS was, indeed, a study of military life. However, its main contribution was the enunciation of a new scientific enterprise, soon to be called the behavioral sciences. This first installment of the series, "Studies in Social Psychology in World War II," presented the findings of three hundred inquiries and over six hundred thousand separate interviews carried out under the auspices of the Research Branch, Information and Education Division, United States Army. The multivolume project was directed by University of Chicago sociologist Samuel Stouffer, who was also the principal author of the first two volumes, collectively entitled TAS. Subsequent volumes included *Experiments in Mass Communication* (1949) by Carl Hovland and associates, and *Measurement and Prediction* (1950), a collection of theoretical articles by Louis Guttman, Paul Lazarsfeld, and other eminent collaborators. The entire series was based on surveys of subjects ranging from the effectiveness of motion picture propaganda, motivation and leadership studies, to critical investigations of race and social stratification among members of America's citizen army.

TAS had the trappings of a revolution. Contrary to the dominant trend in American social sciences, it was the work of an interdisciplinary team rather than of an individual researcher or a group of researchers from one particular discipline. In an academic culture that still endorsed rigid intellectual divisions and descriptive research, TAS offered a multidisciplinary, predictive, quantitative framework. Instead of grand theory, TAS espoused observation and empirically structured research strategies. These organizational and intellectual innovations enjoyed generous funding from the two main sources of postwar "big science": foundations—in this case, the Carnegie Foundation—and the defense establishment.[1]

TAS provoked the immediate reaction of counter-revolutionaries. Wary of disciplinary upheaval, defenders of the traditional social sciences condemned TAS as a haphazard "body of discrete and unordered 'data' . . . reflecting little use of any guiding or meaningful theory." TAS raised fears that a new generation of social scientists would use the study as an excuse to abandon the often lonely and always difficult development of theory and hypothesis, and focus, instead, on lucratively funded but intellectually limiting survey research.[2]

Defenders of the status quo accused TAS collaborators of trivializing the academic calling through a specious reliance on computers. Sociologist Nathan Glazer condemned the study for parodying science with absurd cross-tabulations of totally unrelated variables and an uncritical use of computerized technologies.

We can discover in no time at all—to take a hypothetical example—how many men prefer oatmeal to farina, how many of these have been in the Army one, two, or three years, how many of each of these categories are married, and of these how many have completed college; and thus we may know how many unmarried college men who have been in the Army one year prefer farina. In short, questions that would otherwise never have come to trouble the human mind can now be asked and answered by the machine.[3]

The most impassioned criticism, entitled "The Statistical Soldier," belonged to historian Arthur Schlesinger Jr. In defending the existing academic order, Schlesinger damned TAS as a mediocre and anti-intellectual study, a vulgarization of the academic enterprise. He accused TAS researchers of relying on machines rather than intellectual reasoning, and of producing banal findings instead of provocative observations. The book, he complained, was the work of barbarous hucksters, who had persuaded a gullible public that they had developed "a body of knowledge with the same properties of verifiability and predictability as modern physical theory." Worst of all, Schlesinger protested, somehow, the self-promotion of the "new" social scientists (the term *behavioral sciences* was still uncommon) was amazingly effective. These disciples of statistical reductionism had captured the lion share of government and foundation money; they were about to restructure the universities to suit their agenda, and had relegated the humanities to the status of the poor and not-very-bright-relative. In the final analysis, Schlesinger claimed, TAS was nothing more than a sleight of hand. It had "discovered" nothing new and offered no meaningful observations on American society. At best it was an expensive piece of fluff, pretending to foretell the future, but serving nobody except its authors.[4]

Such criticisms confronted an impassioned defense among leading academic figures. Supporters of the behavioral underpinnings of TAS lauded, in particular, the refreshing notion of interdisciplinary ventures. They celebrated the cooperation of psychologists, anthropologists, and sociologists aimed at transcending the overly descriptive and fragmented social sciences. TAS's multidisciplinary cooperation had produced seminal new concepts for analyzing human behavior and had hastened the development of predictive methods. Admirers emphasized the study's bold moves beyond its ostensible military topic. In addition to its analysis of the nation's citizen-army, TAS provided scientific validation for a new understanding of social role, class, and political change in the United States.

Among the many important methodological contributions of TAS, supporters singled out the analysis of primary groups, the discovery of mechanisms influencing opinion formation, TAS's crucial data on race relations, its documentation of the relationship between individual motivation and social structure, and the development of the concept of relative deprivation.[5] In addition, TAS's attitude scaling and scalogram analysis, its questionnaire designs and interview techniques, were hailed as pathbreaking contributions.[6]

Supporters praised, as well, the political ramifications of the study, noting the impact of TAS's multidisciplinary strategies and innovative quantitative measurements on social justice in the United States. TAS, its partisans claimed, had proven that racial segregation was not only unjust but dysfunctional as well. Science, and not subjective moral values, had demonstrated that discrimination had detrimental effects on military performance in particular and on American society in general.[7]

In sum, TAS appeared to be a harbinger of a new, politically astute and scientifically innovative discourse. In an enthusiastic mixing of intellectual metaphors that he, perhaps, lived to regret, sociologist Daniel Lerner compared TAS's authors to Darwin, Marx, and Freud. TAS, according to Lerner, was a definitive classic of Western civilization and a worthy addition to the proverbial shelf of the Hundred Great Books. The study challenged "its reader to reconsider his recollections of the past, his identifications in the present, and his expectations for the future." TAS, according to Lerner, would have long-lasting intellectual ramifications because it had restructured the academic enterprise from within and had proven that interdisciplinary research could resolve the political and social problems of the nation.[8]

TAS did, in fact, achieve the aura of a definitive study. Its notoriety was, however, fleeting. Throughout the 1950s TAS served as the source for research strategies, hypotheses, and explanations for a wide array of human behavior with only casual links to its original military context. Nevertheless, by the 1960s, TAS was largely ignored. In reviewing textbooks as well as the major works on social and behavioral theory in the 1980s, TAS participant Robin Williams found that the study was conspicuously absent from the footnotes, references, and indexes of most scientific publications. Williams explained that its dissipation was a sign of the times. Beginning in the late 1960s, "widespread disaffection with military topics . . . made TAS disappear from view in mainstream academia." In addition, Williams speculated, TAS's invisibility was, paradoxically, a mark of success; its concepts and research strategies had been internalized and absorbed into mainstream science. Given the profession's poor historical memory, the source of many of these strategies had been forgotten or appropriated by others.[9]

Williams's review suggests that intellectual flaws hastened TAS's untimely demise as well. Relative deprivation, one of the most highly praised of TAS's innovations, serves as a case in point. Defined as "the feeling of personal hardship in comparison to others," relative deprivation was cavalierly used to explain a host of contradictory findings. In TAS, relative deprivation explained why uneducated army troops were less content than the educated; at the same time the term explained why army air corps personnel, better educated and endowed with far more opportunities than regular army draftees, were significantly more dissatisfied than their peers.[10] In subsequent years this gelatinous hypothesis was trotted out to explain a mind-boggling and often conflicting collection of behavioral phenomena, including "revolutions, mass protest and civil disorders, class or ethnic solidarity, individual aspirations, inequality, dissatisfactions with promotions, voting and voting preferences, career decisions, leadership patterns, attributions of locus of control, group boundaries, rates of social mobility, social distance, and others."[11] In providing an explanation for practically everything, relative deprivation explained practically nothing. Its main function was to dismiss contemporary grievances as "relative" and a matter of perception rather than the result of meaningful schisms in American society.

In actual fact, scientific rigor had little to do with TAS's fleeting success. The study's positive reception and its momentary glory were related to its authors rather than its content. At the time of its publication, the veracity of TAS findings was of secondary importance. The medium was the message.

TAS was first and foremost an indicator of a paradigm shift within the academic domain. So long as its authors dictated the norms of the profession, TAS occupied a privileged position on the book shelf of definitive scholarly works. Once the behavioral revolution had exhausted itself, this manifesto lost its lofty status.

TAS reflected several interrelated transitions within academia: the passing away of professional leaders, the replacement of narrow departmental research by large interdisciplinary projects, and a growing clamor for predictive rather than descriptive research. The young, mobilized academics of TAS were the quintessential representatives of a generational and intellectual transition in American academia. They assumed leadership in their respective fields in the immediate postwar years by virtue of prominent wartime experience, their aversion for constraining academic and intellectual divisions, and the departure, by death and retirement, of a previous generation of academic figures trained before World War I.[12] TAS's resonance was a direct product of World War II, when a cohort of young American sociologists, political scientists, and psychologists "temporarily vacated their ivory towers and came to grips with day-to-day political, administrative," and military realities.[13]

TAS, a participant recalled, signaled the arrival of "a unified behavioral science" and the eclipse of the "traditional speculative 'grand theories'" of the divided and divisive social sciences.[14] The empirical, statistically based ballast that accompanied even the most speculative concepts in TAS offered order where previous observers had seen only confusion. TAS framed the issues of postwar academic discourse, identified the pertinent research issues, and produced a consensual knowledge that eclipsed, for a brief historical moment, most alternative interpretations of contemporary social and cultural reality.[15]

While there were different strategies, strains, and schools among these mobilized academics, they shared the presumption that value-free scientific methodology would cut through the "mumbo jumbo of the religion of humanity" and provide objective methods for controlling human behavior.[16] This generation of American academics defined a new epistemological framework based on their wartime experiences and a widespread craving for rational and orderly thought modes to replace myth, superstition, and unverified beliefs.[17] The adjective *scientific*, historian David Hollinger reminds us, meant "disinterested judgments based on exact evidence," and an open-minded culture of inquiry that would neutralize prejudice, and the annihilating, reactionary forces of blood, myth, and tradition.[18] All gods were dead; all faiths were overturned; there could be no poetry after Auschwitz, Berthold Brecht lamented. Into this vacuum stepped advocates of the behavioral sciences, the proponents of a scientific mode of rational skepticism, the representatives of a fundamental departure in both style and content from what they saw as the tyranny of myths.

Defining the Behavioral Sciences

Behavioralists described their vocation as a multidisciplinary departure from the social sciences' preoccupation with the ascriptive bonds of institutions, units, and collective identities.[19] In contrast to the social sciences' preoccupation with "society" as an entity shaping and constraining the behavior of individuals, the behavioral sciences championed classic liberal notions of autonomous individuals. Behavioralists assumed as point of departure that most social phenomena resulted from the actions and interactions of individual agents. In the field of political sciences, for example, the behavioral approach diverted attention from the traditional "concern with institutions" to inquiries on how "individually acquired beliefs and habits relat[ed] to political life."[20] Instead of courts or political parties, behavioral scientists spoke of the electoral behavior, or judicial behavior, of individuals and small groups as the most meaningful parameters for predicting political developments.

Behavioralists distanced themselves from behaviorism, a close, but quite unwelcome intellectual kin. Behaviorism referred to the investigation of observable phenomena generated exclusively and linearly by external stimuli. In contrast to behavioralists, advocates of behaviorism exorcised all reference to opaque mental processes such as purpose, desires, or unconscious motivation. Behaviorists defined the human personality as a collection of habit systems built up by conditioned reflexes. All human action was approached as genetic phenomena, originally laid down in human nature. Behaviorists dismissed the presence of the "black box" of mental processes that intervened between stimulus and response as unsuitable for scientific study.

By contrast, behavioralists approached human behavior as significantly more complex than the physiological, stimulus-response paradigm of behaviorism. The motivational components of human behavior represented the primary area of inquiry for behavioral scientists. Understanding human behavior, they claimed, was not limited to the overt, observable acts that preoccupied behaviorists. The scientific measurement of behavior included the analysis of attitudes, beliefs, expectations, motivations, and aspirations of human action. As such, in constructing predictions of human action, behavioralists did not rely solely on observational technique. The probing of attitudes through questionnaires was equally if not more important than documenting actual behavior, for it provided tools for predicting certain behavioral modes.

Intellectually, the behavioral sciences constituted a break with an academic culture of relativism, the presumption that each society is considered so unique, so particular, that comparisons or generalities are inhibited. Prior to World War II, most American social scientists had limited their search for behavioral consistency to well-contained social units; emphasis was placed on the distinctive and the contextual. By contrast, the behavioral sciences underscored universalism and the search for coherent behavioral patterns beyond the unique and often arbitrarily defined units, such as the nation-state.[21]

Commitment to behavioral regularities did not contradict the notion of free will and individuality. Behavioral scientists claimed that it was possible to accept individual agency and still discover statistically verifiable behavioral patterns. Behavior, they claimed, was neither a random phenomenon nor an expression of ironclad patterns of human action. Nevertheless, aggregates of human behavior could be identified through the creative use of algorithms.

Structurally, the behavioral sciences of the Cold War era referred to a body of knowledge that transcended traditional academic departmental enclosures, and offered, instead, universal research strategies. The underlying assumption was that within any given society the various fields of inquiry associated with the social sciences—individual behavior, institutions, and beliefs—were functionally linked to one another, and that their separation into segregated fields of inquiry was arbitrary.[22]

Given this quest for multidisciplinary science, behavioralists offered deliberately broad definitions of their calling. Bernard Berelson, the director of the behavioral sciences program at the Ford Foundation from 1951 until the termination of the project in 1957, explained somewhat vaguely that the behavioral sciences "can be distinguished from the social sciences as designating a good deal less, but at the same time, somewhat more." Berelson went on to describe the "edges" of behavioral sciences as "fuzzy," and the center of the field as nothing more than "reasonably clear."[23] James Charlesworth, a prominent advocate of behavioralism in American political science, was equally noncommittal. He studiously avoided any firm definition of the term, suggesting that incoherence was the basis for its attraction. Vagueness, he explained, appeared to be an asset, for "whatever behavioralism is, it has generated a great deal of wonderment, controversy, missionary zeal, and scorn."[24] Clarity was not a prerequisite for either support or criticism; in fact it was probably a burden.

The prominent academic centers of the behavioral sciences were equally unwilling to provide exacting definitions. In response to a Ford Foundation request to review its extensive program in the behavioral sciences, a Harvard University report acknowledged that the demand to define the behavioral sciences was "bold," but as far as Harvard was concerned, the behavioral sciences were best defined vaguely as a field encompassing "the general values and objectives which Harvard espouses." A similar University of Chicago report produced equally obscure results. Fully aware of the contradiction between ambiguous definitions of the field and extensive demands for funding, the Chicago report stated that the term defied clarity because it was "a new label for a field still in process of creation and definition." Both the Chicago and Harvard reports implied that commitment and the establishment of boundaries contradicted the raison d'être of behavioralism.[25]

This reluctance to accept finite labels was, in large part, intellectually derived. Partisans of the behavioral sciences advocated a sweeping fusion of the scientific discourse and the removal of supposedly artificial barriers separating the human and natural sciences. The goal of all knowledge, whether physical, social, or behavioral, was the construction of a web of causal explanation by means of scientific techniques perfected by the hard sciences. The possibility of formulating common root terms and strategies shared by all branches of the sciences was, then, the ultimate goal.

Behavioralists were not, however, advocates of what Edward Wilson has called "consilience," the absorption of their enterprise into the natural sciences.[26] Instead, they claimed that the deciphering of human behavior entailed a complementary contribution of genetic factors, on the one hand, and environmental influences, on the other. The "old argument of nature versus nurture ... has been replaced by recognition that both factors interact to varying degrees in different behaviors." A common set of methodological strategies would provide the bridge between behavioral and natural scientists.[27]

Behavioral scientists readily admitted reasons, other than intellectual, for their attraction to the well-endowed physical and natural sciences. Advocates of the behavioralist cause argued that the road to legitimacy and prestige entailed a close association with the manifestly successful natural sciences. Outstanding accomplishments per se would not ensure fame and fortune within academia and without. Robert Merton and Daniel Lerner stated categorically that the chain of events was actually converse. Status was a prerequisite for accomplishment.

> The higher the social standing of a discipline, the more likely it will recruit able talents, the greater the measure of its financial support, and the greater its actual accomplishments. . . . Even a cursory examination of the history of medicine or of physics will suggest the same pattern of interplay between cultural evaluations of the discipline, intellectual development of the discipline, and utilization of the findings.[28]

Under these circumstances, they argued, an affiliation between the behavioral sciences and the prestigious hard sciences would attract talent and facilitate funding.

Part of this quest for both legitimacy and prestige entailed a pandering to public and political trends. In order to accommodate a proverbially anti-intellectual, parochial American public, the founding fathers of behavioralism avoided association by name with politically unwise nomenclatures. In his description of the creation of the behavioral sciences, James Miller acknowledged that there were compelling political reasons for adopting the "behavioral" terminology. Dissatisfaction with the enclosures of the social sciences was not merely an intellectual issue; there were, as well, important political reasons for distancing social inquiry from its traditional namesake. Miller and his associates had foreseen "a possibility of someday seeking to obtain financial support from persons who might confuse social science with socialism."[29] As such, they had created the politically innocuous term *behavioral sciences*. In the immediate post–World War II years, any connotation of radical change— in this case, any variation of the term *social*—appeared politically imprudent.

The Creation Myth

These combinations of politics and science, caution and innovation, formed the basis for a recurring narrative on the origins of the behavioral sciences.[30] This narrative should not, however, be confused with an accurate history of the field. The narrative was, rather, an attempt to distill the essence of the behavioral persuasion by evoking a mythical past that probably never occurred. The construction of a common and consensual version of the past, David Thelen reminds us, serves first and foremost as a guide for conduct in the present.[31] In this sense the creation myth of the behavioral sciences was a representation of the field's professional and political values packaged in a narrative of events past.

The creation myth posits inception as occurring in numerous different places, more or less at the same time. The crucial year, according to the narrative, was 1949, when a working group of University of Chicago social scientists used the term *behavioral sciences* to describe a team effort aimed at discovering a general theory of human behavior. Social psychologist James G. Miller recalled that his colleagues had coined this phrase as a symbol of cross-disciplinary cooperation. Intellectually the term made sense because of the presence of a small number of biologists in the Chicago theory group. The "neutral character" of the term made it acceptable to both social and biological scientists, who claimed that they were on the verge of articulating an empirically testable theory of human behavior, based on a fusionist knowledge of nature and nurture.[32]

Even as the Chicago group was engaged in this imaginative process, the creation myth identifies "similar stirrings" in other academic institutions. Harvard University's newly founded Department of Social Relations (1946) "was in fact, though not in name, a behavioral sciences department," and a "somewhat similar effort was launched" at Yale's Institute of Human Relations. The creation myth claims, as well, that John Dewey, the patron saint of twentieth-century American enlightenment, added his blessing to the enterprise. In 1949, Dewey reportedly came "close to using the term by distinguishing the physical, physiological, and behavioral regions of science." Dewey's stumbling upon the behavioral persuasion was something similar to providential intervention, as he ostensibly knew nothing of the activities of the Young Turks at Harvard, Yale, Chicago, and other places.[33]

The creation myth extends the process of simultaneous inception beyond the groves of academe. At about the same time that university scholars were inventing the term, the new and highly visible Ford Foundation named its program for the encouragement of social knowledge the "behavioral sciences division." Much like the researchers at the University of Chicago, the administrators at Ford emphasized that "the Foundation's use of the term 'behavioral sciences' is not equivalent to the usual definition of the social sciences as a certain group of academic disciplines. Rather, it denotes those intellectual activities that contribute to the understanding of *individual behavior* and human relations, no matter where they may be located academically."[34] Most accounts of the founding of the behavioral sciences have implied that there was no coordination between the scattered scholars and the Ford Foundation. The simultaneous invention of the term was, supposedly, happenstance and, as such, a powerful indicator of its viability.

The significance of the creation myth lies in its central motifs: the insistence on simultaneous discovery and the attendant benefits of free scientific enterprise. The recurring narrative suggests that the behavioral sciences were governed by an ethos of what historian Sam Bass Warner has called in another context "privatism."[35] In describing unplanned and simultaneous invention in different locations, the creation narrative lauds individual ingenuity rather than central planning. The essence of privatism suggests that collective accomplishments are not the result of relentless communal action or a visible hand. Achievement in any field, from business to academia, depends on "the aggregate successes and failures of thousands of individual enterprises," and not on some centralized planning or community action.

Privatism assumes that great advances occur without the heavy hand of government. The role of government, according to this ethos, is merely to provide a creative setting for self-realization. Given this belief in privatism, the impact of government funding—a crucial source of endowment for the behavioral sciences—is conspicuously absent from the creation myth. In its place, the private and supposedly uncoordinated foundations are presented as the main underwriters of the behavioral sciences. When left to their own devices, the seemingly unconnected independent universities, research centers, and private foundations stumbled upon the existence of the behavioral sciences. The supposedly simultaneous and uncoordinated invention of the same term was the ultimate sign of its validity.

The creation myth's paeans to individualism and science were counterpoised by an acknowledgment of hard, contemporary political realities. In addition to its prudent avoidance of any connotation with social upheaval, the creation narrative consciously removes all references to foreign influences. We are led to believe that behavioralism was an immaculate American conception while, in actual fact, the behavioral sciences benefited from the wave of academic refugees who arrived in the United States in the 1930s. The German exiles provided not merely an addition of talent, but talent of an additional sort. These were scholars whose training moved them to pose questions far more ambitious and complex than those that their American counterparts had asked before. Hence, they served as conceptualizers and trailblazers for this new form of multidisciplinary intellectual inquiry.

The omission of government sponsorship and the erasing of cosmopolitan intellectual roots were central components in the behavioral sciences' claims for authority in the post–World War II scientific estate. Behavioralism, so the creation myth leads us to believe, was an example of American exceptionalism. Born and bred by multiple progenitors, the behavioral sciences represented a cultural enterprise as well as a scientific achievement. The authority of the behavioral sciences, according to its guiding myth, resulted from the combination of unique public norms, scientific discourse, and political action that set the United States apart from its adversaries as well as its allies.

The Discursive Framework: Modernization Theory

A study of behavioralism in action is incomplete without recognizing its ties to modernization theory, perhaps the most enduring metanarrative in American intellectual life during the post–World War II years. This overarching theoretical construct of progress and controlled, metered change—at home and abroad—permeated the behavioralist creed. Modernization theory, historian Michael Latham has argued, was "far more than an academic formulation." It was, as well, "an ideology, a conceptual framework that reiterated a much older set of mutually reinforcing ideas and widespread popular notions about the essential nature of American society and its ability to transform a world perceived as both materially and culturally deficient."[36]

Long before it received the lofty label of theory, generic notions of modernization—the inevitable and predictable move from traditional enclosures to rational, economically driven social arrangements—had penetrated most fields within the social sciences and the humanities. The Cold War provided the incentive to turn this implicit truism into a theoretical framework. Political scientist Dean Tipps has suggested that the rise of developing nations and the fatal attraction of Marxism "converged during the 1950s to channel—for the first time, really—substantial intellectual interest and resources beyond the borders of American society" into the study of the emerging political societies. Unable to rely for guidance on any prior accumulated knowledge of these societies, American social scientists turned, by default, to familiar Western notions of change. Hence, the theory of modernization, although its "terminology may be somewhat novel," was deeply rooted in the "conventional wisdom" of Western development.[37]

Modernization theory, much like the attendant behavioral sciences, was an inclusive framework, an attempt to interpret expansion of the individual's rational control over his or her physical, social, and economic circumstances by means of an overarching explanatory principle.[38] The theory posited a series of one-way transitions from tradition-bound subsistence economies to technology-intensive, industrialized economies; from authoritarian political systems to participant-oriented systems; from religious beliefs to secular, scientifically based values. All these transitions were accompanied by an incremental surge in personal mobility, social, physical, and economic. The ultimate sign of modernity, and the most commonly used measurement among theorists, was economic growth. Yet economic development per se could not function as a singular indicator because modernization was a package deal. Transformations in one field were induced by, or induced eurythmic changes in, other fields of human endeavor.

Modernization theory represented a conscious attempt to move beyond racist and ethnocentric definitions of Western progress. Well aware of the political liabilities of previous attempts to explain Western superiority, modernization theorists denied anything uniquely European or American in this theory of comprehensive development. The so-called mental virus that made modern entrepreneurship possible could, and eventually would, strike anywhere. Yet, however earnest was this attempt to universalize the process of modernization, its theorists could not, or would not, avoid the privileged position of the United States. America, according to Seymour Martin Lipset, was "the first new nation," the first national entity to complete in its entirety, the series of stages along the path toward ultimate modernization.[39] A modernized society was characterized by a strong participatory body politic and a rationally structured, industrialized economic basis, not unlike contemporary American society.

The pace and direction of change inherent in modernization theory was unreservedly Western and unmistakably American. Becoming modern, according to sociologist Edward Shils, meant "being Western without the onus of dependence on the West."[40] Given the ability to develop without artificial hindrance—the intervention of subversive, foreign ideologies such as communism, for example—modernization theorists assumed that all societies would eventually converge toward a similar modular format.

Partisans of modernization theory accepted the nation-state as an inevitable and indispensable entity. It is within the nation- state that all crucial aspects of modernization occurred—industrialization, the development of mobile and rational social order, growing political democratization, and the rise of modern technocratic elites. Because theories of modernization were synonymous with changes within the nation-state, this political unit, irrespective of its often arbitrary boundaries and artificial circumstances of creation, was deemed indispensable. The examination of society according to other definitions—class or gender, for example—was dismissed as politically biased or unscientific.

There were, of course, differences and nuances among modernization theorists that were, in large part, a function of the theorists' mother disciplines. Thus, Daniel Lerner, a sociologist and communications theorist, focused on the diffusion of modernization via mass media. Lerner coined the notion of empathy, which he described as "the power to identify with a role, time, place, different from one's own," or "the psychic mechanism" that enables ordinary persons to imagine themselves in a situation that is "better" than their present predicament. Modernization, according to Lerner, worked by diffusion, and the vector was mass media. Empathy, spread by new forms of electronic communications, was, Lerner argued, the ultimate producer of a virtual mobility that inevitably led to material change of one sort or another.[41]

Social psychologist David McClelland sought the impetus for modernization within the family rather than in technological innovations. Always the behavioralist, McClelland described the rise and fall of achieving nations as a function of childrearing practices rather than ideological fervor, economic predicament, technological innovations, or any of the other dominant themes of the day. McClelland called his modernizing vector "the N achievement" factor, a psychological state of mind governed by a high urge for achievement, autonomy, and order. He claimed that the psychological urge to achieve preceded and caused economic development. In contradistinction to Marxism, he argued that "ideas are in fact more important in shaping history than purely materialistic arrangements."[42] Based on a series of cross-national comparisons, McClelland claimed that childhood training for self-reliance rather than material conditions unleashed the achievement impulse. "In a century dominated by economic determinism, in both Communist and Western thought, it is startling to find concrete evidence for psychological determinism, for psychological developments as preceding and presumably causing intellectual change."[43]

Harvard anthropologist Alex Inkeles agreed that "mental and psychic factors" were "key barriers to more effective economic and social development in many countries." However, contrary to McClelland's focus on early childhood experiences, Inkeles claimed that the modernizing ethos could be spread and absorbed in adulthood. The factory, according to Inkeles, served as the "school in modernity." Inkeles rejected the notion of the industrial order as an oppressive experience; factory life, he argued, was benign and offered opportunities for liberating "man" from the deadening forces of tradition. Although he was willing to acknowledge that childhood and diffusion via mass media were important elements in the modernizing process, Inkeles paid particular attention to socialization of the adult. He argued that "the factory, as a particular form of social organization, characterized by rational planning, ready acceptance of new technology, authority based on technical competence, coordination of the efforts of large numbers of individuals, and treatment according to impartial rules" would instill the germ of modernity in the most traditional of men and women. A routinized work regime, teamwork, and the adoption of new technical skills induced a sense of mastery, an openness to change, and an appreciation of the rational order of modernized societies. Inkeles agreed that modernization was first and foremost a psychological factor. Its source, however, was a significant change in the mode of production, a move from Marx's idiocy of country life to the liberating milieu of the factory.[44]

The modernizing process, as a function of positive individual will and desirable personality traits bolstered by a benign industrialized milieu, obviated any meaningful questioning of power relationships both within the United States and between nations. Modernization theorists, whatever their differences, assumed that the United States had reached the successful end of the modernizing trajectory. Their location of "the end of history" in the United States implicitly denied the need for structural domestic reform. The United States's rational and streamlined economic structure, its widespread abundance and functional democratic political system, validated the benefits of modernization. Personality, psychology, and an open economy, not the redistribution of influence and power, were the vital keys for a more equitable and just society. There appeared to be no need for fundamental reforms within the nation.

By the same token, modernization theory provided an authoritative and comfortable explanation for inequality among nations.[45] The privileging of individual psychological traits absolved the West of its liability for underdevelopment in other parts of the world. "Tradition" or mental processes, rather than the legacy of colonialism or material factors, were responsible for underdevelopment. This construct of a generic, retrogressive culture of underdevelopment—the converse of modernization—conveniently "shifted the responsibility for the continued backwardness of much of the world onto the people of those areas," while "denying the historical responsibility of the western world."[46]

Modernization thus offered an ideological framework for an American policy of actively supporting the status quo, even among the most autocratic and ruthless of its allies. The theory promised that change was inevitable and would be evolutionary rather than revolutionary, a psychological process of individual change rather than a violent restructuring of society. Sudden change induced by outside intervention would upset the natural internal transitions. The social and political unrest plaguing significant proportions of developing nations could be explained away as momentary, a transitional stage on the unerring path from tradition to modernization.

In addition, modernization held out the reassuring promise of the demise of adversarial political systems. As historian Carl Pletsch has observed, modernization theorists approached the competing socialist bloc as a proto-modern development, encumbered temporarily by an ideology preventing its "efficient and natural" development. By contrast, the free world appeared to be at a higher evolutionary stage, "guided by invisible hands" and supposedly developing "without ideological prescription or management." The assumption of "the more natural" developmental stage of capitalist democracies implied that the socialist world, once freed from the transitory encumbrance of ideological chains, would "slowly but surely approximate the free world."[47]

Modernization theory had, then, a strong deterministic streak. Much like their Marxist adversaries, its theorists assumed that the route and actual occurrence of transformation was inevitable. Human society was governed by a trajectory of development leading from tradition to modernity. Consequently, the inevitability of political convergence—the growing democratization of the Soviet system induced by the rationalization of its economic structure—appeared to be tantalizingly close.[48]

The Foundations

While modernization theory provided an ideological basis for the field, the behavioral revolution owed much of its initial notoriety to the financial support of the major philanthropic foundations. These institutions were the gatekeepers of academic development during the formative post–World War II years. During the course of the 1950s and early 1960s, foundations were, arguably, the most influential financial backers of university research outside the natural sciences. Foundation policies favored researchers and institutions who were willing to transcend limiting departmental domains, and accept, instead, the multidisciplinary behavioral paradigm.

The impact of foundations on reform within the social sciences was by no means a novel phenomenon of the Cold War period. According to historian Franz Samelson, the first major foray of foundations into this niche of the academic world was the work of Beardsley Ruml, the director of the Laura Spelman Rockefeller Memorial Foundation (LSRM). Dissatisfied by the funneling of money into charitable causes that did little to provide long-term solutions for the country's major ailments, Ruml's LSRM invested in the creation and support of an integrated social science for "the production of a body of fact and principle that will be utilized in the solutions of social problems."[49] LSRM, which in 1929 became the Rockefeller Foundation's social sciences division, fostered "multi-disciplinary knowledge concerning the forces that affect the behavior of individuals and societies." For these purposes the foundation underwrote the creation of the Social Sciences Research Council (SSRC). The major objective of the SSRC during its early formative years was the implementation of the foundation's grandiose plans by means of awards to individual researchers and block grants to enterprising universities. Between

1922 and 1929, the LSRM and the Rockefeller-funded SSRC dispensed over $41 million to American social sciences. Most of LSRM funds were directed toward the University of Chicago, one of the legendary birthplaces of the behavioral sciences and the most interdisciplinary of American universities in the interwar years.[50]

In the immediate aftermath of World War II, the large philanthropic foundations once again offered enticing grants for the restructuring of the social sciences in general and interdisciplinary scientific inquiry in particular. As had been the case in the 1920s, the ultimate aim of postwar foundation policy was to advance mild reform and methods for containing disorder and conflict, while encouraging scientific direction of orderly, controlled progress. "Foundation efforts to advance the social and behavioral sciences," Roger Geiger has observed, "not only played a role in the internal development of research universities but also constituted an important episode in the evolution" of new forms of academic inquiry such as the behavioral sciences.[51]

Numerous critical historians have argued that narrow political interests undergirded foundation support and that the major foundations deliberately removed all controversial issues, no matter how acute, from the agenda of social research. Following World War II, foundations rarely supported organizations or research that implied a significant critique of the American social, economic, or political reality. Critics describe the endorsement of political neutrality and the scientification of human issues as a subterfuge for accepting the status quo.[52] New modes of foundation-backed inquiry, such as the behavioral sciences, avoided troubling questions about the motives of power wielders and the endemic social malaise of American society, and were, in essence, an intellectual endorsement of a conservative social theory.[53] Foundations, according to sociologist Alvin Gouldner, supported an academic culture committed to "making things work, despite wars, inequalities, scarcity, and degrading work, rather than finding a way out."[54] By avoiding any significant challenging of existing social and political arrangements in the United States, foundations and their academic collaborators bestowed a scientific blessing on the status quo.

Not all agree with this damning criticism of foundations. Historically, Dorothy Ross has argued, the foundation-backed scientification of social issues sought, in part, to encourage detachment from political pressures rather than dependency.[55] Sociologist Martin Bulmer claims that innuendoes of complicity and cynic support of the status quo rest on an unsubstantiated politically motivated conspiracy thesis.[56] Even the usually critical Franz Samelson has noted that, whatever their shortcomings, foundations were not "power-hungry conspirators setting out to produce 1984."

Partisans and critics do, however, agree that the most enduring achievement of foundation support was its encouragement of interdisciplinary, team-sponsored, empirical research; projects in theory or the philosophy of science were invariably denied funding. Foundation incentives for positivistic interdisciplinary work were of particular advantage for the burgeoning behavioral sciences with their prudent aura of politically inoffensive objectivity and interdisciplinary relevance.

The Ford Foundation was the most active of a unifying behavioralist creed in the post–World War II academic world. Ford's most conspicuous contribution was the establishment of a generously funded behavioral sciences division in 1951, an ambitious effort to foster and fund the reform of a fragmented social inquiry in American academia. Ford's academic architects dismissed the existing arrangements within the social sciences as counterproductive and unscientific. They criticized, in particular, the social sciences' splintering into isolated departments, overspecialization, the lack of cooperation between discrete fields, and a serious lack of integration between theory and applied science. The foundation's privileging of the behavioral sciences signified the quest for a comprehensive system of social thought claiming to fit every phenomenon, from international relations to social welfare. In accordance with contemporary definitions of the field, the behavioral sciences closed the door to no one. Psychology, sociology, and anthropology served as the anchors of the behavioral sciences division. However, the program was open to experimentation with all other academic specialties. During the course of its seven-year life span the division dispensed $43 million; 37 percent of its funds were designated for the training of a new generation of behavioralists, the bearers of a new interdisciplinary creed.[57]

No less important than the establishment of the behavioral sciences division was its termination—accompanied by the laconic statement that a mere seven years after its inauguration its "mission was concluded." At the most fundamental level, closure signified the limitations of foundation influence on the academic subculture. Termination acknowledged implicitly the ultimate inability to demolish the entrenched departmental structure of the social sciences. The weight of tradition and power structures inherent in departmental divisions stubbornly held ground. In other words, the dismantling of the behavioral sciences division, with its inherent promise of sweeping change, may be construed as a declaration of defeat.[58]

The official closing of the division was, as well, partly the result of political pressures. Foundation support for social knowledge in general and the behavioral sciences in particular resulted in numerous unfavorable congressional hearings during the course of the 1950s. In 1952, a House committee investigated foundation support for projects that tended "to weaken or discredit the capitalistic system in the United States and to favor Marxist socialism." In 1954, another House committee chaired by powerful congressman Carrol Reece of Tennessee denounced in no uncertain terms the "socialism" of the social sciences and the "scientism"—the lack of commitment to values—of the behavioral sciences.[59] This swipe at behavioralism, in particular, was obviously aimed at its major champion, the Ford Foundation.

Somewhat paradoxically, the division's closure may also be construed as an elaborate gesture of success rather than an acknowledgment of failure or capitulation to political pressures. All major foundations in the United States were committed to a policy of aiding "activities only during their initial stages, rather than to continue to support established projects."[60] Symbolically, termination reasserted the foundation's dedication to free enterprise in academia and its commitment to the production of knowledge without abiding entanglements. The short life span of the division implied that the Ford Foundation's massive financial support of the behavioral sciences had been a temporary departure from its commitment to intellectual freedom. Involvement in the structure of the academic enterprise was a temporary strategic intervention to aid an incipient process. Once that project had been launched successfully, there appeared to be no need to maintain a permanent life-support system, such as a separate division for the behavioral sciences. Termination signified the concept's inner strength and autonomy. Thus, the dismantling of the division may be interpreted as a visible gesture of support for the cause, as well as a reiteration of the foundation's faith in academic laissez-faire.

Direct financial support for the behavioral sciences was, of course, picked up elsewhere. Government agencies, in particular those with military connections, were eager for the type of multidisciplinary attempts to decipher complexity that was inherent in the behavioralist creed. Instead of the foundations, the government provided funding for both university-associated and independent research centers.

The most eager clients and most generous benefactors of behavioral sciences research were the various branches of the military and the intelligence community. Having been exposed to the services of behaviorally inclined academic experts during World War II, military clients not only funded a wide range of academic projects; they created, as well, their own behavioral sciences communities.

As subsequent pages demonstrate, the research agenda and academic paradigms that permeated government-behavioral sciences projects were devised and controlled by a small group of important academic figures who had established their reputations during the course of World War II and through their association with the philanthropic foundations in the postwar years. During the course of the Cold War, this cohesive subculture of academic experts demonstrated both intellectual prowess and great political skills. Through a series of interlocking committees and advisory roles, this elite group of academics controlled much of the available funding for research. Predictably, projects that advanced their cause received generous funding, thereby assuring the articulation of a singular, behavioral paradigm for government-ordained research.

This unrelenting control of the academic discourse was neither a conspiracy nor the result of a willful suppression of rivals. It was, in part, a process of mundane social networking. The vast majority of these powerful persons had been associated with the University of Chicago as teachers or graduate students during the 1920s. There, they had formed mutually beneficial ties that would serve them well during their illustrious careers as academic warriors.

Their solutions for resolving the political predicaments of government and military clients were not, however, the result of sequestered brainstorming among the members of this exclusive academic club. Behavioral scientists translated a variety of widely held contemporary values into the language of science. They were guided by a defining ambition to transform American society and control global social trends. While ostensibly focusing on the waging of war and the deciphering of foreign societies, their work reflected and influenced contemporary domestic debates and dilemmas. The reasons for, and the consequences of, a pervasive reluctance to ascribe to others any social or cultural trait that behavioralists could not identify within American society is the subject of the following pages.

The Culture of Think Tanks

The Cold War and Free Enterprise

Throughout his career as university professor and think tank consultant, Thomas Schelling dabbled in numerous, eclectic topics that were far removed from his main field of expertise. Ostensibly a strategic analyst, Schelling published studies on racial segregation, organized crime, and other distinctly domestic issues.[1] This type of checkered research agenda vindicated a new intellectual format in which universities no longer monopolized the production of knowledge. In the burgeoning world of post–World War II academia, scholars frequently wandered between the traditional groves of academe and military-funded civilian research corporations. Such loose arrangements allowed curious scholars to glide between ostensibly unconnected subject matters without fear of territorial poaching.

Situated on private campuses or nominally associated with prestigious universities, the think tanks—officially known as Federal Contract Research Centers (FCRCs)—were sites of feverish and imaginative academic activity. Unlike the university, supposedly suffering from intellectual gridlock and the detached mentality of the ivory tower, the FCRCs appeared to be creative, uninhibited meeting points between government clients and innovative scholars for solving the nation's problems.

Cold War think tanks attracted academia's renaissance men and even the occasional woman. Lavish funding and an intellectual terrain ostensibly unblemished by outmoded divisions of knowledge promoted creative interdisciplinary and intellectually unrestricted investigations. The ramblings of scholars like Schelling and many others were, according to partisans, close to impossible so long as universities monopolized the production of knowledge. University of Chicago sociologist and sometimes think tank consultant Morris Janowitz observed that "nothing short of spectacular revolutionary development" would have enabled the tradition-bound university to have reached a similar intellectual plateau.[2] Universities, he explained, used to value disciplinary borderlines over problem-solving. Politics and tradition had stifled creativity within the traditional academic setting. Now that think tanks offered competition, even the most ossified of universities allowed great leeway for and among its faculty.

This praise notwithstanding, Schelling's accomplishments were as much a sign of the limits of the new intellectual freedom as of its opportunities. The subject matter of Schelling's research was remarkably broad; its content was not. Whether analyzing the strategies of America's global adversaries, domestic economic developments, or social trends at home and abroad, Schelling identified monopoly—economic, political, or ideological—as the source of all evil. In many different forms, he asserted that genuine social justice resulted from pluralism and a minimalist central authority. The paragon of laissez-faire was equally applicable in economics, diplomatic maneuvering, and the back streets of San Francisco's tenderloin district.

Schelling's study of organized crime serves as a case in point. In accordance with contemporary functionalist theory, he accepted that the peddlers of illicit services—drugs, prostitution, gambling—were suppliers of significant, albeit illegitimate services. Trade in illegal substances or services could not be suppressed as long as the market demanded these products. However, contrary to what most analysts of America's underworld economy held, Schelling claimed that organized crime was not a natural part of this marketplace of illicit services. Organized crime, he argued, was not a supplier of services, but a predatory body, imposing extortionatory protection on individual, private merchants of illicit goods. As opposed to ordinary and "far more individualistic" criminals, organized crime infringed upon the activities of individual merchants of criminal merchandise by imposing arbitrary taxation. Organized crime merely monopolized all attempts to market illicit goods, raising its price and in the process corrupting politicians and law enforcement agents. The only way to break the stranglehold of organized crime, he argued, was to challenge its monopoly and enforce competition in the marketplace of illicit goods. The legalization of the illicit marketplace, he stated, would undermine organized crime by destroying the power to cartel. "The consumers will prefer to see the activities become more freely competitive, whether by being released from illegality, or released from the grip of organized crime. So will those who dislike corruption, especially when it is centralized and regularized by large monopoly organizations that can build corruption directly into our institutions, rather than leave it to gnaw away at the edges."[3]

Schelling's studies of segregation offered a similar message. He argued that residential segregation would solve itself, so long as no monolithic power, be it government or any other powerful political force, intervened.[4] Hence, whether analyzing global power struggles, the rise of crime, or racial tensions in American society, Schelling lauded the power of individualism, the advantages of open markets, and the respect of property rights—individual or national—as the tools for controlling all forms of institutions that might otherwise contribute to an imbalance of power—political, social, or military.

Schelling's writings, thematically eclectic but ideologically monotonous, epitomized the successful formula of Rand and its clones. The typical FCRC was, indeed, a haven for unencumbered intellectual curiosity, particularly in the politically sensitive fields of social and behavioral sciences. The underlying assumption behind this freedom to roam far beyond one's initial field of expertise was that identical behavioral codes guided the micro and the macro, the social and the political organism. Hence, solutions discovered in a domestic study of social development theoretically applied to grand global struggles as well. Studies of crime could conceivably enlighten military strategists.

Such intellectual inquisitiveness, was, however, restricted by an unquestioning acceptance of orthodox political values, in particular, the cant of free enterprise. Although the think tank milieu allowed its researchers to challenge the policies of their mostly military clients, the system was never independent enough, or intellectually bold enough, to question the underlying political premises of American society and government. Philip Green, a behavioral scientist who practiced his trade outside the pale of government-funded think tanks, observed that in addition to an unwavering endorsement of laissez-faire, the FCRC intellectuals accepted unquestioningly "that the Soviets posed a genuine threat to Western Europe; that in various corners of the world an American military presence is necessary to halt Communist expansionism; that, in sum, a struggle for the world has been under way since the end of World War II."[5] Such axiomatic assumptions absolved both scholars and politicians from examining or revising the logic of the national security state.

As institutions, the military-funded independent research centers endorsed the same limited notion of pluralism. According to Bruce L. Smith, the author of the first comprehensive scholarly monograph on Rand, the United States was awarded a high return on this academic adaptation of the free enterprise system. "The pluralism of the advisory system, in which Rand is only one institution among many with access to persons in authority, helps assure that no one group will monopolize the attention of policy makers."[6] Yet, as critics of the system pointed out, this endorsement of pluralism was riddled with contradictions. The FCRCs in general and Rand in particular were not equal competitors for the minds of policy makers. By virtue of generous funding, close ties to the various military services, and their acceptance of fundamental axiomatic political and ideological assumptions, a small number of think tanks occupied a privileged position. "To speak of a meaningful pluralism in this connection," critic Philip Green noted, "we would have to believe, first, that independent research groups with no built-in bias toward the military have as an effective an access" as do the military-funded think tanks, or that "the agencies they have access to...are themselves nearly as influential and well-financed as the Air Force" and other privledged branches of the military.[7] The intellectual accomplishments of think tanks—and they were many—were not a sign of pluralism in action; in actual fact they were indicators of the authority of monolithic ideological convictions.

The Quest for a Behavioral Manhattan Project

In order to understand government expectations of its mobilized academics as individuals and the think tanks as institutions, we turn our attention to one of the most fascinating documents of the early stages of the Cold War. On January 15, 1951, the Joint Chiefs of Staff (JCS) issued their periodic "Review of the Current World Situation." This particular review predictably placed the recent outbreak of hostilities in Korea within a global context of predatory Soviet ambitions.[8] The manner of presentation was, however, a marked departure from standard military discourse. Military documents are usually studies in detachment. The most horrific events and cataclysmic expectations are described in dry, clinical terms; the professional, after all, cannot afford to be swept away by emotions. The JCS review of January 1951 had none of these qualities. It was a highly emotional survey of events written by a group of aging World War II veterans, attempting to explain away their momentary blindness by resorting to imagery bordering on the fantastic.

In admitting the anachronism of conventional analyses of the Korean crisis and other global flareups of the early Cold War period, the JCS document offered an apocalyptic vision. The survey described the United States as facing a crisis of religious proportions—a clash of civilizations—the only solution being the waging of a "crusade." In the impending war between "world communism" and the United States, American forces stood alone; the nation lacked reliable allies in all global regions. Consequently, the JCS argued, the

United States would have to retreat to a defense of the Western Hemisphere, described somewhat poetically as the "final citadel."[9]

Perhaps taken aback by the use of such loaded cultural terms in a military document an anonymous hand added an apologetic footnote, explaining that " 'Crusade' is used in the technical sense of a vigorous and aggressive movement for the advancement of an idea and a cause." Nevertheless, the document left no doubt that, according to the JCS, the challenge facing the United States was sui generis, a clash of civilizations rather than a conventional struggle for territory and hegemony between two warring powers.

The JCS survey argued that the current crisis could not be understood by referring to the recent Nazi threat or any other past military challenge, mostly because the Cold War lacked familiar spatial dimensions.[10] In conventional struggles one could locate enemy strongholds and concentrate military attacks according to recognizable geographic parameters. The JCS document explained in great detail that the current enemy could not be pinpointed spatially. Unlike previous adversaries, this enemy occupied a threatening, incoherent domain, bound by neither geophysical boundaries nor political borders. The enemy was sometimes Russian, occasionally Asian, and sometimes an invisible fifth column poised to attack even within the United States. "The basic menace of the United States and its allies from within is as great as the menace from without." Experience promised little guidance for confronting the enemy, as the dimensions of this war were unpredictable; the enemy was everywhere.

In order to address the crisis, the JCS proposed a wistful solution. Six of their seven recommendations for confronting the communist threat focused on "intangible resources" rather than on the buildup of conventional or nuclear military might. The JCS envisioned waging war by means of futuristic psychological barrages rather than bullets. For these purposes the JCS recommended the production of an "intangible" weapons system as awesome and as effective as the harnessing of the atom. Their January 1951 review envisioned national action to "develop and rapidly implement a large-scale program of psychological warfare, including special operations, comparable in scope to the Manhattan District Project of World War II."

The very use of the Manhattan Project analogy implied large investment in research, and of course priceless prestige for its sponsors and participants. Moreover, evoking the atomic analogy for projects other than those associated with the physical sciences opened the door for social and behavioral scientists who, up to this point, were denied access to the inner sanctum of the military-intellectual complex.[11] The JCS document proposed, in effect, an open checkbook for the incipient behavioral sciences.

This generous invitation confronted, however, a series of major obstacles. Institutional reactions to the call for a behavioral Manhattan Project were hampered by logistical problems, political suspicions, and a modest, albeit unexpected display of intellectual integrity. To begin with, designs for a behavioral equivalent of the Manhattan Project were beset by human scarcity. The various disciplines of the social sciences, the building blocks of a unified behavioral sciences, were severely understaffed. A 1952 government report explained that the modest numbers of practicing social scientists foreclosed all grandiose ideas for a government-behavioral nexus. According to government figures, there were 34,000 members of social sciences professional societies as compared to 175,000 in the natural and biological sciences; the United States had only 7,500 registered trained psychologists as opposed to 70,000 chemists.[12] Moreover, few practicing sociologists, political scientists, or psychologists could claim the multidisciplinary expertise demanded by this new job definition; most were inexperienced graduate students.

Mobilization for the behavioral Manhattan Project was beset, as well, by a lack of coordination among government agencies. Government sources listed a dozen separate federal agencies supporting "social science research of potential value to the Cold War" and at least a dozen more projects with partial bearing on the topic. Not only was there no coordination among these agencies. "Overlapping and changing designation of . . . government agencies," as well as obsessive secrecy born out of intragovernmental rivalries, had caused administrative havoc. The federal government had no mechanism for discovering redundancy, and was quite unable to determine where and what research projects were being undertaken within the various spheres of government.

Government efforts to address problems through the establishment of a coordinating agency, the Psychological Strategy Board (PSB), were spectacularly ineffective. Established by executive order in April 1951, the PSB had no operative powers of its own. Its primary mission was coordination and the development of "over-all national psychological objectives, policies and programs" for implementation by other agencies.[13]

Lacking actual executive powers, the PSB proved to be an anemic supervisor for the ambitious task of defining and coordinating "psychological strategies." Initial efforts at coordinating rival bodies were deceivingly promising. The PSB's first director, Gordon Gray, was a personal friend of President Truman. Threatening executive intervention, he managed to cajole the various board members to at least feign cooperation.[14] Gray, however, resigned after a brief six-month tenure, and was followed by a parade of pale successors who matched neither his political acumen nor his managerial skills. Hence, in the long run, the PSB achieved very few tangible results. Bitter rivalries among the Central Intelligence Agency (CIA), the Department of State, and the various branches of the military were more powerful than formalistic demands for coordination.

The most conspicuous product of the PSB was a series of windy strategy papers produced by Edward Lilly, the chief of the PSB's most active division, the Office of Plans and Policy.[15] Lilly, a professor of history and the most industrious member of this office, was after bigger fish than mere coordination among government agencies. Swept away by the tides of McCarthyism, Lilly embarked on a crusade of his own, claiming, among other things, the existence of a communist plot to remove from stores and libraries all copies of anticommunist books.[16]

Dissatisfaction with the PSB's rambling activities led swiftly to its waning prestige. As part of its reorganization of the executive branch, the Eisenhower administration disbanded the PSB in 1954, and established, instead, the Operations Coordinating Board (OCB), a body with somewhat greater authority and access to the president.[17] However, neither the PSB nor the OCB ever achieved any significant coordination of the multiple strands of government social and behavioral inquiry.

Such administrative mishaps compounded the political handicaps of the behavioral and social sciences. As early as July 3, 1946, the U.S. Senate voted overwhelmingly to exclude all variations of the social sciences from the proposed National Science Foundation, the federal conduit for maintaining the country's scientific preeminence. Fearing political repercussions from government funding of what Republican senator Thomas C. Hart called "all the racial questions" as well as "perhaps religion, and various kinds of ideology," the government preferred the grooming and funding of the ostensibly politically safe natural and physical sciences. The invention of the behavioral sciences did little to improve the fortunes of its proponents in Congress. An institutional arrangement by which the behavioral and/or social sciences would become a legitimate and acknowledged element of the "scientific estate" appeared impossible.[18]

These administrative and political obstacles were heightened by a remarkable reluctance among important members of the behavioral sciences movement to accept the Manhattan analogy as a working hypothesis. An early, and very typical illustration of such hesitancy occurred during the course of Project Troy, the first major effort to define the technological, sociological, and intellectual parameters of a strategic psychological superweapon. Project Troy was an ambitious, multidisciplinary project aimed at utilizing the services of science in waging a fully coordinated electronic propaganda campaign against the Soviet Union and its satellites. Inaugurated in 1950, Troy was funded by the Department of State and jointly administered by MIT and Harvard. This project was the first major postwar experiment of what historian Allan Needell has called "the extensive network of government associations with academic and industrial scientists and engineers that the U.S. military had carefully nurtured during and after World War II."[19]

In addition to the primary mission of providing technical solutions for transmitting information and preventing the jamming of electronic communications, the Troy mandate included a study of information theory and other sociopsychological strategies for "perforating the iron curtain." Given this complex mandate, Troy became the first major postwar academic-military project to include a large group of university-based behavioral scientists among its members. The project brought together many of the movers and shakers of the behavioral sciences, most of whom were based in Cambridge, Massachusetts. Harvard participants included psychologist Jerome Bruner and his colleague, anthropologist Clyde Kluckhohn. MIT participants included, among others, psychologist Alex Bavelas and economist Max Millikan. Hans Speier, the director of Rand's social science division, was also among the illustrious and fortunate researchers involved in Troy.

In many ways, Project Troy was the fulfillment of the behavioralist mission. A fortunate group of sociologists, anthropologists, and social psychologists worked together with physicists and engineers in producing a multidisciplinary document aimed at defining the meaning and significance of Cold War strategic propaganda. The final report went beyond the initial mission of providing technical and intellectual solutions for improving the performance of the Voice of America broadcasts. Troy produced, as well, psychological and sociological assessments of alternative means of electronic communication, such as the use of balloons for the showering of enemy countries with propaganda leaflets.

As for the impact of propaganda, Troy's behavioral scientists painstakingly pointed out the fundamental differences between the psychological superweapon and the atomic analogy. Strategic weaponry for hearts and minds did not entail swift and total destruction, but, instead, the gradual erosion of a vulnerable epicenter. As opposed to an actual bomb, the target audience of psychological weaponry could ignore the weapon. A prerequisite from winning the battle for hearts and minds was to gain attention and minimize antagonistic messages that might turn the audience off. Instead of saturating the airwaves with broad "contempt for communism," the report urged that "our line should rather be that 'Stalinism has betrayed certain ideals of Marxism.'" Thus, the report warned against alienating listeners by praising the materialistic success of the West, or by encouraging "hopeless acts of rebellion" by various separatist movements within the Soviet Union.[20]

In the final analysis, the Troy report concluded that the development of any form of psychological weapon was still at the theoretical stage. The complexity of producing messages suited for a wide variety of target audiences demanded further research and greater coordination among experts. In fact, these academic advisors questioned the fundamental premise of a strategic psychological weapon. The behavioral experts involved in the project stated that a psychological superweapon, one that could apply to all countries and all segments of the enemy population, conflicted with empirical data. These experts accepted, more or less, the presence of a fanatical, single-minded, communist threat confronting the United States. However, they acknowledged important political nuances. The Troy report stated that "Communism in China and Southeast Asia does not constitute a simple extension of Soviet power. Mao in China and Ho in Vietnam are not automatic tools of the Kremlin, but men with aspirations for their own countries who have embraced Communist doctrines as a formula for achieving progress in their own countries."[21] Each target, therefore, required a different strategy. Unlike a typical military weapons system, no one psychological strategy could apply to all enemies and annihilate all adversaries in one bold sweep.

Diminishing hopes of achieving the behavioral equivalent of an atomic bomb increased interest in the development of tactical psychological weaponry, tuned and honed to well-defined cultural and political targets, and more in line with the routine of conventional, limited warfare in the Cold War era. Moreover, the growing realization that strategic psychological weaponry was not in the pipeline weakened demands for a grand coordinator. Despite the efforts of national coordinating agencies, such as the PSB and the OCB, the various branches of the military initiated their own programs. Even the military's own initiative to coordinate behavioral and social sciences research achieved little. In the late 1940s, the secretary of defense sought scientific coordination, in general, by establishing the Defense Research and Development Board. The board's arm for coordination in the social and behavioral sciences, the Committee on Human Resources, proved unable to break through aggressive interservice rivalries. The nature of the defense establishment, as a loose coalition of the military services rather than a unified establishment, precluded any meaningful cooperation.[22]

Dissatisfied with political snarls, multiagency gridlock, and interservice sniping, the various service branches cultivated their own research projects in the behavioral sciences. Beginning in the final phases of World War II, and with little fanfare, all of the military services had initiated ambitious affiliations with a variety of sociologists, social psychologists, and political scientists. The sheer number of projects contracted out by the government in the early 1950s and the mushrooming of research institutes feeding off Cold War initiatives defies precise documentation. A significant portion of the research was covert. In addition, the distinction between classic academic research and government contracts was fuzzy at best. Behavioral research related to the Cold War was spread out among twenty different government agencies and organizations. At times it appeared that the sole purpose of most of these projects was to keep prestigious academic personalities on a retainer basis for some future, undefined emergency.

The Rand Archetype

Most military investigations in the behavioral sciences in general and psychological warfare in particular were carried out in civilian think tanks funded by the various service branches. The air force, the youngest and most aggressive of the services, led the way, funding an array of research institutes engaged in both theoretical and applied research in psychology, sociology, political sciences, and communication theory. As the self-claimed patron of academic inquiry, the air force opened its doors to all academic branches claiming scientific ambitions. The most conspicuous of these efforts was the establishment of a social science division at the prestigious Rand Corporation, the major think tank associated with the air force.

The Santa Monica–based Rand Corporation, where the best and the brightest plotted doomsday scenarios of nuclear warfare, was also home to a comparatively reclusive group of behavioralists who were members of Rand's social science division. The marginality of social and behavioral sciences at Rand was perhaps best illustrated by its geographical location. During its early years the division worked out of a distant Washington office. This territorial and institutional marginality was finally abolished in 1956, when the division moved to Santa Monica. However, as a disciplinary field, the division never achieved the notoriety of physics, mathematics, or economics.[23]

Research at Rand was governed by a scientific pecking order. The most important projects dealt with weapons development and strategic planning. By default, these were propositions and plans associated with nuclear warfare. Most nuclear-related strategic planning took place within Rand's prestigious physics and economics divisions. The privileged position of the physics division was a direct outgrowth of the field's World War II triumphs and the subsequent development of the hydrogen bomb. Only trained physicists had the know-how to plot the destructive capabilities of nuclear weapons. The shift from the physics division's studies of technical capabilities to investigations of strategic and military implications was inevitable. "Given the central role that bombing played in American military strategy," historian Stephen Waring notes, "there was little difference between studies to improve the tactics of strategic bombing and research to improve the strategy itself."[24]

The extraordinary status of the economics division was derived, in part, from the successful experiences of World War II. Economic analysis had played a major role in World War II, dealing in matters of crucial logistical importance, from transportation scheduling to the planning of weaponry and civilian production. However, historian Michael Bernstein notes, its privileged position in the ensuing Cold War was related above all to the development of game theory, the mathematical simulation of confrontational decision dilemmas. The attraction of game theory, Bernstein argues, lay in its focus on the crucial area of conflict and decision making. The coup of Rand economists was their ability to market this useful tool for analyzing competitive economic behavior as an indispensable item for strategic problems and national defense planning.[25]

Rand's air force clients demonstrated an unqualified willingness to develop this line of mathematical inquiry, particularly because it introduced a semblance of order and an illusion of predictability into a confusing state of affairs. Reducing the enemy to a ruthless, expansionist, predictable calculator, rather than a complex adversary, had a distinctly calming effect on planners. The air force, Rand's major sponsor and the leader among the services in strategic nuclear warfare, was the most avid consumer of game theory, designating Rand as its crucial center for research and development of this field.

The attraction of mathematical rigor was precisely the reason for the uncertain status of the social science division, where Rand's sociologists, psychologists, and political scientists were grouped together. Inaugurated in 1948 at about the same time as the economics division, the social science division found itself on the defensive from the very beginning. Hans Speier, the division's founding director, was either ignored or dismissed as "that Prussian officer." Colleagues from physics and economics described Rand's experts in psychology, sociology, and political sciences as "essayists," the producers of journalistic assessments that one could find in the New York Times.[26] In their eyes, the behavioral and social sciences, despite their ostensible acceptance of statistical methodology, were still anchored in anachronistic, impressionistic strategies.

Critics of Rand's social science division lashed out, in particular, at the division's simulation games, a species of game theory for the mathematically challenged. As far as Rand's mathematicians, economists, and physicists were concerned, these games, based on role-playing rather than mathematics, lacked analytical rigor and were unscientific, and, as such, were useless policy tools. The strategy of communication in the division's simulations was vernacular language, supposedly laden with ambiguity and lack of clarity. By contrast, game theory imparted its results in the rigorous, standardized, and universal multidisciplinary language of mathematics. Personal judgment, however seasoned, was deemed unscientific, thereby banishing the social science division from Rand's prestigious thermonuclear guild.[27]

Behavioral scientists were further marginalized by their attitude toward war. According to the reigning "realism" among most of Rand's strategic planners, war was a natural, recurrent, inevitability; violence, whether domestic or international, was an unavoidable element of human nature, controlled only by the fear of retaliation or coercive authority. War was approached as a social or institutional modification of innate, instinctive conflict behavior, part of human nature.

The epistemological community of behavioral scientists in general and the behavioral scientists at Rand's social science division in particular disagreed. Whether war resulted from individual or collective immaturity, anxieties, neuroses, maladjustments, or a combination of such factors was a matter of contention.[28] However, behavioralists agreed that war was a pathological form of behavior and should be approached in the manner that a physician approaches a disease. Preventive intervention or the treatment of the ailment appeared preferable to accepting its festering existence.

During the early stages of the Cold War, behavioralist analysis of international conflict was dominated by psychoanalytical concepts. At Rand in particular and among behavioral scientists in general war was attributed to emotional maladjustment. Critics derided and dismissed such analysis as both misinformed and disguised pacifism—a contemporary euphemism for uncertain political loyalties within academia.[29] In reality, behavioralists were anything but pacifists. Behavioralists argued that pacifism and aggressive, warlike behavior were equally destructive and deviant forms of behavior. "Self-immolating impulses"—pacifism—and "aggressive impulses"—warmongering—were two sides of the same coin, the sources of which lay in the unconscious. Both instincts were the result of "repression" and destructive "intra-psychic conflicts."[30]

Such psychological ruminations did not improve the fortunes of behavioral and social scientists. Quite the contrary. The social science division aroused animosity when, every now and again, its esoteric research strategies attracted unwanted, negative public attention. A case in point was Paul Kecskemeti's notorious study, *Strategic Surrender*.[31] Published commercially in 1958, this investigation of surrender in wars past and future unleashed a flurry of negative press reports, culminating in a congressional resolution prohibiting public funding of "defeatist" projects such as "when and how, and in what circumstances" should the United States surrender to its enemy.[32] It was work such as the Kescksmeti study that attracted undue and damaging legislative attention. Powerful forces in Congress periodically condemned Rand and its funders for undermining American values by "empiricism," the pseudoscientific evaluation of all aspects of American life, both sacred and profane. Congressional critics argued that empiricism, as practiced by Rand and supported by foundations, dismissed "moral precepts, principles, and established or accepted norms of behavior." They condemned the much-acclaimed empiricism of behavioralism as subjective, politically biased, and fundamentally un-American.[33]

Congressional critics did not find similar faults with the published work of Rand's physics division, such as Herman Kahn's doomsday studies of survivability rate in the event of nuclear warfare.[34] Criticism was rare because the studies of the physics division always assumed that the United States would emerge as victor, even when faced by attrition rates of tens of millions of casualties.

Thus ostracized for suspicious political loyalties, questionable intellectual credentials, and minimal political savvy, Rand's behavioral scientists were excluded from the inner circle of nuclear strategy during the early stages of the Cold War. By default, the members of the social science division focused on the supposedly secondary issues of conventional warfare. Perhaps because of its inferior status within Rand, the social science division never abandoned the futuristic search for the ultimate psychological weapon. Hans Speier, the director of Rand's social science division, described the task of his division as the development of psychological weaponry "to realize the aim of war—which is victory—without acts of physical violence, or with less expenditure of physical violence that would otherwise be necessary."[35] Once the Korean War erupted, these theories had a distinctly attractive ring.

The Other Think Tanks

In addition to Rand, the well-funded and ambitious air force developed other wings for behavioral research. Its most visible efforts occurred under the auspices of the Air University, Maxwell Base, Alabama. This think tank, known as the Human Resources Research Institute (HRRI), was the most active of three in-service behavioral science research centers run by the air force.[36] HRRI proposed projects quite similar in nature to the Rand inquiries in the behavioral sciences. Rand relied primarily on its own staff for its research. HRRI, by contrast, worked mostly on a contractual basis with prestigious academic figures from the country's major universities.

HRRI enjoyed a short, yet quite spectacular life span. Established in 1949 as the air force's main center for research in the behavioral sciences, HRRI was particularly active during the Korean War. Together with other minor air force research centers, HRRI was the senior participant in the air force's Far East Research Group, aimed at studying a wide range of behavioral issues, from the behavior of POWs to analysis of enemy negotiation tactics. The most ambitious and most fateful of HRRI's research projects was the analysis of the Soviet social system, prepared under contract by Harvard University's Russian Research Center.[37] According to Raymond Bowers, a University of Arizona sociologist and former director of HRRI, the final report of this investigation "was required reading at the Command and Staff and War Colleges of the Armed Services for a number of years," and its interview protocols set the standard for much of the intelligence community throughout the Cold War.[38] However, congressional attacks on the Harvard center in general and military-ordained behavioral sciences research in particular led to the dismantling of HRRI in 1954.[39]

The navy, the air force's closest rival in the search for the development of nuclear weaponry, developed a much more circumspect attitude toward the behavioral sciences. Despite auspicious beginnings in the final phases of World War II, the navy chose not to establish an independent civilian research institute for Cold War behavioral sciences. Such research was confined to the Office of Naval Research (ONR).

Founded in 1946, the ONR spent over $2 million annually on behavioral research during the first years of its existence. These projects were performed mostly by offering contracts to outside researchers. Behavioral research at the ONR was tightly controlled by a supervisory staff of naval officers and, as of 1950, was all but abolished. All key positions within the ONR were manned by career officers whose interest in anything beyond weapons development was peripheral. The navy had established the ONR primarily to further its main objective of building a nuclear fleet, as well as winning the interservice race for future technologies of warfare. In the eyes of the ONR, research in the behavioral sciences—other than the specific issues of logistics, human relations, and enhancing the performance of battle crews—would invite adverse political scrutiny. Moreover, with the outbreak of the Korean War, navy brass increased its pressure for "relevance"—by which they meant research directly related to weapons systems. The ONR's officers were unwilling to risk losing funding for advanced weapons projects by maintaining research in fields of research with direct political implications.[40]

During the early 1960s the navy renewed its behavioral research, albeit very modestly, by establishing Project Michelson, a research initiative dedicated to inquiry into deterrence theory, the signaling to an enemy of a commitment to defend an ally. In Cold War terms, deterrence theory meant the use of credible nuclear threats as a means of containing the enemy; it is this nuclear component that renewed navy interest in behavioral research.[41] Here, too, the navy chose to contract out research to a small group of renowned behavioral scientists rather than set up a think tank of its own. Studies included "Comparison of Soviet-American values," contracted out to Robert Angell of the University of Michigan, and Stanford University's Wilbur Schramm's inquiry into "Public Opinions as a Limiting Factor in Deterrence."[42]

Not to be outdone by the other services, the army funded Rand-compatible research in the behavioral sciences as well. During the early Cold War years, the army's two most visible institutes were the Human Relations Research Office (HumRRO), affiliated with George Washington University, and the Operations Research Office (ORO), associated with Johns Hopkins University.

Established in 1948 as an independent channel for research free from the salary and seniority limitations of military life, the ORO was a military-funded civilian research center run on a contractual basis by Johns Hopkins University. Despite its nomenclature, the ORO could hardly be classified as a typical operations research unit. This term referred primarily to the mathematical appraisal of data, ranging from the streamlining of routine technical and engineering operations to the development of game theory for strategical analysis.[43] A very small portion of research at ORO dealt with the technical issues of operations research, and no significant work in the area of game theory was ever undertaken by the center. The major function of the ORO was behavioral research. However, the ORO endorsed none of the free-thinking type of investigations that characterized Rand. The role of the behavioral sciences in the ORO was defined and restricted to specific tasks.

Army expectations from ORO emerged during the course of Project Clear, an ambitious investigation of racial integration within the army. Following the outbreak of the Korean War, the army ordered the ORO "to initiate a project to determine how best to utilize Negro personnel within the Army."[44] For these purposes the ORO contracted with the New York-based International Public Opinion Research (IPOR), one of the many private consortiums of university-based behavioral scientists offering their services to government and industry. There is little doubt that both the army and the ORO knew that their civilian contractors were morally committed to racial integration, and that their report would inevitably call for the swift dismantling of all racial barriers. Leo Bogart, the principal IPOR investigator, stated that the researchers "embarked upon their task with no illusions that 'objective facts' existed without reference to 'moral and compassionate' aspects." Bogart recalled that "although the question of the investigators' private opinions on the subject was at no point raised as a prerequisite to employment on the project, . . . they all shared an utter abhorrence of segregation, a sentiment which is universal among qualified social scientists familiar with its origins and consequences."[45]

Bogart's recollections suggest that as far as both the army and the investigators were concerned, the importance of the report lay not in its preordained results, but in its scientific apparatus. A scientific report, reduced in large part to a verifiable statistical analysis, promised to sway at least wavering supporters of integration. As Project Clear suggests, the primary purpose of the ORO in the army's eyes was to provide scientific legitimization for its policies.

Like Project Clear, much of the ORO's research was potentially controversial. And, as was the case with Clear, the army sought to restrict publication and circulation of its politically vulnerable findings. Such restraints were a source of constant friction between the rigid army hierarchy and its civilian researchers. In 1961, clashes over army restrictions on publications led to the severing of ORO ties with Johns Hopkins, the dismissal of ORO director Ellis Johnson, and its reestablishment as a new nonprofit corporation known as the Research Analysis Corporation (RAC).[46]

Following the ORO debacle, most of the army's covert research in the field of conventional warfare was handed over to the newly established Special Operations Research Office (SORO), an organization run under contract by the American University in Washington, D.C. SORO's primary activity was the development of counterinsurgency doctrine. As part of this effort, SORO was responsible for the infamous Project Camelot, an ambitious investigation of sources of instability in Third World nations. Camelot sought the development of formulas for the army for coping with "potential instability" in global trouble spots. When leaked to the press due to the indiscretion of a Camelot associate in Chile, the project aroused furor; critics accused the army of undermining the political regimes of foreign countries, as well as encroaching upon areas that had little to do with military affairs.[47]

After perfunctory apologies for the Camelot debacle, the army disbanded its association with American University, changed the name of SORO to the Center for Research in Social Sciences (CRESS), and continued with greater secrecy and caution the same type of work that it had sought to do in Project Camelot. From 1958 to 1966, CRESS prepared a series of twenty-seven area-handbooks on Third World countries that historian Paul Dickson has described as "guides to the conduct of psychological warfare in nations throughout the world." Writing in 1972, Dickson added that the books were so highly classified that they were unavailable for even congressional scrutiny.[48]

HumRRO, another army-funded independent think tank, focused almost exclusively on projects linked to the behavioral sciences. Established in 1951, HumRRO owed its existence to the grand sociological studies of Samuel Stouffer and associates, published in TAS. Army officials envisioned the center as a continuation of the Stouffer project. Its primary mission was defined as research in "psychotechnology," a term that encompassed "research into training methods, GI motivation and morale, and psychological warfare."[49] In 1960, HumRRO severed its administrative ties with George Washington University, and established itself as a nonprofit corporation in Alexandria, Virginia. Most of HumRRO's early work dealt with the analysis of GI combat performance under the stress of both nuclear and conventional warfare. Following the outbreak of the Korean War, HumRRo shifted its agenda from investigations of American troops to analyses of enemy armies.

Unwilling to delegate all research responsibilities to the various military branches, the Department of Defense established its own prestigious think tank. Founded in 1956, the Institute for Defense Analysis (IDA) was a nonprofit membership corporation supported by some of the leading universities in the country: California Institute of Technology, MIT, Stanford, and Tulane. In subsequent years, IDA expanded its membership to include Columbia University, the University of Michigan, Pennsylvania State University, the University of Chicago, Princeton University, the University of Illinois, and, last but not least, the University of California. In 1968, IDA discontinued its restrictive membership-only policy, and began recruiting members from the academic community at large.

IDA's founding charter suggests that the secretary of defense was seeking a Rand-compatible organization. As such, researchers were given much freedom to engage in almost every conceivable topic. IDA's most prestigious research group was the JASON division, established in 1958 "as an attempt to expose outstanding university scientists—mostly physicists—to critical defense needs." Initially Jason members dealt with the theoretical issues of thermonuclear warfare, much like their colleagues in the physics division at Rand. In accordance with Rand trends as well, these physicists soon turned their attention to "such problems as counterinsurgency, insurrection, and infiltration," providing "fresh insights into problems that are not entirely in the realm of physical science," yet worthy and important enough for the attention of its practitioners.[50]

The Invisible Humanist

Even in the 1950s, prior to rising criticism of the military-intellectual complex, the network of academic institutes and military patrons was beset by doubters from within. The power of military-funded academic centers reminded MIT historian Elting Morison of Harold Lasswell's prophecy of the Garrison State, the transition from an open political culture, based on the principle of compromise, to a tightly controlled, secretive government dominated by experts in coercion and violence. Morison feared, in particular, the inherent clash between secrecy and free intellectual inquiry. Universities were threatened by the "classified idea." Creativity, he explained, demanded "the unobstructed flow of information and ideas" that in many ways contradicted the nature of much government research.[51] Such fears did not, however, persuade Morison to abandon the government fleshpot. Both Morison and his university were heavily involved in government-funded Cold War behavioral research.[52]

Moreover, Morison failed to point out that not all academic fields were accomplices in this secretive government-academic network. Even though many of the topics lent themselves to analysis by experts from the humanities, inquiries into other cultures remained the exclusive domain of social and behavioral scientists. The invisibility of the humanities was all the more curious given the fact that humanists had been active participants in the intellectual enterprises of World War II.[53] Yet, unlike their colleagues in the behavioral and social sciences, humanists and practitioners of the liberal arts were not recruited by Cold War think tanks in significant numbers.

Henry Loomis, a senior official at the PSB, tagged the political climate as the main reason for avoiding association with cultural experts. Writing in 1951, he explained that "by definition, the scientists most informed on Communism are most suspect." Cultural experts, by their very nature, "read subversive literature" and associated "with many Communists, ex-Communists, and fellow travelers" in order to acquire an intimate knowledge of the cultural dimensions of communist society. Such associations turned the cultural expert into a security risk. Loomis explained that "in the case of chemistry, a chemist is expected to completely immerse himself in his subject and his political beliefs have little or no effect on his ability as a chemist." Cultural experts could not expect any such leeway in the politically uncertain 1950s. Fearing such political landmines, government clients preferred the behavioralist—a scientist who, like the chemist or physicist, claimed technical, supposedly value-free, skills.[54]

It would appear, as well, that the humanist discourse was inappropriate for the purposes of the national security state. The contemporary humanist rejected universalist underpinnings, preferring to focus on the uniqueness of space, time, and culture. Behavioralists had no such intellectual reservations. A case in point was the ONR-funded analysis of domestic social arrangements within the United States. In the late 1940s, the ONR contracted with the private, Philadelphia-based Institute for Research in Human Relations for a study on "the identification of and acceptance of leadership in urban communities." Needless to say, this project was not a study of urban leadership in some distant enemy country; the data were drawn from Philadelphia, and their implications were first and foremost American.[55]

Critics of this creeping intrusion of a military service into the ostensibly forbidden domestic domain have noted the obvious dangerous implications of a military service engaged in the collection of data on domestic issues. The navy could, and did, claim that such a study represented nothing of the sort. The navy was concerned with understanding the abstract dynamics of leadership and other behavioral traits that, supposedly, were not culture-specific. Indeed, the underlying assumption of the Philadelphia study was that urban behavior, and the demise of traditional forms of political alliances, were universal sociological phenomena. Philadelphia merely served as a case study to "explore the patterns of local leadership as they exist in a large urban community" irrespective of a specific national or geographical setting. Such breathtaking liberties obviated the services of humanists who were beset by what sociologist Morris Janowitz called their "mystical concern" with cultural uniqueness.

Several technical factors contributed, as well, to the triumph of behavioralism, and conversely, the invisibility of humanists. To begin with, behavioral scientists tended to work in interdisciplinary teams. There was something extremely attractive and very persuasive in teams of advisors who marched among sociology, psychology, and political science and, yet, were able to reach consensual opinions. Such harmony had never characterized the workings of humanists, who were unaccustomed to teamwork and intellectual conviviality. In contrast to humanists, behavioralists dismissed boundaries as vestiges of Victorianism. Humanists respected hierarchies and supported intellectual borders. Unlike behavioralists, who considered divisions and hierarchies detrimental to the scientific enterprise, humanists, for both methodological and social reasons, staked out territory and defended the separation of powers within academia. Moreover, the humanities prized the past and placed a premium on experience. Such concepts had no place in the military-academic complex. The civilian academic expert, Rand Corporation's Bernard Brodie explained, plotted strategy "beyond history—i.e., beyond experience," a task for which humanists were either ill-prepared or were unwilling to accept.[56]

Thus, the niche of conventional warfare, in particular following the outbreak of hostilities in Korea, provided opportunities for those whose intellectual world recognized no limits. Predictably, Rand's social science division led the way. The major figures in this division shared a common background. They had participated in the grand social sciences projects of World War II. They had been affiliated, in one way or another, with the University of Chicago, as faculty or as graduate students. Needless to say, they were partisans of universalism, the explaining of social realities by theories assumed to possess unlimited validity. Rand's behavioral scientists were advocates of psychoanalytical personality studies of elite political groups. At various points in their careers they had all been associated with Harold Lasswell, the leading exponent of the University of Chicago's behavioral school of political science and a practitioner of a Freudian analysis of political motivation. There was a touch of poetic justice in the fact that the feverish Lasswell, who spent most of his productive years without a tenured position and many of the other perks of academic prestige, would hover in the background as his friends, disciples, and colleagues from graduate school gained prominence in the military-intellectual complex.

Psychopolitics and Primary Groups

Theories of Culture and

Society in Cold War Academia

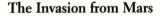

The Invasion from Mars

On October 30, 1938, a CBS radio dramatization of H. G. Wells' *War of the Worlds* provoked widespread fears of a Martian invasion in New Jersey. Radio listeners exhibited acute signs of panic, ranging from spiritual preparations for the end of the world to actually fleeing their homes. In subsequent years, similar broadcasts in other countries suggested that the power of radio to provoke extreme reactions was not a uniquely American phenomenon.[1] These extraordinary media events were, according to contemporary commentators, remarkable demonstrations of the ability of electronic media to manipulate the minds of the masses.[2]

The burgeoning behavioral sciences community disagreed. In a seminal study of the original broadcast, published in 1940, Hadley Cantril, Hazel Gaudet, and Herta Herzog revealed that, indeed, a sizable minority of the audience had confused fiction with reality.[3] The radio broadcast had attracted an audience of somewhere between six million and nine million listeners. Approximately a million members of the audience were either frightened or disturbed by the broadcast; a minority—the study never mentioned exact numbers—actually panicked. The majority of listeners swiftly discovered that the broadcast was fiction. They employed simple modes of verification, ranging from consulting program listings in the newspapers, monitoring other stations for similar broadcasts, paying attention to the disclaimers interspersed throughout the program, or simply recognizing the obvious imaginary nature of the broadcast—the preposterous physical descriptions of the aliens, the frantic pace of events, and so on. Given the many and mostly simple strategies for verifying the authenticity of the alien onslaught, the authors of *Invasion from Mars* argued that the believers were not victims of a manipulative radio dramatization. No text, however artful, could have ignited such extreme modes of panic. The broadcast was either accepted or rejected because it confirmed preexisting psychological dispositions and/or resulted from a variety of social factors rather than from the content of the performance itself. Those who believed that a Martian invasion had occurred did so because such an event was consistent with their social expectations or psychological state of mind; by the same token, skeptical listeners rejected the authenticity of the dramatization because nothing in their worldview encouraged belief in extraterrestrial life.

In this refutation of the "magic bullet" paradigm—a communication master-theory that assumes a high level of susceptibility among the audiences of mass media, regardless of background—the authors of the invasion study argued that listeners of all political, social, and economic backgrounds were highly discriminating in the type of communication they accepted. They believed information that supported personal convictions, but, by the same token, ignored, discarded, or overlooked contradictions of their social, emotional, and psychological preconceptions. In other words, those who believed that an extraterrestrial invasion was under way did so because it reinforced "preexisting mental sets."

Invasion from Mars offered a counterintuitive analysis of the power of words in an era in which electronically amplified propaganda appeared to induce pathological behavioral patterns. While acknowledging the artful nature of the performance, the disorienting impact of technology, and the authority of radio, the study paid particular attention to the psychological and social predicament of the listeners. Cantril and his colleagues insisted that texts had no mystical qualities. Radio had enlarged the scope of the audience, and its broadcasts were considered to be a reliable source of information. However, words, whether electronically relayed to vast masses or spoken within more intimate circumstances, had no independent authority. The significance of this or any other text lay in its interpretation, which was governed primarily by the psychological and social predicaments of the listeners. Pathological behavior, whether the panic induced by the *War of the Worlds* or the extreme behavioral patterns supposedly triggered by government-ordained propaganda, was the result of the private psychological or social predicaments of the audience, and not a predictable, uniform response to a text, however artful.

In offering explanations for the susceptibility of believers, the authors of the invasion study alternated between sociological factors, such as the level of education of informants and their social networks, to psychological factors, ranging from a clinical lack of self-confidence among believers to underlying destructive impulses that led certain types of listeners to expect catastrophes. Published in 1940, *The Invasion from Mars*, with its mixture of personal and public, social and psychological, as well as its circumspect assessment of the manipulative power of technology, was a harbinger of the two major trends within postwar American behavioral sciences.

The most significant of these models assumed that all forms of public and political behaviors were displacements of subjective psychological events; society was a collection of individuals, each with a personal psychological profile. This psychocultural approach, according to social psychologist Gordon Allport, asserted that "the mainsprings of conduct were hidden from the searchlight of consciousness."[4] Adult motives were sublimated or projective responses to mainly unconscious childhood traumas. "This prevailing atmosphere of theory," Allport explained, "engendered a kind of contempt for 'psychic surface' of life. The individual's conscious report is rejected as untrustworthy, and the contemporary thrust of his motives is disregarded in favor of a backward tracing of his conduct to early formative stages."[5]

A competing school of sociologically oriented behavioralists offered a sometimes opposing, sometimes complementary point of departure. This alternative model claimed that behavior was determined by fundamental social factors, such as membership in primary groups and social networks. Contrary to conventional sociological models of atomization in modern societies, behavioralists assumed that primary groups—cohesive and autonomous clusters of individuals governed by an informal codex of rules regulating the behavior of members—survived and thrived in modern societies.

Conventional sociological models had characterized modernization as a rupturing shift from the organic community of the gemeinschaft to the impersonal society of the gesselschaft. Behavioralists, by contrast, argued that primary groups, supposedly an exclusive feature of the premodern gemeinschaft, continued to play a pivotal socializing role in modern societies. Neither the onslaught of technology nor the erosion of tradition had affected the role of the primary group in governing opinion formation, assigning the terms of involvement in society, and defining the relationship between the individual and the formal hierarchical structures of modern society. Despite the eroding effects of modernization, the sociological variant of behavioralism asserted that people's actions were derived from a primary and stable form of social networking rather than the cumulative actions of self-seeking individuals.

The Primary Group

The sociological variant of behavioralism was nurtured, funded, and promoted by defense-related projects during and immediately following World War II. In their attempts to assist the military in shaping the morale and motivation of recruits, behavioralists offered a creative analysis of the beliefs, values, and behavior of mobilized Americans. They argued that the nation's citizens in uniform exhibited weak to nonexistent political commitments and that, paradoxically, the conspicuous absence of ideological underpinnings had no meaningful effect on the soldiers' fighting spirit. Conscripts reported a shallow understanding of the war aims and professed benign neglect of its ideological significance.

Such disinterest in the meaning of the war did not, however, affect loyalty or motivation. American soldiers accepted "momentarily any plausibly worded statement of the interpretation of the war," Samuel Stouffer stated in TAS.[6] Stouffer and his colleagues claimed that American soldiers absorbed and adhered to the symbols of the state out of loyalty to their "primary groups," rather than devotion to the ideological underpinnings of the symbols.

The privileging of the primary group was by no means an invention of the war years. Throughout most of the early twentieth century the term was a staple analytical concept of the Chicago school of sociology. As early as 1920, W. I. Thomas's monumental study, *The Polish Peasant in Europe and America,* focused on the waning of the primary group among uprooted Europeans and the disorienting consequences of its disappearance. Other major studies approached primary groups as a pathological phenomenon. A series of Chicago gang studies described primary groups as facilitators in the development of delinquent careers among marginal youth.[7] The primary group was, then, either a thing of the past or a harbinger of dysfunctional behavior in modernizing societies.

A decisive turn in the fortunes of the primary group occurred with the publication of Elton Mayo's *The Human Problems of an Industrial Society* (1933), the seminal study of productivity in a Western Electric factory in Hawthorne, Illinois. Contrary to previous assumptions that the primary group was either a holdover from traditional societies and/or a facilitator of deviant behavior, Mayo claimed that primary groups had a crucial functional role in industrialized societies. In his Hawthorne studies, Mayo argued that the performance of workers on the factory floor could not be explained simply by their individual or collective desires for increased wages, improved working conditions, or even technical skills. He identified the primary group as a crucial determinant in shaping the actions of factory workers.

Mayo stated that productivity and positive responses to managerial objectives were linked to a series of informal micro-organizations among factory workers. The individual's attitude toward the workplace was determined in large part by the informal codes of an intimate group of co-workers belonging to the same team. The Hawthorne investigations suggested that primary environmental influences—a sense of pride in the intimate working team and positive relations between the primary group and representatives of management—had a meaningful impact on productivity rates. To the degree that such primary groups received the respect of management, their productivity increased. Ignoring the presence of primary groups or actually discouraging their existence induced alienation, disinterest, and a resultant reduction in productivity.[8]

Having assumed that a modern army shared many of the attributes of a modern industrial complex, the nation's wartime behavioralists discovered a functioning primary group in the most unexpected of places. They claimed that this primary group, governed by its own internal dynamics and informal rules, was an indispensable element in enforcing and regulating behavior in military organizations, the most formal institution of the modern nation-state. World War II studies of the American soldier in battle claimed the relative unimportance of the soldier's identification with the concrete political mission behind the war, or even the larger abstract ideological question at stake. They portrayed the modern conscript in the United States "as typically without deep personal commitment" and unconcerned with the "values underlying the military struggle."[9] There was a pervasive "absence of thinking about the meaning of the war" that did little to effect the efficient execution of military mission as long the goals and orders coincided with the objectives of the primary group.[10]

These investigations claimed that an efficient military chain of command could not rely exclusively or even primarily on a mechanism of unremitting discipline and coercion. The effective enforcement of commands occurred only when it coincided with the expectations and rules of conduct within the informal, primary groups, which in the case of the armed forces was the soldier's basic unit. A code of masculinity, loyalty to one's immediate comrades, and various other aspects of male bonding within the primary group were responsible for the social cohesion of a fighting force, the formation of morale, and, ultimately, an efficient combat performance.[11]

Behavioralists described the motivation of enemy soldiers in similar terms. They claimed that neither the coercive power of the totalitarian state nor blind acceptance of a fanatic ideology was responsible for the outstanding fighting spirit of enemy soldiers. In marked departure from conventional wisdom, the sociological branch of the behavioral sciences argued that fanaticism and indoctrination were marginal behavioral factors, even in the enemy camp.[12] The authors of these inquiries were, of course, well aware that the actual behavior of enemy soldiers appeared to contradict their assumptions. Even when faced with certain defeat, enemy soldiers fought tenaciously for the ideological symbols of their respective causes. However, behavioralists argued, such professions of devotion had no ideological underpinnings. "Identification with the stern authority associated with state power was a means for ordinary soldiers to re-affirm their acceptance of the code of military honor, but should not be seen as an endorsement of the political system which it upheld." As long as soldiers enjoyed the esteem, support, and affection of a functioning primary group, they remained faithful to their social systems. Loyalty to the group was displayed by an indiscriminate acceptance of ideological symbols. The individual's squad "offered him affection and esteem from both officers and comrades" and empowered him with a sense of belonging, thereby diminishing "the element of self-concern in battle which would lead to disruption of the fighting unit." Ideology, by contrast, was a marginal or even nonexistent factor in motivating enemy troops.[13]

The privileging of the primary group permeated studies of civilian life as well. The eminent Paul Lazarsfeld set the dominant tone by arguing that neither ideology nor the rational calculations of well-informed citizens affected elections, even in the most democratic of societies. The primary group, he argued, was the most important factor governing political choices. In his analysis of the U.S. presidential elections in 1940 and 1948, Lazarsfeld claimed that the vast majority of voters displayed both ignorance of and disinterest in substantive political issues. Contrary to common wisdom, Lazarsfeld and his colleagues argued that voting patterns in democratic countries were best understood by reconstructing primary groups among voters rather than attempting the futile task of deciphering their innermost political beliefs.

In The People's Choice (1944), a study of the 1940 U.S. presidential election, Lazarsfeld developed the concept of the "two-step flow of communication" as a counterpoise to models of an omnipotent mass media and/or the atomized citizen. The "two-step" model suggested that opinions flowed from the mass media to influential persons who served as opinion leaders within primary groups. These pivotal individuals filtered, modified, and passed on opinions to the less informed group members. In other words, the ordinary rank and file of citizens only rarely absorbed opinions directly from the media. According to Lazarsfeld, the technological advances of modernity—in particular, the innovations of mass communications—had not destroyed the social bonds of primary groups. He argued that the "discovery" of opinion leaders was ample proof that modernization had not transformed once-stable societies into a maelstrom of alienated individuals. Lazarsfeld's theory questioned the very existence of the so-called rootless mass that had supposedly sprung out of the urban-industrial landscape of Western society. Blaming technology for the psychopathology of modern society was, therefore, unwarranted.[14]

In *Voting* (1954), a study of the American election campaign of 1948, Lazarsfeld and his associates described the act of voting as a tribal affair, an occasion to express solidarity with one's primary group. They concluded that Americans "vote not for a principle in the usual sense but 'for' a group to which they are attached. The Catholic vote or the hereditary vote is explainable less as a principle than as a traditional social allegiance."[15] Much along the same lines as the military studies that discounted the role of ideology, Lazarsfeld argued that there was no such theoretical beast.

> The upshot of this is that the usual analogy between the voting "decision" and the more or less carefully calculated decisions of consumers or businessmen or courts, incidentally, may be quite incorrect. For many voters political preferences may better be considered analogous to cultural tastes—in music, literature, recreational activities, dress, ethics, speech, social behavior. Consider the parallels between political preferences and general cultural tastes. Both have their origin in ethnic, sectional, class, and family traditions. Both exhibit stability and resistance to change for individuals. . . . While both are responsive to changed conditions and usual stimuli, they are relatively invulnerable to direct argumentation and vulnerable to indirect social influences.[16]

The studies of primary groups in both military and civilian contexts strengthened the case for the "end of ideology." In all instances, civilian or military, behavioralists argued that individual members of large and complex social structures were not motivated by ideas and values, nor did they react mechanically to the directives of a central authority. These studies implied that within modern societies, manifestations of political values and ideological conviction were mere veneer. As far as military organizations were concerned, the colors of the flag could be changed without affecting the efficiency and fighting spirit of the well-trained soldier as an individual or the army as an institution.

If even the soldiers of a totalitarian state were not the captives of an all-encompassing ideology, one could not expect ideology to play a significant role in democratic societies. Behavioral patterns were controlled in large part by individuals within primary groups who transmitted expectations to and from the larger social structure. The informal code of the primary group, rather than the ostensible ideologically saturated objectives of the nation-state, were, according to this group of researchers, the key to understanding human behavior.

The Pyschopathological Model

Irrespective of its wide resonance, both in academia and beyond, the modular primary group was not the predominant research strategy of Cold War behavioral sciences. Prominent researchers advocated alternative, powerfully attractive psychoanalytical theories. Contrary to their colleagues from the sociological school, these researchers argued that manipulation by words was, indeed, possible, by means of tapping into the psychological infirmities of the target audience.

The intrusion of psychoanalytical concepts into the behavioral sciences was intimately tied to the presence of Harold D. Lasswell who, almost single-handedly, introduced the disturbing world of the unconscious into Cold War behavioral sciences. Lasswell's influence was quite curious, for he was a general without an army. Harold Lasswell had none of the social connections that one associates with successful scholarship. Key members of his profession considered him arrogant and personally unpleasant. University of Chicago sociologist Edward Shils described himself as "put off" by Lasswell's "deliberate pose of omniscience" and the manner in which he "affected intimacy with all . . . social science."[17]

Reviews of Lasswell's book in the flagships of American social sciences described him as shallow, pompous, and speculative ad absurdum. In reviewing his *World Politics and Personal Insecurity* (1935) for the *American Sociological Review*, Princeton University political scientist Walter Lincoln Whittlesey ridiculed Lasswell's leaping "about the cosmos of sociological-psychobiological-obstetrical-psychiatric political science with the abandon of a flock of sparrows at a horse-show." Lasswell burdened the reader with "a cluttering of casual allusion," like "William E. Borah clerking in a mental canned goods chain store."[18] Across the street, in the *American Journal of Sociology*, Lasswell's psychopolitics fared no better. The eminent sociologist Everett C. Hughes accused Lasswell of hiding his problematic, often weak ideas behind "fantastic formations of words." Lasswell had abandoned science for a cosmic, yet poorly substantiated "search for the fate of the world."[19]

In addition to, or perhaps due to, the contempt of influential peers, Lasswell suffered from perennial professional insecurity. During the formative years of his career, he practiced his calling without the benefits of tenure, a prestigious academic position, and the traditional entourage of doting graduate students. Having entered the University of Chicago as a precocious youth of sixteen, Lasswell swiftly completed a B.A. in economics in 1922. After receiving a Ph.D. in political science in 1926, his career at Chicago appeared to be assured with his appointment as an assistant professor. By 1937, his meteoric career at Chicago came to an abrupt halt, when President Robert Hutchins refused to offer him tenure; Hutchins considered Lasswell a "faddist" and a "monument" to "passing whims."[20]

Following his unceremonious departure from Chicago, Lasswell remained without a tenured academic position during his most productive years. During the particularly harsh period from 1938 until 1946, most of Lasswell's financial support came from the General Education Board of the Rockefeller Foundation, and his appointment as the director of the Rockefeller-funded Wartime Communications Research Project at the Library of Congress. Only in 1946, and through the energetic lobbying of law professor Myres McDougal, did Lasswell receive a tenured position at Yale law school. Boxed into a law school, partly by choice and partly by circumstances, and hampered by his pseudoscientific writing style, an estranged and condescending Lasswell was doomed to spend the remainder of his academic career in the golden cage at Yale.[21]

Despite these obvious handicaps, Lasswell was arguably the most influential behavioral scientist in American academia. His many writings, spanning a period from his precocious youth until his death in 1978, inspired an entire generation of behavioral scientists, in particular those who specialized in politics and communications.[22]

Lasswell's first major attempt at weaving politics and psychoanalysis was his "The Psychology of Hitlerism" (1933), in which he attributed Hitler's success to the dictator's ability to alleviate the personal insecurity of many Germans.[23] In this and other articles published throughout the 1930s Lasswell demonstrated a propensity for applying psychoanalytical explanations for the unsettling tide of political events following the Great War. More than any other scholar of his generation, he provided the conceptual basis for using psychology in general and psychoanalysis in particular as a tool for deciphering political behavior.

Prior to Lasswell's prominent work, most scholars of politics had approached political behavior as the outcome of conscious processes. Conventional political science focused on the mechanism of government and institutions as the key to understanding the dynamics of politics and society. Lasswell, by contrast, assumed that private and mostly unconscious processes governed the political process. He argued that all human motives, private or public, social or political, were dominated by childhood sexual and excretory experiences. Lasswell approached all forms of ideologies—patriotism, class struggle, racial superiority, or whatever symbol might happen to be psychologically or socially acceptable at a given time—as the rationalizations of private fantasies generated, in large part, by childhood experiences. He described the conscience as "an introjected nursemaid," and the adult mind as "only partly adult."[24]

Lasswell explained that the role of the scientist of human affairs was to trace the manner in which such personal experiences were unconsciously displaced into public causes. "It has become something of a commonplace that politics is the arena of the irrational," Lasswell observed. "But a more accurate description would be that politics is the process by which the irrational bases of society are brought out into the open."[25] In his influential *Psychopathology and Politics*, Lasswell explained that "political movements derive their vitality from the displacement of" personal psychotic disturbances "upon public objects." Always the scientist, he attempted to translate this provocative assumption into a pseudomathematical formula.

The general formula for the developmental history of the political man employs three terms:

$$p\}d\}\ r = P$$

p equals private motives, d equals displacement onto public objects, r equals rationalization in terms of public interest. P signifies the political man, and } means "transformed into.". . . The distinctive mark of the 'homo politicus' is the rationalization in terms of public interests.[26]

Lasswell argued that politics, more than any other aspect of human affairs, was a natural arena for "displacement," partly because of the great visibility of public affairs and partly due to the ambiguity of most political symbols. The symbols of politics were invariably vague and given to multiple interpretations. Like the inkblots used in projective tests, the ambiguity of political symbols aroused the unconscious through a process of free association, and induced the displacement of private psychotic disturbances onto public affairs.[27] The source of such unconscious disturbances, was, of course, in childhood. Lasswell argued that whenever an individual "runs for office or passes judgment, his behavior is overdetermined by motives, conscious and unconscious which were organized in successive patterns during infancy, childhood, and youth."[28]

Lasswell insisted that a rational evaluation of events had little to with the dynamics of politics. The key to understanding, and perhaps controlling, political events, he argued, was to recognize the irrational basis of politics, and to accept psychoanalysis as a legitimate tool for understanding public affairs. As a Neo-Freudian, Lasswell asserted that psychoanalysis should not be reserved for the treatment of the mentally ill. Political scientist Arnold Rogow explained that the essence of Lasswell's innovation was "that political behavior as such cannot be understood without the psychoanalysis of leaders and followers, revolutionaries and conformists, the sick and the well."[29] The differences between the sick and the healthy were not as sharp as conventional wisdom assumed. "Neurotic symptoms and traits are never entirely absent from any life history," Lasswell argued.[30]

While all participants in the political process deserved analysis, Lasswell urged special attention for elites. In *Politics: Who Gets What When, How*

(1936), his most readable discussion of the political process, Lasswell described the study of politics as "the study of influence and the influential." His point of departure was the blunt dictum that "government was always government by the few, whether in the name of the one, the few, or the many."[31] Lasswell claimed that in every type of political system only a small group of elites was aware of developments or was able to influence the flow of events. Thus, he argued, behavioral scientists should restrict their study to the techniques used by elites to maintain their power, "by manipulating symbols, controlling supplies, and applying violence."[32]

Among all the tactics employed by elites to perpetuate power, Lasswell was most fascinated by the "manipulation of symbols," by which he meant propaganda. Contrary to most of his colleagues in the formative 1920s and 1930s, who either dismissed or feared the persuasive powers of propaganda, Lasswell approached propaganda as an effective and benign tool for maintaining power. In fact, his Chicago dissertation, later published as *Propaganda Technique in World War I* (1927), represented the first major American study to question the conventional view of propaganda as the insidious tool of devious political regimes. As far as Lasswell was concerned, propaganda was "no more moral or immoral than a pump handle."[33] All modern governments used propaganda as a tool for furthering their policies. As far as Lasswell was concerned, nonviolent persuasion by means of propaganda was more humane than the conventional tactics of coercion. As such, the role of the responsible scientist was to analyze how propaganda functions instead of delving into its moral qualities.

Effective propaganda, Lasswell explained, was based on the assumption that in times of personal and collective vulnerability human beings are controlled through their emotions rather than their rational faculties. Under these circumstances, the successful propagandist seeks to arouse base emotions, ranging from hatred to affection, in order to further national goals.

Lasswell was not the only scholar of propaganda of his day. He was however, one of the most politically astute, always fashioning his research to meet the concerns and fears of potential funders. During the course of World War II, Lasswell offered analysis of communist societies, foreseeing well before others that this revolutionary doctrine appeared more threatening to many Americans than the Nazi specter. In *World Revolutionary Propaganda* (1939), Lasswell and his associate, Dorothy Blumenstock, offered quantitative techniques for effective measurements of communist propaganda in Chicago over a four-year period.[34] In a display of great ambition, Lasswell and Blumenstock quantified how many people had been exposed to communist propaganda, and also attempted to describe in statistical terms how much time they spent thinking about such propaganda. The stroke of brilliance was, of course, in their focus on communism, the enemy of the future, rather than on the very crowded field of fascism and Nazism.

World Revolutionary Propaganda convinced Lasswell's Rockefeller benefactors to finance his Wartime Communications Project at the Library of Congress, where, as historian Mark C. Smith has noted, "Lasswell assured his already convinced listeners" that the quantification of communications ensured "scientific and policy gains."[35] Various studies conducted under the auspices of the Wartime Communications Project and eventually published in *Language of Politics* (1949) demonstrated Lasswell's astute grasp of the academic-policy nexus. Lasswell explained that useful scholarship had to reduce complex arguments to the universal language of numbers. The central theme of much of Lasswell's wartime work was that "political power could be better understood in the degree that language is better understood, and that the language of politics can be usefully studied by quantitative measures."[36] Lasswell argued that quantitative content analysis was far more useful than traditional impressionistic methods of reading and interpreting language. By reducing the significance of language to a set of measurable symbols, the researcher could claim the importance of certain political trends on the basis of frequency. Repetition signified relevance.

The psychopolitics of Lasswell and his followers should not be seen as a total rejection of the sociological strategy and its focus on primary groups. Lasswell's point of departure was political science, while his counterparts were fundamentally sociologists who were concerned mostly with social networks. Of course, differences were quite significant. Social psychologists and sociologists were unwilling to accept the lack of reason behind much of the traumatic events of the twentieth century and sought, instead, cognitive explanations. Psychotheorists, by contrast, accepted irrational behavior, and sought explanations in the unconscious. Central to Lasswell's approach to language in general and propaganda in particular was the premise that through skillful use of linguistic symbols, the scientist could tap powers of control that were quite different from cognitive social processes. Sociologically oriented behavioral scientists studied the cohesive mechanisms of society and investigated the micro-organizations of ordinary people; the psychological school focused on elites. Partisans of psychoanalysis in the behavioral sciences placed great importance on language and its methodic decoding, while the social psychologists preferred to count and quantify observable behavior, rather than investigate linguistic evidence.

Yet far more important than these differences were the common links between these competing behavioral strategies. Both schools of thought placed no value on ideology as a motivating factor in political and social process. Whether loyalty to ideology was the result of collective response to an observable social phenomenon or triggered by pathological childhood experiences was a matter of contention, of course. However, both schools of thought agreed that grandiose ideological convictions were smokescreens for something else. Both of these behavioral strategies placed great emphasis on quantitative measurements and were fundamentally ahistorical. Their historical assessments covered, at the very most, the life span of their subjects and informants. Any sense of primordialism was absent from their work. Both American society and the societies of adversaries were, in their minds, synthetic creations that had little to do with far-reaching cultural and historical origins.

"Trust in Numbers"

The most intriguing common bond among behavioralists of all persuasions was their distrust of raw qualitative data. Having dismissed their humanist colleagues as captives of the vagaries of language, behavioralists of all persuasions endorsed a quantitative discourse. They believed that a positive reception of their disciplinary innovations hinged upon a strict avoidance of the imprecision of conventional language. Thus, the most speculative and the most mundane suppositions of behavioralists were numerically encoded. When forced to use words rather than mathematical representations, behavioralists resorted to technical jargon—the linguistic equivalent of numerical precision. Numbers, according to behavioralists, offered transparent presentations of difficult problems. There was a symbiotic relationship among objectivity, openness, and "trust in numbers." Damned for its superficiality by critics and praised for its openness by partisans, this reliance on measurement was a hallmark of behavioralism.

Quantitative measurement offered, as well, a semblance of unity for the intellectually fractured world of contemporary science. Historian Theodore Porter has observed that "firm statistical rules" promoted a sense of order by suppressing the unruly, diverse forms of interpretation associated with ambiguous qualitative data. Quantification standardized the governing intellectual concepts of separate investigative fields.[37] Numbers permitted comparison of people, places, and problems that were otherwise different and ostensibly incomparable. Quantification enabled the codifying, unifying, and, above all, simplification of large and diverse bodies of information.

Statistical knowledge was a particularly appropriate political tool for furthering the nation's global objectives and justifying its imperial enterprises. According to anthropologist Arjun Appadurai, quantifiable strategies created manageable and familiar political, economic, and social classifications for the exercise of power in foreign lands. Statistics, he argues, are to foreign "bodies and social types what maps are to territories." Numerical vocabularies, like cartographic conventions, flattened idiosyncrasies and created neat classifications. "The unruly body of the other is recuperated thorough the language of numbers."[38] Classification by numbers explained away the inscrutable and transformed ostensibly chaotic phenomena into recognizable, measurable, and controllable features.

The transposition of language into numbers was, as well, a reaction to the mistrust of outsiders. A reliance on statistics was, Theodore Porter explains, a response to external demands for accountability, "an adaptation to public exposure" rather than an intellectual "achievement of a well-insulated community of researchers." Shawn Parry-Giles's analysis of the Voice of America (VOA) congressional hearings in the 1950s serves as a case in point. Called upon to prove the effectiveness of the VOA, officials responded by presenting Congress with "anecdotal evidence"—written testimonies and circumstantial evidence such as Soviet jamming—as proof of the effectiveness of the broadcasts. Congressional critics rejected the evidence, claiming that it was vague and unmeasurable. The VOA responded, and ultimately satisfied Congress with a barrage of statistical data, "proving," by numbers, that the VOA had triumphed in the war of words. Parry-Giles suggests, as well, that the very "use of the 'war of words' metaphor by propagandists" was significant in itself. "Just when 'body counts' or land measurement were used to determine the success of a war, congressional leaders expected evidence of conversion rates brought about by America's propaganda."[39]

Here, then, lay the seeds of the widespread, positive reception of content analysis, one of the most popular strategies of the behavioral sciences during its formative years.[40] Harold Lasswell, both an inventor and skilled practitioner of content analysis, argued that the task of the behavioralist was to demystify language by reducing its untidy qualities to measurable categories. In terse prose that reflected his contempt for conventional language, Lasswell explained that all texts could be reduced to a series of measurable symbols. He argued that the most promising method for neutralizing linguistic imprecision as well as tracing the links in the chain of communication "between the psyche of the audience and the text" was the employment of quantitative procedures. The conversion of language into numerical representations promised to dispel the cloud of qualitative, impressionistic, and conjectural analysis. Precise measurements of the parts, rather than impressionistic speculations about the whole, diminished the margin of uncertainty often associated with the woolly "hunches" of traditional methods of textual analysis.

The widespread trust in numbers led eventually to the privileging of game theory, the mathematical simulation of confrontational decision dilemmas. Military clients were attracted to this format of mathematical inquiry because it introduced a semblance of predictability into a confusing state of affairs. Reducing the enemy to a ruthless, expansionist, and predictable actor, rather than an inscrutable adversary, had a distinctly calming effect on strategical planners.

From the vantage point of hindsight, this embracing of game theory in particular and mathematical formulas in general makes for easy target practice. Mathematical models were heavily laden with ideological assumptions dictating their final outcome. Game theorists assumed, but never challenged, the premise that the Soviet adversary was a predatory, expansionist power. By the same token, these experts defined the United States as a "defensive status quo power," whose objectives were evident to the Soviets.[41] Moreover, practitioners of game theory tended to confuse the artificial order of the mathematical world with the disorderly world surrounding them. They arbitrarily dismissed problems that were not quantifiable, and ignored the chaotic elements of history and culture and their effects on decision making.[42]

In the confusing period of the early 1950s such issues were overlooked, mostly because the mathematicization of human behavior in general and Cold War decision making in particular fulfilled a crucial need. The Cold War was terra incognita and in need of a map, however tenuous; the application of a grid of mathematics fulfilled this cartographic lacuna. Moreover, mathematics provided a unitary lingua franca among disciplines, allowing physicists to converse with economists and members of other mathematically oriented disciplines. In addition, historian Theodore Porter observes, numbers were especially appealing to persons in position of power, who lacked the mandate of democratic election or divine right. "A decision based on numbers (or by explicit rules of some other sort) has at least the *appearance* of being fair and impersonal."[43]

Whether endorsing methods of measurements such as content analysis, or offering strategies based on game theory, the importance of behavioral scientists resided in the willingness to accept, if not actively seek, roles outside academia. Following their activities in World War II, most behavioralists did not return quietly to their academic callings. Some became full-time associates with research institutions. The master practitioners returned, at least nominally, to academia, but retained crucial ties with nonuniversity research institutions. Once settled in the world of research institutes, theories and warring schools lost their exclusiveness and blended into a variety of fused compromises that were meant to meet the demands of clients and the sometimes untidy reality of conventional war during the Cold War period. At numerous think tanks funded by, or associated with, the defense establishment the theories of behavioralism became praxis.

The Korean War offered the first and most comprehensive attempt to test behavioral theory in crucial real-life situations. An army of behavioralists entered the Korean theater armed with intellectual weapons aimed at controlling, manipulating, and predicting the behavior of both friend and foe. As advisors on the battlefront, at truce tents, and in prison camps, behavioralists offered crucial advice and counsel for a confused military and political establishment.

PART TWO
NORMAL SCIENCE

4.

The Obstinate Audience

The Art of Information
Management in the Cold War

Visiting Professors

During the Christmas season of 1950, three American professors wove an erratic path along the Korean battlefront. Unaware of the changing fortunes of the war, they turned toward the North Korean capital of Pyongyang, only to be blocked by a massive jam of troops and refugees fleeing south in the wake of advancing Chinese forces. These consultants of the Air Force University's HRRI settled, instead, for a brief visit to recently liberated Seoul. With the sounds of battle in the background, they mustered the remaining strands of their academic composure and set about analyzing the social impact of communism on Korean society.

The visiting professors were not novices seeking fame and fortune by means of exotic field research. They were senior academic figures who, in an unusual gesture, had waived the privilege of analyzing the fieldwork of underlings from comfortable and distant groves of academe. The leader of the Korean expedition was Wilbur Schramm, the dean of the communications division at the University of Illinois, who would later become the director of the Institute for Communication Research at Stanford University. Schramm, the author of the definitive mass communications textbooks throughout most of the 1950s and 1960s, was accompanied by John W. Riley, chairman of the Department of Sociology at Rutgers University. Riley was a major figure in the burgeoning field of applied behavioral sciences. He moved freely among the spheres of academic world, government, and private sector, eventually settling for the job as vice president of a large insurance conglomerate. The junior member of the team was John Pelzel, an assistant professor of anthropology at Harvard, who joined the expedition because of his mastery of "oriental languages." The American visitors were accompanied by a hovering squadron of twenty-five South Korean social scientists, who functioned as translators, cultural guides, and political seers.

Schramm's conspicuous presence, rather than participation by proxy, suggests that the HRRI mission was not a routine exercise in applied research. He arrived in Korea with impressive academic credentials. In 1943 he was appointed as director of the University of Iowa's school of journalism. During the course of his Iowa tenure, Schramm founded the country's first independent Department of Communications. In 1947 he received the appointment of vice president of the University of Illinois, where he established the university's Institute of Communication Research and laid the foundations for the nation's first doctoral program in mass communications. The 1950 Korean sortie was part of a large air force grant to his Illinois research center. Schramm had, therefore, no compelling reason to jeopardize his physical well-being for an additional line in his curriculum vitae. He lingered in the vicinity of the actual fireline because the geographically distant Korean conflict offered unusual intellectual and political opportunities, both personal and institutional.

Schramm, who is nowadays considered one of the founding fathers of mass communications research, approached the Korean trip as a station on the journey toward this lofty status.[1] His institutional achievements—in particular, his defining of communication studies as an independent academic discipline—gained him the reputation of a skilled administrator. However, at the time of his Korean trip, he still lacked the aura of a pathbreaking researcher. Schramm carried, as well, the additional burden of a Ph.D. in English literature, a poor recommendation for entering the behavioral sciences. The Korean trip promised to dispel such uncertainties. The HRRI mission offered Schramm opportunities to engage in applied, interdisciplinary research, and to establish himself as an important contributor to the theory and praxis of communication studies.

Schramm and his colleagues defined their Korean trip as an exercise in both theory and applied research. Prior to the HRRI mission, American inquiries into communist societies—the ultimate expression of applied research in the behavioral sciences in the 1950s—ranged from the textual analysis of political documents to the interrogation of defectors. American penetration into North Korean territory represented the first significant unmediated contact with a Cold War enemy society. Such physical proximity provided opportunities to evaluate the universal relevance of theories developed exclusively in the West.

As members of the self-conscious guild of mass communication scholars, Schramm and his colleagues were actively engaged in defining the emerging orthodoxy in this academic field. They were advocates of so-called weak or limited theories of communication. Contrary to fears, both popular and academic, of audience manipulation by powerful electronic media, the various weak theories assumed that mass communications merely reinforced preexisting attitudes; even under the best of circumstances mass media could not induce changes of opinion. Advocates of weak theories shifted theoretical attention from the media to the audiences. They argued that the effect of media messages was more a function of the psychological and social status of recipients than of the message itself. Testing such theories under the extreme conditions of a "Soviet" society, which lacked the communicative cacophony of Western societies, promised to be the ultimate test for limited theories.

The HRRI Report

The final report of this brief research trip, entitled "A Preliminary Study of the Impact of Communism on Korea" was an exhaustive study of "the institutional patterns used by communists in North Korea," and occupying communist forces in the Seoul area.[2] Throughout the manuscript, Schramm and his collaborators argued that a skillful application of key behavioral theories, tested and validated in the Korean laboratory, could undermine the enemy from within. The Korean research trip identified "the causes of tensions, stresses, and strains in a communist society" and provided the basis for a plan to "exploit such tensions to the disadvantage of Communist control systems."[3]

Wilbur Schramm, the senior member of this research expedition and a committed Cold Warrior, was the author of three of the report's five chapters. These portions of the document dealt primarily with patterns of "Sovietization" in North Korea and occupied Seoul respectively. John Pelzel, the junior member of the team, was the author of the chapter on land reform and political life in rural "Sovietized Korea." His study, entitled "The Sovietization of Two South Korean Rural Communities," was by far the most meticulously prepared segment of the study. John Riley edited the section entitled "Flight from Sovietization," a series of interviews and statistical analyses of refugee motivation for fleeing communism.

At its most superficial level, the report reflected the impact of Cold War political priorities on academic research. Moral aphorisms and judgmental condemnations of communism permeated the entire manuscript. However, when placed in the discursive framework of the time, and when read as a document written for and by behavioral scientists sharing unsaid, yet explicitly clear frames of common reference, "A Preliminary Study of Communism" is transformed from a mercenary, political document into an important examination of American social and behavioral paradigms in a foreign context. The significance of the HRRI report lay in its translating of a distant foreign experience into the familiar terminology of the metropolis. All forms of supposedly alien behavioral patterns were explained as variations of an American original.

The HRRI report's point of departure was to disprove the relevance of economic class and ideology for understanding the internal rifts in Korean society. John Pelzel's segment on rural communities—where the vast majority of Koreans resided—fullfilled this function. According to Pelzel, popular discontent and the political schisms of Korean society were not organized around contemporary ideological or economic issues. Instead, they were the result of primordial traditions, in particular, the division between the descendants of first and second wives in the traditional Korean core village. Pelzel argued that the inferior status of the descendants of second wives was the major cause of civil strife in Korea. Social stratification Korean-style, and not economic class distinctions, separated Koreans, he claimed.

In this ethnographic narrative of rural life during the Korean War, Pelzel offered plausible generalizations that refuted any meaningful economic or ideological analysis of the Korean crisis. Korean peasant society, he argued, was torn by an "irreparable schism" between "those descended from the first wife and descendants from the second wife" of the original village founder. This schism lived on and was compounded by opportunistic communist interlopers. "Where the descendants of the first wife were conservative politically," the descendants of the second wife were unfailingly liberal. "When the Communists came in, this division became irreparable."[4] Ideological differences were trivial, economic differences were nonissues; only an inexplicable clinging to an outmoded tradition defined the divisions of Korean society.

The HRRI report implied, as well, that contemporary Korea was locked into a struggle with no meaningful historical roots. The legacy of Japanese colonialism, as well as the historical significance of Korea's symbiotic ties with powerful Russian and Chinese neighbors, were dismissed as irrelevant. The report assumed that pertinent historical developments began with the imposition of communism in the north.

In contrast to this limited historical time frame, the report dwelt in great detail on the life span of informants. In accordance with concurrent behavioral theory, the HRRI report presumed that personal time, as opposed to historical time, and more than any other social, economic, or cultural variable, affected the typical Korean's response to communism. North Korean refugees were significantly more aggressive than their southern peers in their reaction to communism because "persons who have had experience with communism for a matter of years rather than months are more likely to feel intensely about it and take aggressive action against it."[5]

The authors' spatial understanding of the conflict was equally sharp and selective. Historian Bruce Cumings has noted that American observers such as these HRRI investigators consistently avoided interpretations of the Korean War as a precursor of "what we now call a 'North–South' conflict, the main agenda being decolonization and a radical reconstruction of colonial legacies." Instead, the HRRI report placed the conflict on an exclusive East–West axis, thereby rendering irrelevant Korea's geographical circumstances as crossroads between powerful and often warring civilizations. As far as the report was concerned, the occurrence of "Sovietization" in Korea, rather than somewhere else, was insignificant; "Sovietization" was part of a global blueprint that had already occurred in Eastern Europe and would presumably materialize in other corners of the globe as well. Cumings notes that such spatial displacement allowed for the development of an interpretation of the Korean War based on "the barest knowledge of the internal Korean milieu."[6]

Thus insulated from Korea's historical and geopolitical legacy, the HRRI report could claim by declaration that the North Korean political system was an imposition of a Soviet model, devoid of legitimate, indigenous credentials of its own. The visiting professors stated that Korea's Communist Party had no authentic Korean roots, and was, as such, totally reliant on a tight, Russian-inspired system of social control for its survival. Schramm and his colleagues proclaimed, rather than proved, that "the forces attempting to Sovietize South Korea were working from the same blueprint which had been used in North Korea. The North Korean blueprint, in turn, resembles the patterns in other Sovietized states closely enough to make one suspect the existence of a master blueprint."[7]

The American researchers summarily dismissed North Korea's revolutionary-nationalist credentials and its capacity for independent action. They described the main features of communist political reform as socially subversive, while defining South Korean society as an authentic culture suffocating from the grasp of the "tentacles of communism." The report claimed that most of the seemingly liberal legislation in Sovietized Korea was, in fact, destructive rather than progressive. The political and social reforms instituted by Communists were aimed at annihilating primordial forms of cultural interaction, and replacing them with allegiance to a foreign, synthetic social system.

The authors' extensive analysis of gender relations serves as a case in point. By their own account, the women in South Korean society were the dispirited and ill-treated "work-horses" of a "man's world." Legally and socially they were marginal persons whose fate and fortune were controlled by husbands, fathers, and other male members of the extended family. The HRRI report acknowledged that the communist regime, both in North Korea and in the briefly occupied areas of the south, had induced revolutionary changes in the status of women. The Communists liberalized divorce laws, outlawed concubinage, and introduced women into positions of economic and social power. However, Schramm and his colleagues found no redeeming qualities in these reforms. They interpreted these changes as attempts to undermine a stable and, therefore, competing social system rather than achieve social justice.

In communist-occupied Seoul women had "held jobs of honor" and prestige, and adopted the habit of addressing "each other as 'tong-mu'—comrade."[8] However, the HRRI report warned against interpreting such moves as fundamentally progressive. The changing role of women had undermined the extended family, the backbone of Korean society. By practicing a gender-specific form of divide and conquer, communist perpetrators had upset the indigenous stability of Korean society. Quoting an unnamed Korean sociologist, Schramm and his collaborators argued that women's emancipation, Korean-style, had exposed Korean society to foreign contamination. Emancipation eroded the indigenous defense mechanisms of "order" and "tradition."[9]

Such broad declarations on Korean society and culture, derived mostly from secondhand knowledge, did not encounter any major theoretical obstacle. The conceptual framework of this study assumed that all human behavior, in all societies, and at all times, abided by common undergirding principles. This universalist creed assumed that the branding of certain societies as distant or foreign was superficial and unscientific. The unique or alien were figments of the imagination or the products of faulty methodology.

In a typical contemporary comment on this approach to the behavioral sciences, Harvard sociologist Alex Inkeles explained that "there cannot be one social science for the study of one's country and a different one for the study of other nations." All human behavior, regardless of time and place, could be reduced to a common web of abstract relations. Thus, the primary task of investigations such as the Schramm report was "not that of making our research methods more adequate for the study of foreign societies, but of improving our conceptual tools and methodological equipment . . . [for] the study of *any* society."[10]

The Obstinate Audience

The most significant implementation of such theoretical underpinnings appeared in the HRRI report's main focus, the analysis of mass media and social control in "Sovietized Korea." All of the study's chapters dealt in one way or another with communication and control in "Sovietized" societies. Theories of mass communication were, in fact, the thread linking the many subjects raised by the report, from land reform to gender relations. This first major exemplar of Cold War fieldwork presumed that the "Soviet" format of social control — in Russia, Korea, or any other Iron Curtain satellite — differed from Western practices in its intensity only.

The analysis of communications and control in a totalitarian ecology began with the somewhat predictable description of repression employed by communist masters. Both the original report and subsequent articles published after the fact explained that Communists attempted to control the flow of information by monopolizing the mass media and blocking all channels of alternative information. Efficient social control in Sovietized Korea entailed an exclusive, hermetically sealed control "of communications sufficient to shut out opposing propaganda and to saturate the people of the state with ideas and attitudes predisposing them to sovietization." Schramm, an indisputable leader in the field of communication research, reduced Soviet technique to its three most basic elements:

Monopoly: As far as possible every non-Communist source of information was to be excluded. . . .

Concentration: Their propaganda was based on a relatively simple line, which was repeated over and over again.

Reinforcement: As propagandists, they believed in shotgun rather than rifle methods. They used every channel to din their propaganda line into their audience. . . . The careful matching of media to message was apparently less important to them than the need to saturate the information channels.[11]

This somewhat predictable explanation concluded, however, with an unusual twist. Schramm and his collaborators stated that astute Soviets were well aware that repression, intimidation, and monopolistic control of electronic media promised limited returns only. Neither physical repression nor a simplistic belief in the effectiveness of "monopoly," "concentration," and "reinforcement" by mass media could ensure social control in Sovietized Korea, or elsewhere. While maintaining that the monopolized media in "Sovietized" societies had powerful agenda-setting functions, Schramm and Riley argued that a tightly managed system of mass communication could not manipulate the minds and behavior of its audience. Their report shifted attention away from the faulty concept of an omnipotent media and focused, instead, on the active, and at times, recalcitrant receiver. They claimed that Soviet experts were aware of the limits of persuasion by mass media. As such, they had employed alternative techniques of face-to-face persuasion, a concept that was on the cutting edge of contemporary communication research in the United States of the 1950s.

Such provocative observations on the limited effects of mass media in Korea reflected the predominant trend in American communication theory. World War II research had led to the renunciation of the "magic bullet" model, the assumption that an active communicator manipulated the mind of a passive receiver. By the late 1940s reigning communication theory assumed that effective persuasion—the changing of an individual's opinion—was only partially and very tenuously related to monopolization of mass media. Significant shifts in opinion occurred only among those who were predisposed to change. Mass media served as an agent of reinforcement or a catalyst, rather than a direct stimulus.[12]

Schramm and his colleagues sought Korean examples in support of this communication paradigm that they themselves had helped fashion. They methodically gathered indications that Koreans, like Americans or any other national group, reinterpreted, ignored, or distorted communication data that did not support their preordained worldview. Their interviews with refugee-informants suggested that Korean peasants, like distant American urban dwellers, were not the helpless victims of mass media propaganda.

The HRRI report analyzed the North Korean mass media as an agent of reinforcement rather than of change. Exposure to communist propaganda could not in itself bring about ideological conversion in Korea, or, for that matter, anywhere else. The audience, captive or otherwise, did not confront the media in a state of psychological defenselessness; they were protected by cultural predispositions, selective retention, and social networks that neutralized the media attempts to convert. The report concluded that, given the prejudicial resentment of communism among large portions of the Korean population, the Soviet monopolization of mass media was of limited effect.

Basing their case on the contention that individuals retain messages that support their own point of view, while forgetting, ignoring, or distorting adverse opinions, Schramm and his colleagues argued that the Soviet communication blitz had caused, in itself, little social or political disruption. The retention of their informants had been extremely selective. Their investigation claimed that "general public reaction to the mass media was less than favorable during the occupation period. 'Uninteresting' was the usual reaction of Seoul respondents."[13]

Reporting on the opinions of Korean peasants following months of exposure to communist propaganda, John Pelzel, the junior member of the HRRI team, concurred. He stated that "there was little evidence that the pro-Soviet line was believed, and much to show that a considerable reservoir of trust remains in the United States." By contrast, Pelzel reported that anti-Rhee propaganda had "fallen on fertile ground" mainly because Korean peasants were already negatively predisposed toward the South Korean dictator.[14]

Schramm and his collaborators acknowledged that certain elements in Korean society had, indeed, changed sides in this battle for hearts and minds.

However, they argued that neither intimidation nor relentless exposure to a monopolized, and highly politicized, mass media could explain conversions to communism. For some, conversion could be explained by their marginality. Women and other disaffected members of Korean society were liable to change opinion because they did not particularly value their membership in the primary group.

For others, the diffusion of new ideas came through contact with opinion leaders. Based on research carried out exclusively within the United States, the authors of the HRRI report called attention to key community members who exerted significant influence on their peers' opinion formation.[15] They claimed that the diffusion of ideas via respected members of an individual's social network—the opinion leaders—was more effective than the mechanism of mass media. Opinion leaders, according to American theorists, were more likely to affect change in opinion because "a person, unlike a mass medium, is likely to raise issues and arguments of immediate personal relevance to the listener. And . . . when someone yields to personal influence in making a decision, the reward, in terms of approval, is immediate."[16]

The Schramm report adopted with modest variation the American-derived models of opinion and personal persuasion. The Korean study accepted the presence of opinion leaders as indisputable fact, rather than a contentious theoretical generalization derived from a specifically American political context. The authors of the HRRI report claimed that Soviet experts in communication and persuasion privileged personal contact over mass media as well. The Soviet equivalents of American opinion leaders were the Party "agitators." Leaning on the comfortable crutch of contemporary Sovietology, Schramm and his colleagues explained that Soviet societies differentiated between agitation and propaganda.

There is a basic difference in Soviet terminology between *propaganda*, which in Leninist terms is the presenting of many ideas about a single subject to a small number of people, and *agitation*, which is defined as the presenting of a few ideas to the mass of people. In the advanced Communist schools of North Korea and neighboring China, the curriculum was propaganda. The mass media and the many face-to-face channels to the Korean people were used for what the Communists called agitation, and the content of these channels was kept simple and direct.[17]

The drawing of analogies between communist agitators and American opinion leaders demanded a certain amount of intellectual acrobatics. The making of an opinion leader in the American milieu was an informal process. Informality was such that opinion leaders, as well as their disciples, were often unaware of their political power. Moreover, American theoreticians assumed that the spontaneous creation of such opinion leaders was the epitome of a healthy, democratic society. Opinion leaders were usually close associates of the people they influenced and tended to hold the same socioeconomic status as their audiences; their designation as opinion leaders was spontaneous; no government agent or official manipulated or controlled this process.

Unlike their democratically selected American counterparts, Soviet agitators did not achieve their preferential status informally. They were the groomed communicators of the Party line. While never fully grappling with such fundamental differences, the HRRI report implied that informality and spontaneity were of secondary importance. Skilled Soviet manipulators of public opinion were meticulous in choosing agitators who commanded the respect of their peers. South Korea's agitators under Northern occupation were crypto-Communists who had enjoyed communal prestige well before the invasion. "Many occupied respected positions (doctors, lawyers, executives, public officials) and gave no hint of their Communism" before "crawling out of the underground."[18] Moreover, the HRRI report claimed that communist agitators and American opinion leaders relied on the same channels and techniques of influencing public opinion. Schramm and his colleagues explained that Soviet methods of information management placed heavy emphasis on personal contact as its primary instrument of influencing opinions. Agitators, the disseminators of the single idea, worked on the basis of face-to-face interaction.

The most promising targets of agitators, and, therefore, the human elements most susceptible to change in Sovietized Korea, were society's marginal members. Korean agitators issued a string of promises to the dispossessed and deprived. They promised equal status for women, land distribution to the landless Korean peasants, and an eight-hour day for Korean laborers. The HRRI report made particular note of how the first group of agitators went about their mission following the occupation of South Korean territory. Agitators "were specially trained in the way they should treat civilians; when they shook hands with South Korean women they used the occasion to emphasize the Communists' promise of equality for women. When they redistributed the land, that too was a text for teaching."[19]

Whatever the similarities, the HRRI report did not, of course, presume that communist agitators and American opinion leaders were identical twins. They described the formal choosing and training of agitators, as opposed to the spontaneous rise of the American-modeled opinion leader, as a fundamental weakness. Agitators were superimposed on Korean society; they were not natural creations, but foreign grafts. Their success hinged upon a continuous and relentless monopolization of their audience's attention, as well as the eradication of alternative and competing channels of information. The synthetically created Soviet agitator succeeded due to a "meticulously organized power structure, capable of suppressing every effort to form a counter-elite; upon a monopoly of communications, capable of saturating the people of the state with ideas and attitudes persuading them to sovietization while suppressing opposing propaganda."

The HRRI Report: Recommendations

The HRRI report's recommendations focused on "Sovietized" Korea's unwavering obliteration of any competing form of communication. Monopolization, as practiced in Korea, contradicted the essence of persuasion theory, an investigative area residing in the intersection between mass communication studies and social psychology. Based on the work of Yale University's Carl Hovland, the HRRI report assumed that monopolization was a weak weapon for persuasion. Hovland and his associates in *Experiments on Mass Communications* (1949) claimed that, when trying to win over those who "were initially opposed to the point of view being advocated," the presentation of "arguments on both sides of an issue" appeared more effective in producing at least short-term changes in attitudes.[20]

The HRRI report asserted that the enemy's communication experts rejected, or were unaware of, such findings. North Korean officials single-mindedly closed off potential avenues of alternative communication, even at the price of hampering their propaganda effort. In a seemingly counterproductive act of desperation, communist officials confiscated radio receivers in occupied Seoul, "despite the fact that the Communists had possession of Radio Seoul, the most powerful broadcasting station in Korea." Schramm and his colleagues explained "that the Communists were willing to forgo the opportunity of speaking to South Koreans on their own radio in order to be sure that the South Koreans were not able to listen to the Japanese radio!"[21]

Thus, the HRRI report concluded, an American undermining of opinion management in "Sovietized Korea" hinged upon a successful manipulation of this weakness. Based on the Communists' fear of any conflicting message, the report urged a skillful use of radio as the most efficient medium for counteracting the enemy's communication strategy. The HRRI investigation mustered oral testimony to prove that information management via radio could foster the rise of authentic opinion leaders who might eventually undermine the authority of synthetic agitators. In a typical segment, a democratically inclined South Korean informant explained how he had used radio under communist occupation:

We would take a little radio receiver and go down under the floor and wrap the receiver and ourselves in quilts and listen to the news, usually from Japan, sometimes from San Francisco. After listening to the news,

each of us would go and tell the news to people around his home. . . .
When we got a leaflet we would memorize it and pass the information
along the same way.[22]

Schramm and his colleagues did not argue that radio could transform opinions. They did, however, expect that radio broadcasts would reinforce the
inherent anticommunist views of authentic opinion leaders and, through
them, affect the vast majority of Koreans. They speculated that "Communist
efforts to achieve an information monopoly were at least 90 percent successful,
but the leaks in their dike (U.N. radio and U.N. leaflets) were highly important."[23]

Neither the brevity of the report's fieldwork nor the unquestioning application of poorly tested theoretical generalizations was cause for qualification or
cautionary advice. As politically astute individuals, the authors of the HRRI
document were presumably aware that reports of this nature demanded crisp,
comprehensive observations and decisive conclusions. The paradigm of limited effects and the concurrent theory of opinion leaders offered well-defined
options for waging successful psychological warfare against the communist
enemy. By underscoring the resistance of audiences to mass media messages,
and by dismissing the notion of audience defenselessness, Schramm and Riley
identified the area of mass communication as perhaps the most vulnerable
link in Soviet methods of waging the Cold War.

The HRRI Report: Its Ramifications

Despite the personal participation of Wilbur Schramm as well as the unusual
circumstances of his team's battlezone fieldwork, the report had a surprisingly
light impact. Its most immediate influence was limited to the confines of
HRRI. The theoretical linchpins of the Korean investigation provided the
foundation for analyzing Asian communism in all major studies emanating
from the Air University. A series of reports entitled "Studies in Chinese Communism" adapted the concepts of limited effects, opinion leaders, and the
obstinate audience as their theoretical foundation. Under the auspices of two
University of Southern California political scientists, Theodore H. E. Chen
and Frederick T. C. Yu, and a cohort of Chinese-born, American-educated
researchers, HRRI presented the air force with "Studies in Chinese Communism." This multivolume analysis of the communist Chinese propaganda apparatus bore striking resemblance to the Schramm report.[24]

The researchers' Chinese background and explicit distaste for the People's
Republic elicited a detailed and alarmist picture of communist propaganda
onslaughts by saturation and monopolization. However, their training in
communication theory led them to discount the enduring ramifications of a

gargantuan Chinese propaganda machine. Adapting the concept of limited effects, they claimed that the use of mass media to divide and conquer confronted formidable social obstacles. They asserted that "exposure of the masses to the Communist propaganda does not necessarily mean their acceptance of the propaganda." Chinese resistance to indoctrination occurred in all strata of the population. Peasants feigned miscomprehension, city dwellers displayed indifference, and intellectuals stubbornly resisted these manipulative attempts to restructure Chinese society. No matter how efficient, no onslaught of mass media could alter the predisposition of the obstinate audience.[25]

Another joint report issued by HRRI and Harvard University's Russian Research Center accepted the Korean study's privileging of limited effects as well. The report claimed that officially ordained mass media in Soviet society competed with face-to-face communication, which was much more effective given its reliance on genuine, naturally cultivated opinion leaders. Unofficial oral communication networks were not merely a reaction to Soviet monopolization and communist oppression. "The Soviet system of word-of-mouth communications exhibits many of the distinctive characteristics. But, at the same time, it has many elements in common with both highly industrialized societies and backward areas, resulting from the fact that this is a recently industrialized system overlaying a peasant society."[26]

The resonance of the Korean HRRI report was mostly confined to such internal documents. As far as the academic publication circuit was concerned, Schramm and his senior collaborator, John Riley, published some of their findings in two scholarly articles on techniques of communication and control in "Sovietized Korea."[27] Even though the original Korean report was swiftly declassified, these two very enterprising scholars never published a scholarly monograph.

Such modest academic results were due, in part, to the study's lack of originality. Schramm and his colleagues offered no meaningful innovations. They had faithfully followed a path blazed by Harvard sociologist Alex Inkeles, whose *Public Opinion in Soviet Russia: A Study in Mass Persuasion* (1950) was published during the midst of the HRRI Korean research trip. Even though the Harvard study was based on the interviewing of political refugees—a far less reliable source than the informants of the HRRI study—Inkeles's focus on the main enemy and primary source of all secondary manifestations of "Sovietization" diminished the academic market value of the Korean report. Moreover, Inkeles had the additional advantage of writing under the auspices of Harvard University's prestigious Russian Research Center, one of the most fashionable centers of the military-academic complex.[28]

Much like the Schramm report, Inkeles's objective was to dispel the mystique of the Soviet political system and describe even the most threatening aspects of its political culture as nothing more than variations of well-documented behavioral phenomena. In an effusively positive foreword, Clyde

Cluckhohn, Harvard anthropologist and director of the Russian Research Center, explained that the Inkeles study contributed to a better understanding of the Soviet system by applying a "general theory of mass communication." He stated that Inkeles "had made excellent use of generalizations which have been developed . . . in the United States" in his deciphering of Soviet society.[29]

While acknowledging the power of coercion in the Soviet system, Inkeles was also a strong proponent of the limited effects of mass communication. Much like the Korean-based HRRI report, the Inkles study focused on agitators as the Sovietized variation of Western opinion leaders. Inkeles explained that "Bolshevik thought and practice continue to place the heaviest emphasis on daily face-to-face contact between the masses and representatives of the party, as a fundamental instrument of . . . influencing opinions and shaping attitudes." In comparing Bolshevik agitators to American opinion leaders, Inkeles, like his colleagues at HRRI, noted that agitators, as the primary disseminators of Party doctrine to the masses, were chosen in light of their high "personal standing with their audiences."[30]

The Schramm study of Korea echoed these ideas almost verbatim. Presumably, the main objective of the Korean model was to check in the Korean context ideas and theories developed elsewhere; by Schramm's own admission, Korea was a duplication of the Russian original. This fundamental lack of originality probably led Schramm and his collaborators to forgo an academic monograph. They turned, instead, to the less prestigious, but more lucrative commercial market. Rather than addressing their peers and students, they recast their academic report as a pseudoscientific publication. Less than a year after their semester abroad, Wilbur Schramm and John Riley transformed their original document into a popular form of anticommunist literature. Entitled *The Reds Take a City* (1951), this narrative of communist repression and the "Sovietization" of South Korea was translated into numerous languages and distributed worldwide by the United States Information Agency.

The Reds Take a City was built upon a series of interviews with overtly Western Korean informants selected from the original HRRI report. The interviews included the lengthy monologues of a Christian clergyman, an actress, a university professor, and a journalist. Reader recognition of the persecuted transformed Korea's civil war into a familiar story. Therefore, representatives of the laboring classes and other Koreans of unfamiliar backgrounds and professions were conspicuously absent from this tale of the communist threat. Permeating the entire book was a sense that even the most draconian techniques of Sovietization could not induce more than superficial political acquiescence.

In the best of traditions, the book had a happy ending. Schramm and Riley offered their readers the hope that "the experience of Koreans under communism was progressively disillusioning and . . . only small minorities, be they north or south of the 38th parallel, were completely taken in by the stratagem and machinations of the invaders." Here, then, was an easily digestible version of the "limited effects" paradigm of communication theory.

With the same ease with which they had superimposed a civilian-American communication paradigm on a foreign military subject matter, both Schramm and Riley returned effortlessly from Korea and communism to a uniquely American media context. Together with his spouse, Matilda White Riley, the Rutgers chair of the Sociology Department offered variations of limited effects in explaining the reaction of children to violence in the mass media. As early as 1951, the Rileys absolved the television industry for disseminating a culture of violence. They argued that violent programming only affected children who were predisposed to violence, those who were "most likely to feel insecure and inadequate" in their relationship with parents and peer groups.[31] Riley's growing reputation as a leading advocate of limited effects and as a skilled practitioner of applied behavioral research led him away from pure academic studies to the private sector. In 1960, he accepted the position of senior vice president and director of social research at the Equitable Life Insurance Society. Even after accepting this position, Riley remained a major consultant for the military on such areas as psychological warfare.[32]

Schramm, too, turned his attention to the growth industry of mass communications research and television. Much like Riley, Schramm argued that television had little direct impact on attitudes and opinions. Its major effect resided in providing what he called "image material," the social construction of situations and ways of life quite different from those directly experienced by the viewer.[33] Like most of Schramm's work, the notion of media as an image builder was not an original contribution. It was a simplistic adaptation of the concept of media-generated "empathy" — the psychic mechanism that enables individuals to identify with a role, time, and place different from their own. This seminal concept was the intellectual property of media scholar and modernization theorist Daniel Lerner.[34]

Other portions of Schramm's subsequent work were devoted to dispelling supposedly asymmetrical concern with the power of manipulative communicators, focusing, instead, on the freedom of the receiver to decipher, ignore, or distort media messages. Here, too, Schramm offered no meaningful departure from concepts developed by others. When asked during the course of an oral history to identify his major intellectual contribution to the field, Schramm stated that "it would be for one paragraph in *Television in the Lives of Our Children* (1961). It said: 'Perhaps the most important way to look at the effects of television on children is not what television does to children but what children do to television.' Children are not inert. You don't shoot television at children. They fit into what they know, what they are doing."[35] Schramm's intellectual legacy to future generations was, of course, nothing more than a summary of received knowledge on the theory of limited effects.

As the HRRI report and subsequent work suggests, Schramm was a pedestrian scholar. Even though he was, perhaps, the most prolific writer in the field of communication research, his intellectual accomplishments were mostly derivative. If Schramm's academic work was somewhat conventional, his administrative accomplishments were unique. By 1955 he had moved from the relative obscurity of developing mass communication programs and research institutes at midwestern public universities to the major leagues of private campuses. At Stanford, where Harold Lasswell, Daniel Lerner, and other river gods of communication studies had performed some of their most influential work, Schramm accepted the position of professor of communication and director of Stanford's Institute for Communication Research.

Schramm's impressive organizational accomplishments compensated amply for his modest intellectual achievements. By the early 1970s, Schramm was enshrined in the pantheon of communication studies. Everett Roger's recent history of the field places Schramm at the top of a short list of great contributors to the field of communications research. According to Rogers, "Schramm was so influential. . .that when he published a book about some new research direction, say, television effects and children, he set the agenda for communication study."[36] Emile McAnay's eulogy of Schramm places him even above the great theoretical contributors of the field. "Communications was a crossroads where many passed but few tarried." Unlike sociologist Paul Lazarsfeld, political scientist Harold Lasswell, or social psychologists Kurt Lewin and Carl Hovland, "Schramm was *the* founding father because he remained at the crossroads" and built an academic empire.[37]

The Canon of Cold War Communication Studies

At first glance, the placing of Schramm alongside Lasswell, Lazarsfeld, and other intellectual giants appears curious. Even those who have enshrined him as founding father offer only faint praise for his intellectual achievement and have focused, instead, upon his role as an institution builder. Such organizational feats were not, however, the reason for his lofty professional reputation. Others, besides Schramm, founded important communications research centers. It would appear, then, that the source of Schramm's aura lay elsewhere.

Media historian Christopher Simpson argues that Schramm's most favored status was due to his publication of the defining textbooks of the field.[38] Given the power of these textbooks, Schramm became the gatekeeper of communication studies. Media theoretician Steven Chaffee describes Schramm as "the principal disseminator of that Zeitgeist . . . those paradigms and that knowledge yielded by mass communication research."[39] His virtual monopoly of basic reading material in communication studies allowed him to either anoint, or dispose of, the theoretical innovators of the field. His textbooks attributed enduring scientific value to some of the theories and their producers, while banishing others to oblivion.

In his most widely distributed textbook, *Process and Effects of Mass Communication* (1954), Schramm approached the study of mass communication as primarily a modified species of social psychology. He provided ample space for quantitative experimental studies of attitude change carried out in the course of World War II, in particular the work accomplished under the auspices of *TAS*. Here, Schramm included studies of persuasion undertaken in laboratories or within the context of small primary groups. As a behavioralist he saw no need for communication studies to include analyses of larger social systems, or to grapple with historical variables and their impact on attitudes and persuasion.

An entire section of his influential textbook was devoted to "communicating to another culture." All the articles in this section focused, in one manner or another, on familiarizing the unfamiliar by quantification. The fuzzy fields of language and psycholinguistics were not part of Schramm's definition of mass communication.[40]

Schramm devoted inordinate space to the limited effects of communications. Those who offered contrary opinions had no place in his compilations. Despite the fact that the principal studies on limited effects of mass communications were carried out on small, homogeneous communities and before the advent of the television age, they appeared in his textbooks as the "dominant paradigm."[41] In seeking personal corroborating evidence for studies on limited effects, Schramm trotted out anecdotes from his Korean War experiences.[42] He found no inherent problem in comparing studies derived from an American context with his interrogations of enemy POWs in Korea.

At an epistemological level, Schramm's canon of communication studies was an exercise in fusion. His textbooks ignored distinctions between the foreign and the familiar, or between military and civilian spheres. All articles on "communicating to another culture" were in one way or another tied to psychological warfare and government propaganda. Carl Hovland's studies on persuasion, all of which were carried out in a military context, appeared as contributions to persuasion, in general. Schramm did not offer any qualification of results due to these special circumstances.

In comparing American or Western strategies of social control with "Sovietized" societies, the canon implied that propaganda and information management were normative aspects of modern society. The techniques of information management in "Sovietized" societies were neither exceptional nor novel. They existed in modern democratic societies as well. The Schramm collections condemned the political themes of information control in "Sovietized" societies and the ruthlessness of its implementation. However, Schramm's compilations studiously avoided any criticism of the very attempt to orchestrate or manipulate public opinion. Condemnation of communist strategies never shrouded implicit, yet clear convictions that information management—a polite term for media manipulation—was inevitable in all modern political regimes.

The Schramm compilations did not identify clear-cut, unbridgeable differences between democratic and totalitarian societies' uses of information control; condemnation was reserved for the content or abuse of certain techniques. In its denunciation of "Sovietized" political systems, the communication canon actually identified a narrowing gap between American management of opinion and totalitarian techniques. As the case of the striking similarity between American-style opinion leaders and Soviet agitators suggests, the information politics of democracies and totalitarian powers appeared, at times, to converge.

Schramm's mapping of his field was corroborated and copied by others. The influential *Public Opinion and Propaganda* (1954), edited by University of Michigan social psychologist Daniel Katz, offered its readers a similar format. The underlying premise of this collection of essays, hailed as the ultimate compilation of definitive articles on social psychology and persuasion, was the irrelevance of distinguishing between democratic and totalitarian techniques of communication. Differences were merely quantitative rather than qualitative. All forms of "public opinion," a term associated with democratic societies, were affected by "propaganda," an expression that the uninitiated mistakenly associated with totalitarianism or warfare. Tactics used in inherently totalitarian or confrontational situations were integral parts of the democratic agenda as well.

The architecture of the Katz collection demonstrated a determined effort to move beyond the constraints of politics and ideology toward a more scientific exposition of persuasive techniques. Thus, an article on "Propaganda Techniques in Institutional Advertising" in American society preceded an exposition on German short-wave propaganda broadcasts to the United States. By the same token, the renowned "Cohesion and Disintegration in the Wehrmacht," written by Morris Janowitz and Edward Shils, appeared alongside a discussion of "personal contact or mail propaganda" for encouraging voter turnout in American elections.

The book erased outmoded distinctions between propaganda on the battlefield and in the marketplace. Differences of strategy were mostly technical; the theoretical underpinnings of persuasion were the same, only the intensity of the message was adjusted to suit different military and civilian settings. Projects designed for war could be tested on civilians, and lessons derived from battles were adopted by civilian advertising strategists.[43]

Whether the assumptions and theories undergirding these collections were scientifically valid is beside the point. The importance of the canon lay in its epistemological authority and its validation of contested strategies for understanding the process of communication both at home and in foreign lands.

The power of the canon was not, of course, restricted to university campuses. Beyond the world of textbooks and classrooms, this type of fusion between the familiar and foreign would manifest itself in numerous formats during the course of the Cold War. Privileged American concepts of human behavior affected the texts of psychological warfare and the management of POW compounds and even transformed negotiation strategies with the enemy.

America's academic warriors were neither naive nor unaware of alternative strategies for understanding the world. There was a method to their madness. By collapsing distinctions between the familiar and the foreign, by limiting historical analysis, and by superimposing American-derived strategies on foreign cultures, they conceptualized distant and incoherent landscapes in a manner that made them susceptible to a comfortable, familiar style of crisis management. Behavioralism in general and communication theory in particular were not only instruments for the methodic mapping of the unfamiliar culture. They were also active strategies for imposing order on, and legitimizing an American worldview of, a cultural and political terra incognita. The superimposing of American-made theories of behavioralism on the Korean reality allowed policy makers to suppress the genuine differences of this distant land and pursue policies with only casual links to reality.

5.

The War of Ideas

Ideology and Science in

Psychological Warfare

When war broke out in Korea on Sunday, June 25, 1950, Harry Truman was back home in Independence, Missouri. Dean Acheson, his secretary of state, was enjoying an idle weekend on his family farm in rural Maryland.[1] Although resting, the country's leaders claimed in their memoirs that they were not caught entirely off guard. Surprise, they implied, was mostly of a geographic quality; they had expected conflict, but not in Asia. America's military and civilian leaders had anticipated that the test of wills would occur on familiar European battlefields. "For some months, as tensions had mounted . . . we had run exercises on danger spots for renewed Soviet probing on our determination," Dean Acheson recalled. "Korea was on the list but not among the favorites. Berlin, Turkey, Greece," perhaps even faraway Iran all seemed to be more likely venues for a Soviet test of wills.[2]

This Eurocentricity defined, by default, the meaning of the Korean War. Despite the distinctly Asian contours of the conflict, America's decision makers interpreted the Korean hostilities as a sideshow of an eventual European

showdown. Whether Korea was a testing ground for American resolve in anticipation of a Soviet-led offensive somewhere in Europe, or whether the Russians had devised the war in order to divert American resources and attention
from the main European theater was almost beside the point. The nation's
leaders were convinced that the most dangerous consequence of conflict in
Asia was its effect on Europe. President Truman and most of his close advisors
"felt certain that if South Korea was allowed to fall Communist leaders would
be emboldened to override nations closer to our own shores."[3]

Such spatial fixation resulted, in part, from the fact that the architects of
America's Korean policy were still basking in past triumphs. The country's
military and civilian leaders had established their careers on European battlefields and in political affairs; they saw no need to seek new fields of glory in
unfamiliar terrain. The "loss of China"—the supposedly bungled support for
American allies in the Chinese civil war and the ensuing triumph of an inimi-
cal regime on the mainland—merely strengthened preoccupations with Europe, where most American government and military figures could claim familiarity and success. Hence, they planned, hoped, and expected that the
military and diplomatic challenges in the offing would occur in Europe.

The academic experts involved in the Korean War never challenged this
Eurocentricity. Most of these consultants had also established their reputation
in the European theater of World II. Moreover, as true believers in universal
patterns of behavior, they had no compelling reason to adjust their inherently
Western theories to unfamiliar Korean circumstances. In addition to this pervasive cultural and spatial bias, these mobilized academics expressed a deep
and somewhat counterintuitive contempt for the power of ideas. Despite the
allegedly mesmerizing powers of totalitarian enemies, past and present, they
dismissed ideology as a motivating force in human behavior.

By the early 1950s, a dominant cohort of American intellectuals had declared their "emancipation from ideology" whether right, left, or center. The
major paradigm guiding these American intellectuals was the "baselessness of
ideological pretensions" of all types and colors.[4] Thus, Cold War academics
assumed that communism—the most salient and intimidating of contemporary ideological rivals—would not be subdued by other, more attractive Western ideological alternatives because all ideologies were subterfuges for something else.

American behavioral and social scientists reduced ideology to a rationalization of the thirst for power, a psychological defense mechanism for screening
information that might challenge a person's status, or a displacement of psychologically disturbed minds. Consequently, the solvent for the communist
threat was not a counterideology espousing socialism, laissez-faire, or anything
else. It was, rather, what David Riesman described as the fostering of the
natural defenses people have against the stranglehold of totalitarianism in
general and ideological frameworks in particular. The most lethal enemy of

totalitarianism and ideologies was not the attractiveness of other ideas, but the narcissism of human nature. No ideological system, however powerful, attractive, or intimidating, could resist the corrosive force of "people in pursuit of their private ends." Pervasive apathy, endemic corruption, a thriving black market, and rampant crime in communist countries were signs of the inability of ideology to tame and subdue human nature. "We need to re-evaluate the role of corruption . . . with less emphasis on its obviously malign features and more on its power as an antidote to fanaticism," Riesman declared. He argued that the encouragement of personal desires—the "anti-social, anti-societal" self-seeking behavior of citizens in totalitarian enemy societies—was the most efficient weapon for combating the communist threat or, for that matter, any overtly oppressive ideological regime.[5]

Psychological Warfare: The World War II Legacy

During the early stages of the Korean War, the most visible transformation of the "end of ideology" into policy occurred within the domain of psychological warfare, a futuristic strategy for defeating the enemy by words rather than bullets. When called upon to design a modern campaign of psychological warfare, the country's mobilized academics defined effective propaganda as a simple variation of conventional behavioral paradigms rather than a battle of ideas.[6]

This trivialization of ideas was by no means a by-product of the Cold War. During the course of World War II the designers and architects of psychological warfare had dismissed rational persuasion or concerted bombardments of ideas as a waste of resources. A residue of skepticism underlay the conventional interpretation of World War II as a battle of competing ideological titans. The enemy, they argued, was not mesmerized by ideas. By the same token, they did not assume that ideology played a significant part in Western society, either.

World War II psychological warriors held a fundamentally pessimistic assessment of human capacity for altruism and public concern. They approached the human species as, first and foremost, a self-seeking organism, dominated by egotistical cravings for survival, sexual gratification, and the diminishing of hunger and fear.[7] These academic advisors, most of whom espoused the behavioral persuasion, argued that contemporary social circumstances had repressed and tamed these primitive, basic instincts. Consequently, the task of the efficient psychological warrior was to devise a mechanism for circumventing the repressive devices of modern civilization in general and military life in particular in order to tap into the individual's natural state of narcissism. The exploitation of socially subversive primal drives was the main, if not the only, task of efficient psychological warfare.

In accordance with the master theories of mass communication, World War II psychological warfare doctrine emphasized its limitations. Propaganda, according to prevailing orthodoxy, was a conservative rather than a subversive tool. At best, propaganda tended to reinforce existing opinions rather than convert. As far as battle line psychological warfare was concerned, the soldier, much like his civilian counterpart, employed defensive mechanisms for suppressing or modifying irrelevant or unwanted information. A campaign of truth was, then, an insufficient weapon because the conversion capabilities of propaganda were limited.

Standard World War II psychological warfare doctrine shunned politics, made no attempt to promote democracy, and did not condemn the enemy's worldview. "Praising the excellence of our product is not only secondary but rather beside the point," Martin Herz argued in his seminal analysis of World War II leaflet propaganda. Herz explained that "it would be difficult to sell" the American way "to potential customers who are day in, day out, told that" the enemy is a "danger and a menace." Thus, Allied propaganda during World War II had invested little energy in convincing "German soldiers of the iniquity of the Nazi system," thereby running the risk of alienating members of the potential audience. Instead, the ultimate goal was merely to remind the enemy "that they were being defeated and that it was sensible to give up."[8] The ideal text for psychological warfare was, then, ideologically innocent.

Psychological warfare focused primarily on offers of physical survival, and was deemed productive only when the enemy confronted chaos, catastrophe, or imminent defeat. Functional propaganda, according to World War II doctrine, played upon the material benefits of surrender, the deprivation of families back home, the cravings for creature comforts, and the arousal of sexual instincts.

The centerpiece of this doctrine was the surrender leaflet, an official-looking pass, with instructions on prudent surrender procedures, accompanied by detailed visual or textual descriptions of food, medical aid, and the safety from death and mutilation available during captivity. No denigration of the enemy nation or extravagant claims appeared in these leaflets. The leaflets were mostly descriptions of minimal creature comforts and protection against personal annihilation. "Germans like things done in an official and formal manner," Paul Linebarger informed the readers in his authoritative book on psychological warfare. "The Allies obliged, and gave the Germans various forms of very official looking 'surrender passes,' . . . printed in red and (with) . . . banknote-type engraving which makes it resemble a soap-premium coupon."[9]

In addition to the limiting of themes, the academic experts of World War II psychological warfare urged a limitation of targets as well. They argued that most individuals were not concerned with the weighty issues of ideas and values, and few had the power to influence policy. Rand Corporation's Hans Speier explained that because "the mass of the population cannot overthrow, or actively influence the policies of despotic regimes . . . the population at large is no rewarding target of conversion propaganda. . . . Any notion to the contrary may be called the democratic fallacy."[10]

The primary targets of efficient psychological warfare were either "marginal men" or persons experiencing a life-threatening crisis. Attacking the self-assured person or the member of a stable social system was dismissed as "a waste of time." The ideal targets were potential waverers, "the men who despaired of victory but were reluctant to draw the consequences, the men who were still willing to fight, but who fought without determination, who would 'never surrender' but who might submit to capture 'if the situation were hopeless.' "[11]

These influential conclusions regarding both propaganda content and targets were codified in the seminal World War II studies of Morris Janowitz and Edward Shils, both of whom were leading figures in the military-academic network at mid-century.[12] Their fieldwork had been carried out in POW camps in Europe, where informants reported that loyalty to the group and camaraderie, rather than ideology, were the main reasons for their fighting spirit.

The major thrust of these World War II studies was to prove that the seemingly irrational behavior of human beings—such as the allegedly fanatical disposition of Germans to continue fighting even when faced with imminent defeat—could be explained in logical, scientific terms. Shils and Janowitz argued that ideology had not effected the fighting spirit of the Wehrmacht; commitment to the cause was the result of social cohesion within the German fighting units. Their POW informants described their daily life as dominated by a supportive group of close comrades-in-arms and parental officers. Most of the study focused on the marginal role of ideology among the rank and file. Harsh discipline and/or fanatical indoctrination were presented as peripheral aspects of the Wehrmacht code. Shils and Janowitz claimed that the presence of indoctrination officers was "regarded apathetically or as a joke" because "for most of the German soldiers, the political system of National Socialism was of little interest." By the same token, the German soldier-informants rejected Allied counterideology as well. It was all "bunk," regardless of the source. "We need only repeat the statement of a German soldier, 'Nazism begins ten miles behind the front line.' "

The implications of such findings for psychological warfare were crucial. As far as Shils and Janowitz were concerned, the use of propaganda for breaking the enemy's will to fight was effective only when the soldier was faced with a personal existential crisis. Propaganda could pierce the unwavering loyalty of German soldiers when the "primary unit" disintegrated "due to breaks in communication, and the lack of food or medical supplies." Under these circumstances, soldiers reverted to a primal "narcissistic format of behavior," a preoccupation with personal survival, and a discarding of concerns for one's comrades. Propaganda was effective upon the crumbling of a constraining social unit, and constructive propaganda focused on fundamental concerns only: promises of food, warmth, comfort, and survival. Following the disintegration of their social frame of reference, German soldiers resorted to basic fears of isolation, personal "concern about food and health," and a "fear of castration" derived from "their narcissistic apprehensiveness about damage to their vital organs and to their physical organisms as a whole." The inundating of the enemy with political and ideological messages was, under these circumstances, a waste of resources.

This influential study was based on questionable empirical evidence. To begin with, Shils and Janowitz ignored entirely the indoctrination of German youth prior to their mobilization. Schooling and mass media had fashioned a worldview prior to induction into the military; ideological commitment was, perhaps, latent but presumably potent. In addition, their informants were hardly representative of the entire Wehrmacht. The POWs were mostly infantry troops, with only sporadic informants from the armored corps, artillery units, or other army personnel; their study did not include the interrogation of navy or air force personnel. Moreover, all informants had been captured in the final stages of the war in Africa, Italy, France, and Germany. Shils and Janowitz apparently had no access to German captives from the eastern front. This meant, a critic has pointed out, "that the article inadvertently ignored most German ground forces."[13]

Such caveats were of little consequence because Shils and Janowitz disarmingly implied that their dismissal of indoctrination was not a great discovery but, rather, a mobilization of science to bolster preordained conclusions. Their research did not bring sudden clarity to a confusion of opinions regarding German motivation. Instead, it was derived from the codex of existing knowledge. The fundamental thrust of their study was to seek corroborating evidence for, and not test the validity of, their belief that the German army, like any other modern army, was "sustained only to very slight extent by the National Socialist political conviction of its members."[14] In this sense, their interrogation of recent enemy captives made sense. Considering the mental disposition of German POWs, historian Omer Bartov has observed, the enemy captives "could hardly be expected to reply sincerely to questions posed by their interrogators regarding their commitment to a regime and ideology deemed criminal by the enemy."[15]

Despite these obvious problems, the findings of Shils and Janowitz had an enduring effect. Given the aura of these two prominent men, their conclusions were accepted as scientific facts. The dismissal of ideology, the importance of social cohesion, and, conversely, the resort to instinctual drives when faced with social disintegration became central conceptual frameworks for analyzing military performance in both Korea and Vietnam.[16] Critics would occasionally challenge some of Shils and Janowitz's technical points. However, the axiomatic assumption was that ideological explanations of motivation were unconvincing. In a typical comment, the authors of a study of American military performance in Vietnam asserted that "we know that military cohesion exists quite apart from politics and ideologies. . . . Specifically, a sense of active patriotism, nationalism, or other ideologies is not necessarily central to military discipline, and cohesion."[17]

The Korean Context: Project Revere

The most notable academic fine-tuning of World War II theories for the Korean theater was Project Revere, a military-civilian investigation of communication processes carried out between 1951 and 1953. Funded by the air force and directed by University of Washington sociologist Stuart A. Dodd, Project Revere represented an ambitious attempt to codify in mathematical terms the "reception" of airdropped leaflets and the "diffusion" of their content. For these purposes, the air force provided Dodd and his associates at the University of Washington with a budget of $300,000, a particularly large sum by early 1950s standards.[18]

Dodd's mandate was to increase the affectivity of military psychological warfare in Korea. However, he chose to carry out his research in markedly different surroundings. Sensing no contradiction in terms, Dodd targeted a variety of American towns in Washington State and elsewhere.

Initially, the scientists of Project Revere focused on what they called "interpersonal message diffusion," or in lay terms, the spread of messages contained in leaflets by word-of-mouth. Choosing a rural town of about one thousand inhabitants in Washington State, the project workers devised a strategy for motivating leaflet recipients to learn the contents of the leaflets and subsequently pass on the message to others.

For these purposes they developed the "Coffee Slogan Experiment." In what one of the participants called "happy, if unusual" circumstances, the project directors received the collaboration of a local coffee company, producers of the Gold Shield brand. In return for several hundred pounds of coffee, Project Revere chose as its experimental message for diffusion the company slogan of "Gold Shield Coffee; Good as Gold." In order to stimulate the learning of the slogan, as well as its diffusion, the Revere staff offered some of the local households a free pound of coffee. This group of "starters" was required to learn the slogan, and pass it on to other residents. Later that day a plane dropped thirty thousand leaflets on the community, informing town residents that one out of every five households knew the slogan, and promising free coffee for all those who managed to discover and learn the Gold Shield message.

The second stage of Revere involved a civil defense theme. Leaflets appealed to respondents to "be modern Paul Reveres" by passing on extra copies to other town residents and mailing back an attached postcard. This portion of the project produced mathematical formulas for the optimal amount of leaflets per capita. Revere research produced, as well, a host of banal conclusions, suggesting that family ties and social networks were the primary channels of message diffusion. The study confirmed contemporary theories regarding the role of opinion leaders in the dissemination of information, and corroborated World War II studies on the distortion of oral information.

The significance of Project Revere was not, however, in its predictable results. The major implication of the project was the assertion that communication techniques developed in distinctly American surroundings were reproducible. Revere provided rules for the diffusion of messages, reduced to mathematical formulas and purged of cultural qualifications. As far as Revere associates were concerned, diffusion could be measured objectively; elements such as ratio of leaflets per person or channels of diffusion were not culturally specific. The substitution of commercial messages hawking coffee with civil defense warnings implied, as well, that the content of the messages was unimportant. It was the persuasive technique that counted. The use of an American civilian population to devise a strategy for the diffusion of messages among enemies and in war zones had produced no major concern for correctives; these were details to be worked out in the field.

Psychological Warfare in Korea

For the most part, the army, the service that bore the brunt of the Korean conflict, executed the actual business of waging psychological warfare in Korea. Once the protracted nature of the Korean War had sunk in, the army resurrected its defunct propaganda mechanism, by creating the Office of the Chief of Psychological Warfare (OCPW). The program for psychological warfare in Korea included grand plans for the exploitation of radio, the ultimate technology of mass communication at mid-century. Radio broadcasts, in both Chinese and Korean, offered about one-and-a half hours of original programming a day beamed from relay systems spread throughout Korea and Japan. In addition to radio, the OCPW devised plans for broadcasting tactical propaganda by means of airborne and motorized loudspeaker units.

The most significant obstacle facing Korean War psychological warriors was the low-tech state of the enemy. Radio broadcasts, the weapon of choice of the early 1950s, were deemed problematic given the low ratio of radio receivers per capita in Korea. The army's most optimistic assessments reported about two hundred thousand civilian radio sets in Korea, approximately one set per one hundred persons. The thin distribution of receivers, together with the disruption of power in most parts of Korea, rendered this medium all but useless.[19] An alternative to radio, the use of loudspeakers at the front, as well as airborne loudspeaker broadcasts, floundered due to the lack of native-speaking personnel.[20] Somewhat reluctantly, American psychological warriors turned their attention to the low-tech dissemination of propaganda by leaflets.

Even though leaflets were somewhat of a primitive means of communication, this form of psychological warfare reaped the benefits of modern technology. Aerial leaflet drops employed a cluster-type of bomb, using a mechanism that jettisoned its cargo at about 1,000 feet. Each bomb had a capacity ranging from 22,000 to 45,000 leaflets; aircrafts could carry thirty-two bombs per mission. In addition, the army used a modified version of 105 mm howitzer shells for artillery barrages of leaflets. Although each shell held only 400 leaflets, the advantage of this method was its accuracy, as opposed to the typical and haphazard carpet bombing of leaflets. By January 1952, the volume of paper raining down from Korean skies had reached staggering proportions. In an operation controlled from Tokyo, the Far East Command (FEC) inundated Korea with over 2 million leaflets per day using 400 different texts for dissemination among Chinese and North Korean troops, as well as North Korean civilians. Within the first 18 months of the Korean conflict American aircrafts and artillery had disgorged a billion leaflets, the work of 400 creative personnel.

In defining the content of its psychological warfare program, the OCPW employed academic advisors who were associated with the Rand Corporation and the army's two major think tanks, ORO and HumRRO. Armed with the positive experiences of World War II and strengthened by the growing prestige associated with the behavioral sciences, the academic consultants of OCPW descended on Korea immediately following the outbreak of hostilities.

Upon assuming their Korean duties, these academic advisors confronted an existing psychological warfare operation that was inconsistent with accepted behavioral theory. Ostensibly, the debate concerning psychological warfare focused on Harold Lasswell's classical statement of "who says what to whom and to what effect." However, the actual defining of content for psychological warfare was rife with controversy. Proposals for a campaign based on values clashed with counterarguments claiming that ideological messages merely cluttered the landscape with meaningless verbiage.

Following the outbreak of hostilities, early efforts at organizing psychological warfare were executed by the staff officers of General Douglas MacArthur's Japanese-based FEC. Under the guidance of Major General Charles A. Willoughby, MacArthur's chief of intelligence operations, early propaganda proposed overtly political themes, such as singing the praises of democracy or attacking communism in strong ideological terms. In its plans for disseminating propaganda among Chinese troops, the psychological warfare branch of FEC proposed direct attacks on the very nature of communism, as well as assailing enemy leaders. Early themes included: "Chinese soldiers are being used to fight battles . . . to impose communism on all of Asia. Are you one of those to be sacrificed for a foreign country?" as well as attacks on the Chinese-

Russian nexus, claiming that "the USSR plans to separate Inner Mongolia, Tibet, Sinktiang, and Manchuria from China, as it has already done with Outer Mongolia." The ultimate objective of such leaflets was not to encourage mere surrender. MacArthur's propaganda had the far-reaching objective of destroying the mesmerizing hold of communist doctrine by "exposing Communist plans for exploitation and subjugation of China."[21]

This challenge to the thematically limited behavioral doctrine of psychological warfare was by no means confined to MacArthur headquarters or to the radical fringes of the American body politic. As early as 1946, Harvard social psychologist Donald McGranahan, who had collaborated with Shils and Janowitz in their study of cohesion and disintegration in the German army, categorically rejected the conclusions of his colleagues. McGranahan admonished his collaborators for their "advertising complex" and their rejection of ideas. Good commercial advertising entailed the avoidance of debate and controversy and, conversely, "appeals to attitudes that are widespread and non-controversial—desire for physical comfort, health, beauty, popularity, love of home and children, etc." The superimposing of such concepts on the struggle with totalitarian regimes was, according to McGranahan, a grave mistake for both moral and practical reasons.

A brief glance at history, both recent and distant, proved that ideological campaigns had achieved impressive results. The "evangelic propaganda" of Christianity had succeeded by "direct attack on pagan beliefs" and openly declaring "conversion to be its ultimate goal." By the same token the Russians, "who undoubtedly discovered the same trend of loyalty to Hitler among their German prisoners, found this no argument against" what McGranahan considered a very successful "frontal attack on the Nazi cause." The United States, he argued should "openly avow" its purpose of converting the enemy to democracy.[22] Evasion of crucial ideological issues unnecessarily yielded a large portion of the field to the enemy. Moreover, camouflaging the philosophical foundations of the United States' participation in the war against totalitarianism raised unwanted questions concerning the country's ideological integrity and commitment to victory.

McGranahan cited, as well, a politically prudent reason for introducing ideology into propaganda. Well aware of the climate of anti-intellectualism in mid-century America, he argued that the inclusion of explicit ideological statements would dispel innuendos of academia's doubtful political loyalties. It was perhaps for these political reasons that Brigadier General Robert A. McClure, the chief of the army's OCPW, refused to take sides in this fundamental rift. As a veteran and direct beneficiary of the World War II propaganda mechanism, he, of course, advocated using "the best advertising techniques," a euphemism for standard behavioralist techniques. On the other hand, his political instincts led him to declare that "at least we ought to expand our effort in the ideological field and see if we can't change the attitude of the people on the other side."[23] McClure's solution was to permit the simultaneous dissemination of leaflets adhering to the two conflicting approaches to psychological warfare. Given the political climate of the United States at mid-century, this fusionist strategy made sense.

Fusion, however, was not a simple issue; the philosophical differences separating the two strategies were sharp. As point of departure, the authors of the behavioralist leaflets approached their mission as an exercise in persuasion techniques derived from the world of advertising, rather than the presentation of conflicting ideologies. Their texts promoted a social order in which persons were encouraged to think primarily of themselves and their private concerns. The behavioralist approach inspired no devotion to causes or collectives beyond one's self or family. The major themes, both literary and graphic, focused on the private things that people held dear—survival, family, and personal security—and encouraged them, by contrast, to ignore the public interest. (Figure 1)

These leaflets concentrated on the immediate and personal, waiving aside the impact of encompassing economic, political, and social structures on behavior and attitudes. They dismissed politics and urged their audience to forgo the security of group loyalties in favor of private gratification. The war in this material was translated into a private dilemma rather than a common struggle. Surrender offered the fulfillment of personal and intimate concerns: individual security, personal relief from hunger and fear, and sexual gratification. Concern for others was either removed from these leaflets or else presented as a species of false consciousness.

The leaflets of ideologists, by contrast, preached a social rather than private message; they appealed to a sense of the nation as a whole. (Figure 2) The texts honored tradition, called for altruistic sacrifice, and invoked a collective heritage and the restoration of a golden age. There was little that one could call "capitalist" in these leaflets. If capitalism is a system promoting the private pursuit of happiness, these leaflets were explicitly noncapitalist and, at times, anticapitalist. They demanded deferment of private gratification and invoked, instead, communal values. In contrast to the behavioralist offerings of useful tips for personal survival, these political texts promoted altruism and sacrifice.

The uneasy coexistence between these two competing strategies led to occasional crosscurrents. At times, the behavioralists would address larger political issues, and at times the ideologists would attempt to link personal benefits with larger causes. The conflict over the portrayal of Kim Il Sung, leader of North Korea, serves as a case in point. In departure from standard procedure, the behavioralists attacked the popular leader of their nemesis. However, in accordance with World War II doctrine, they avoided direct assault on the North Korean leader's political persona, so as not to arouse the antagonism of Koreans who admired and trusted him. Rather than waging a frontal attack on political loyalties, these leaflets sought only to induce suspicion and confusion. In accordance with contemporary behavioralist doctrine, the texts did not condemn Kim Il Sung but, instead, called into doubt his very existence. In cartoons and in texts, these leaflets announced that "the man who calls himself Kim Il Sung has deceived the people in Korea in many ways, but the most dishonorable is his pretense to be Kim Il Sung, the great hero of Korea." The leaflet identified the imposter as "Kim Sung Chu, a Communist who was sent to Korea from Russia in 1945" and had entangled Koreans in a civil war for the benefit of outside forces. Lest the message get lost, the text was accompanied by a cartoon showing the " 'the false Kim Il Sung' looking at his faceless reflection in a mirror, and remarking on his loss of face in Korea." (Figure 3)

The premise behind this curious attempt to undermine the people's trust in their leader was derived from the experiences of World War II. In preparing the content of their anti-German propaganda, Allied psychological warfare operations had assumed that "the steadfastness with which the German soldier held to his loyalty to Hitler, for example, indicated that a frontal attack on this particular ideological symbol was less likely to succeed than appeals based on non-ideological considerations."[24] Following in the footsteps of their World War predecessors, Korean War behavioralists refrained from attacking Kim Il Sung, preferring, instead, to cast doubt on his actual existence.

Advocates of the direct ideological frontal attack had no recourse to such hesitations. The Kim Il Sung in their leaflets was a cruel despot as well as a groveling servant of Russian masters. A typical leaflet showed Kim Il Sung handing over the agricultural products of the suffering Korean people to his Russian masters. (Figure 4). Such leaflets, according to proponents, would further "North Koreans' resentment toward their communist regime."

Partisans of the political approach sought to arouse antipathy toward communism by underscoring its dystopian aspects. In literature aimed at Chinese troops, their leaders were portrayed as puppets of Russian interlopers (Figure 5), and communism appeared as the destroyer of authentic Chinese traditions. The ideological approach portrayed "Russian inspired communistic influence" as shattering the Chinese family, and encouraging children to inform on their parents and forsake their ancestors. (Figure 6)

The behavioralist approach, by contrast, focused on the personal, rather than the institutional consequences of the communist presence. The poorly clad, ill-equipped soldier, pictured alone, rather than as part of a group, had no chance of survival when confronted by overwhelming enemy firepower. (Figure 7) The sexual themes focused on the rape of defenseless wives. Evil Communists, both Korean and Chinese interlopers, unleashed their sexual appetites on innocent spouses of frontline soldiers. (Figure 8)

As had been the case in World War II, the centerpiece of the behavioralist campaign was the surrender leaflet. Creature comforts—food, cigarettes, and medical treatment—were used as enticements for surrender. (Figure 9) Here,

FIGURE 1. Holiday leaflet "designed to create dissension between the NK people and the NK government."

Frame 1: Two dispirited NK soldiers in the snow.

Frame 2: Korean spouse with miserable children. Two cranes hold a banner inscribed "1953 Lunar New Year." The accompanying text notes that "it is the Communists who force you to spend such a miserable Lunar New Year."

(Courtesy MacArthur Memorial Archives, Norfolk, Va.)

1102

FIGURE 2. Surrender appeal to ex-ROK soldiers in North Korean ranks. The illustration portrays Tangun, the legendary father of the Korean nation, standing against a backdrop of the ROK flag as he welcomes ex-ROK soldiers back into the fold. The caption reads: "One father, one blood, one undivided nation." (Courtesy MacArthur Memorial Archives, Norfolk, Va.)

FIGURE 3. Leaflet claiming Kim Il Sung is an imposter. *Frame 1*: A figure, labeled "the false Kim Il Sung," gazes at his faceless reflection and remarks on his "loss of face." *Frame 2*: An advisor tells the leader-imposter that "The people are clamoring for peace." Kim replies "Yes, but the Communist party must have war in order to keep its power in Korea." (Courtesy MacArthur Memorial Archives, Norfolk, Va.)

FIGURE 4. Leaflet designed to foster North Korean resentment toward communism.
Frame 1: A supplicant Kim Il Sung offers his meager gift of Korean agricultural products to a Russian master who demands more.
Frame 2: A harsh Kim Il Sung demands from "North Korean people" the entire stock of their agricultural products for Russian masters.
Frame 3: Contrast between a well-fed, gluttonous Russian and the empty-handed Korean peasant. (Courtesy MacArthur Memorial Archives, Norfolk, Va.)

FIGURE 5. Leaflet designed to arouse resentment of Chinese leaders. Illustration shows "Soviet advisor" manipulating marionettes labeled "Soviet Puppet Liu," "Soviet Puppet Mao," "Soviet Puppet Chou." Chinese Text: So-called Soviet advisors are Russian special agents sent to control China. Under the domination of Chinese communist Soviet puppets, China has no independence. Stay safe and keep fit for fighting against the communist Soviet puppets. Korean Text: This is a UN message to the CCF Place it for them to see. (Courtesy MacArthur Memorial Memorial Archives, Norfolk, Va.)

FIGURE 6. Leaflet designed "to arouse animosity of CCF toward Russia for destroying the traditional family."
Frame 1: Son: I will testify that he is a reactionary. Mother: But son, you cannot testify against your Papa! Son: Stalin is my Papa!
Frame 2: "Russian reforms wreck Chinese homes." Russian soldier: Her husband has been away from home too long. Now according to the new marriage laws, she is to be *your* wife. Bottom statement: Don't fight Russia's war! Stay safe to free China from Russian domination. (Courtesy MacArthur Memorial Archives, Norfolk, Va.)

FIGURE 7. Leaflet demonstrating a single North Korean soldier confronting overwhelming American firepower. The caption reads: "The sky thunders . . . the earth rocks . . . human flesh cannot stand against tanks and planes!" (Courtesy MacArthur Memorial Archives, Norfolk, Va.)

Figure 8. Leaflet "designed to create dissension between North Koreans and CCF." Accompanying text: NK people and soldiers! The Chinese communist dogs, by meddling in the Korean War, not only prolong the war and kill your blood brothers. They also rape your women while Korean men fight at the front! (Courtesy MacArthur Memorial Archives, Norfolk, Va.)

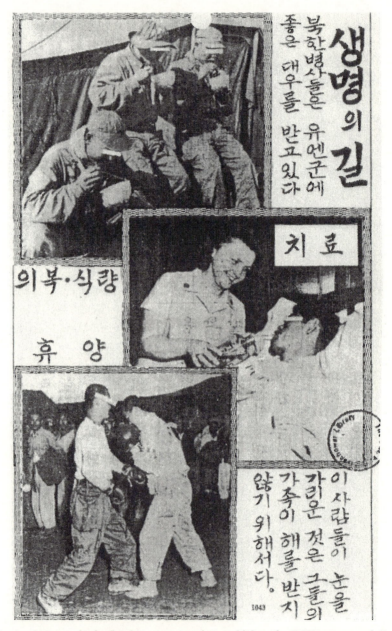

FIGURE 9. Surrender leaflet demonstrating the good life at the POW compound. Reverse side contains a surrender leaflet in Korean. (Courtesy Dwight D. Eisenhower Presidential Library, Abeline, Kans.)

FIGURE 9 (cont.). Reverse side of POW leaflet. The final paragraph of the leaflet promises that "food, warm clothing and cigarettes are provided for all. And you will given the opportunity for health-restoring recreation."

FIGURE 10. Leaflet aimed at supposedly literate Korean opinion leaders. The cartoon strip demonstrates the manner in which students were promised only "a few weeks" of military service before returning to school. The final frame shows a communist officer screaming at his reluctant student-soldiers: "Advance dogs, or I will shoot you myself. Fight for communism!" The accompanying text is a wordy discussion of communist duplicity. (Courtesy MacArthur Memorial Archives, Norfolk, Va.)

Figure 11. Chinese "antimorale" leaflet. A Russian pushes a Chinese Communist, who, in turn, pushes a Chinese soldier. The caption reads: "Why die for Russia?" (Courtesy MacArthur Memorial Archives, Norfolk, Va.)

FIGURE 12. Gulf War leaflet appealing to private concerns of the Iraqi soldier. The caption reads: "Fellow Iraqi soldier. It hurts us that you may return to Iraq dead or maimed." (Courtesy private collection of John Arps, Middelburg, Holland)

too, the surrender leaflet focused on the individual rather than the collective. Enticements were personal, devoid of any reference to a cause beyond the personal.

In accordance with reigning doctrine in communication studies, behavioralists aimed at two different audiences. The first major strain of leaflets targeted the ordinary enemy soldiers, whose literary skills were somewhere between minimal and nonexistent. Pictures and cartoons, rather than text, were the major tools for persuasion. Moreover, these leaflets were single-minded attempts to induce the most basic of "behavioral modification," capitulation and demoralization of the rank and file. A meticulously detailed leaflet on procedures for surrendering was the main item of this particular format. This leaflet used a cartoon strip set of directions attached to a formal-looking letter, instructing American troops to provide safe passage for surrendering prisoners.

A second format of behavioralist leaflet propaganda was explicitly literate. Contrary to simple pictorial format, they did not target the ordinary soldier. Instead, these leaflets were aimed at what communication theorists called opinion leaders. The leaflets were based on comic strips as well. However, in contrast to the pictorial leaflets aimed at the rank and file, the decoding of these pictures demanded literary skills; the illustrations were complex and meaningless without accompanying written commentaries. (Figure 10) Based on the concept of the "two-step flow" of communication, behavioralists assumed that the rank and file did not arrive at complex opinion on an individual basis; the source of their views were opinion leaders, respected members of their community or immediate social circles whose interpretation of events was the source of mass opinion. Working under the unfounded assumption that opinion leaders were literate, these leaflets offered detailed texts.

Evaluating the Leaflet Campaign

Throughout the course of the Korean War, the army commissioned studies of leaflet effectiveness. These inquiries, written primarily by academic consultants associated with army-funded think tanks, did little to affect the internal difference of opinions. The reports had more to do with defending disciplinary turf than anything else. They were, for the most part, partisan attacks on the use of ideological material and, conversely, enumerations of the advantages of simple behavior modification.

Based on a selective debriefing study of POWs, ORO reports claimed that "leaflets dealing with immediate and practical situations . . . appear to be better understood than, and preferred to, leaflets dealing with abstract concepts such as independence and national unity." When confronted with contradictory findings, such as enthusiastic response to literate and overtly political leaflets, these reports dismissed the results as untrustworthy. The data on "self-declared literacy" among the POWs were, according to the ORO, "suspect." Prisoners responded favorably to political or complex leaflets due to cues, unconscious or otherwise, from interrogators and collaborators. Their inability to answer specific "questions concerning the leaflets" suggested incomprehension and group pressure more than anything else. The ORO claimed that over two-thirds of a test group indicated that political leaflets were "easy to read," a figure that was "inconsistent with the number of literates (48 percent) found among these POWS."[25]

OCPW internal audits offered similar criticism. A November 1953 report asserted that "psychological warfare operations in Korea . . . ranged from the unplanned . . . , the unorthodox, and all the way to the inept." The report reserved particularly unpleasant words for the leaflet campaign's waste of resources. This operation had reached the $1 billion a year mark, with little tangible results, even though "the enemy is walking about in piles of leaflets up to his ankles." Leaflet ineffectiveness was attributed to inaccurate drops, the use of too many themes, and the urge to focus on "quantity rather than quality. The target has seen so many leaflets hurled at it . . . that the attention value of the message flying through the air has been largely lost." The "law of diminishing returns" appeared to affect "leaflet dissemination as it does every other form of human activity."[26]

The report argued that diminishing results were caused, in part, by the breaching of accepted doctrine of simple behavioral messages. Hinting at the abundance of political messages contained in this paper storm, the report claimed that the enemy was "overwhelmed and numbed" by the sheer number of themes pouring out the skies, the result of ideological misconception and poor supervision of overzealous indigenous personnel. The campaign was too political, and too complex.

> Both Chinese and Korean personnel . . . could not or would not bring themselves down to the level of the target audience. . . . (T)o do so, in their minds, would have been to seriously lose face. Eight Army leaflets and loudspeaker scripts produced by native Chinese were . . . dissertations on the history of Soviet occupation of Manchuria with much learned comment on Soviet politics. PWS leaflets were of the same nature. . . . The Chinese employees especially, had the inferiority complexes of White Chinese, exiled from their native hearth and were ever prone to grind their own political axes rather than conduct straight psywar. They, as well as the Koreans invariably considered it a loss of face to indulge in any but higher-than-the-lowest language.[27]

In contrast to the harsh criticism aimed at ideological propaganda, the behavioralist approach generated only mild exhortations for technical improvements and more thorough scientific investigations of the communicative process. The reports urged investigation of communicative strategies with an audience characterized by a "high incidence of illiteracy." For want of a better alternative, their solutions were mostly formulaic. The analysts employed by the ORO and HumRRO concluded that solutions lay in uncovering the channels of communications between opinion leaders and the rank and file. "We need to know the extent to which, despite intimidation by political commissars and superior officers, the illiterates in the target audience rely primarily upon the literates for information, for new ideas, etc." The reports offered, as well, technical advice, such as seeking information on the "characteristics that a drawing of the face must have in order to be recognized by a Chinese audience."[28]

The simplification of leaflet propaganda was the subject of an ORO report written by Paul Linebarger, the author of the definitive textbook on psychological warfare. A political scientist with an impressive resume of books on politics in Nationalist China, Linebarger was very much a partisan of World War II strategies of avoiding politics and complex motives. Given the distortion of messages, due to the prejudices of the receiver or the cultural illiteracy of the producer, Linebarger urged focusing most, if not all, efforts on the simple surrender leaflet, the most unambiguous of all propaganda tools. Among the various options for riveting attention to this crucial text, Linebarger suggested that the leaflet should resemble a banknote. "Few Chinese would throw it away. *It would look too valuable.*" Linebarger urged, as well, the use of colored paper instead of plain white sheets because "psychologically" people assume that colored paper has more value than the mundane white. "Vivid red or yellow paper might stand a much better chance of attracting attention."[29]

The only meaningful criticism of behavioralist strategies was produced by consultants of the air force's HRRI. Absolved of the need to take sides in intramural army squabbles, the HRRI document identified fundamental faults in the behavioral format. The supposedly simple designs of behavioral appeals, according to the HRRI report, were undecipherable when placed outside their original Western context. Enemy captives were unable to decode even the most uncomplicated of cartoon strips because this particular visual-verbal transmission of information had no perceptual meaning to Koreans and Chinese. POWs approached each picture as a separate entity and did not comprehend the continuous narrative format of the strip. The placing of graphic thoughts or texts in a balloon above the heads of the cartoon characters was, as well, a cryptic device that induced confusion rather than clarification. As for the pictures themselves, they, too, unleashed misunderstandings. One of the most pervasive leaflets of Korean psychological warfare portrayed Stalin kicking a Chinese leader who, in turn, booted a soldier. (Figure 11). Chinese POWs did not, however, recognize themselves in this picture. They interpreted the scene as Stalin kicking an American rather than a representative of the People's Republic. Due to the high incidence of illiteracy, the insertion of subtitles identifying the figure as Chinese did little to dispel this confusion.

A particularly vivid example of the misuse of Western strategies for a non-Western audience appeared in the leaflets' representation of women. In accordance with Western conventions, women in the leaflet campaign of both the ideological and behavioral formats were not persons, but symbols: pure, passive objects. Male soldiers—members of the most regimented of social organizations—were presented as persons of free will, capable of deciding their personal destiny and influencing the political fate of their country. Women—ostensibly free-willed civilians—were not active social agents but, rather, passive representations subordinate to the shaping influences of active males. Women appeared as the objects of invidious sexual appetites of enemy soldiers or the beneficiaries of their husbands' positive decision to break with communism. As representations of the national entity or symbols of communist intrusion into authentic native cultures, they lacked free will of their own. Men could identify themselves in the leaflets, as either supporters of a common cause or rational individuals seeking personal survival. Women were invariably something other than flesh or blood: symbols of the nation, representations of tradition, objects of fantasy and desire.

To a certain degree this gendered division made sense; after all, men waged war, and women were mostly distant fantasies. However, no effort was ever made to comprehend whether the employment of women as symbol for the health or crisis of the nation—a decidedly Western convention—made sense to Korean and Chinese audiences. Whether this use of a Western model to capture the imagination of a foreign audience was, indeed, workable or exportable remained a mystery.

No meaningful examination of conventions, graphic or otherwise, ever took place. Both schools continued to churn out their particular worldviews simultaneously and appeared to be more engaged in discrediting each other than confronting the communist enemy with culturally meaningful propaganda. In the long run, the behavioralist format triumphed. Standard doctrine, as formulated after the Korean War, reconfirmed the golden rules of World War II, in particular the avoidance of politics and the focus on the individual's self-seeking behavior.[30] Following the Korean War, the behavioralist format became standard doctrine. Even the 1991 Gulf War employed the behavioralist themes as defined on Korean battlefields.[31] (Figure 12)

As far as the Korean War was concerned, the impact of behavioralists was not confined to the contentious field of psychological warfare. Their greatest triumph occurred in the final phases of the war. During the course of armistice negotiations, behavioral consultants influenced fateful decisions and crucial policy issues. The fortuitous circumstance of a charismatic advisor and a series of provocative and readable Rand Corporation publications led the American negotiation team to adopt behavioral strategies for outwitting the enemy at the truce encampment.

Success was somewhat more elusive in other Korean War episodes. The contentious rift between ideologists and behavioralists shifted to the inhospitable shores of Ko Je Do, a prison island where both Chinese and Korean POWs were incarcerated in very close quarters. There, a concerted campaign of ideological indoctrination turned the prison stockades into a veritable battlefield. The riots that shook the island were triggered and, to a certain degree, encouraged by a cohesive group of American reeducation officials who cared little for the concept of the "end of ideology." The dramatic battle for the hearts and minds of enemy prisoners of war appeared to demonstrate that ideology had more than a perfunctory role in the political struggles that ensued in the camps. In addition, reports of "brainwashing" and the ideological conversion of American POWs suggested that predictions of the demise of ideology were premature, if not invalid.

6.

Deus ex Clinica
Psychopolitics and Elite
Studies of Communism

The Rand Corporation and the Korean War

Upon returning from Korea in late November 1951, the Rand Corporation's senior analyst, Herbert Goldhamer, recorded his impressions on dictaphone "in order to fix memories and impressions before they disappear."[1] Published posthumously by Rand in 1994, Goldhamer's Korean memoirs were an unusual record of intellectual assumptions and the role of the behavioral sciences in the military-academic complex. Goldhamer and his colleagues had arrived in Korea charged with the limited mission of assessing weapons effectiveness by debriefing enemy POWs. An astute reading of local circumstances led them away from this pedestrian mission and toward the more intriguing issues of enemy morale and psychological warfare.

Herbert Goldhamer, the most energetic and politically astute of the Rand team, scored a great personal triumph as well. By late August 1951, he had assumed the unofficial position of coach and confidant at the armistice talks.

His active participation in the negotiations during the fall of 1951 removed the stigma of irrelevance from Rand's social science division and thrust this hitherto marginal unit into the eye of the storm. At Panmunjon he successfully promoted the esoteric field of psychoculture. This psychological analysis of political processes became, for a brief historic moment, a key strategy for deciphering the early political and military crises of the Cold War.

The initial presence of Rand advisors in Korea was inauspicious. Goldhamer and his colleagues, Alexander George, Paul Davison, Jay Hungerford, and Ewald Schnitzer, were assigned on a rotating basis to Korea to assess the air force's "interdiction" campaign, the destruction of enemy infrastructure by massive fire power.[2] Unwilling to waste their time on such an unspectacular assignment, these Rand advisors initiated a series of studies on enemy morale, indoctrination techniques, and psychological warfare.

Goldhamer, the anchor member of this rotating Rand team, had even more ambitious goals. He spent at least some his time interrogating friend rather than foe. During the course of his Korean junket, he became aware of acute frustration among the theater commanders. American military personnel complained that civilian overseers had imposed unrealistic, self-defeating political restrictions on the execution of the war. Washington, according to this common complaint, had forced a reluctant FEC to engage in armistice talks rather than pursue a military solution to the war.

Sensing this general atmosphere of frustration, Goldhamer offered his military clients in Korea a provocative analysis of the Korean dilemma. Goldhamer claimed that, contrary to conventional wisdom, the enemy had not initiated armistice negotiations from a position of strength. Even though the enemy had managed to rout American troops and push the battle back from the Yalu River to the 38th parallel, Goldhamer discovered weakness where others had found strength. Based on his interrogations of POWs, Goldhamer argued that the enemy's military infrastructure was on the verge of collapse. Command and control as well as logistical capabilities had been stretched beyond their limits. "I felt that the Communist bid for a ceasefire towards the end of June was in considerable measure not the result of physical military losses (manpower and material), but the result of their incapacity to maintain adequate control over their troops."[3] Thus, Goldhamer claimed that by agreeing to a truce and ceasefire negotiations, the United States had literally snatched defeat from the mouth of victory.

Goldhamer's analysis apparently impressed his superiors. In a striking display of self-promotion, he convinced the commanding officers of FEC to appoint him as advisor and debating coach to the armistice talks. His new assignment was particularly impressive given the fact that the JCS had previously vetoed any form of civilian advisory team for the armistice talks. When General Matthew Ridgway, at the time the commander in chief of the UN Command in Korea, had proposed assigning American ambassador to Korea

John J. Muccio and State Department political strategist William Sebald as advisors to the armistice team, his superiors had refused. They feared that the enemy would interpret the presence of civilian advisors as a sign of American willingness to discuss issues other than a strict military armistice.[4] The revision of this policy, and Goldhamer's new mission, was presumably in response to distress signals emanating from the armistice team. The daily reports from the talks raised the uneasy suspicion that the American team, comprised of high ranking officers with no prior negotiating experience, were outclassed and in desperate need of some form of guidance. Thus, on August 24, 1951, Gold-hamer joined the armistice team, the only civilian member ever to participate in this exclusively military mission.

Goldhamer offered his untutored companions at the armistice talks a plan to salvage at least some semblance of victory from the Korean predicament. To begin with, he coached the negotiators in the art of bargaining. Unskilled in negotiations, they had ceded a series of easy propaganda victories in the early stages of the talks.

In addition to his bargaining skills, Goldhamer claimed other important intellectual weapons in his arsenal. Since its inception, the major project of Rand's social science division was the deciphering of the "behavioral codes" of political elites: the beliefs, values, and perceptions underlying choices in political action. Rand had compiled a series of comparative studies of elite behavior in crisis, ranging from analysis of Nazi hierarchy to Soviet-American negotiations in the final stages of World War II.[5] Moreover, Rand's chief expert on Soviet Affairs, Nathan Leites, had recently completed the first of a series of studies on the behavioral code of the Soviet elite. These Rand studies, together with Goldhamer's credentials as an expert on bargaining, offered opportunities for reclaiming at least a symbolic victory from the truce tents.

Goldhamer's memoirs, as well as the diary of Admiral Turner Joy, the commander of the UN delegation to the armistice talks, indicate that Gold-hamer influenced events in the encampment. He became the confidant of the senior delegates, writing memos and drafts for the actual talks, settling disputes among the team, and offering advice on how to deal with both com-munist adversaries and distant, but interfering, military overseers in Tokyo and Washington.

Psychoculture

Goldhamer's most important legacy was his insertion of the concept of the "operational code" into the strategical thinking of American negotiators. Armed with papers and books published by Rand's social science division, Goldhamer explained that enemy policies and tactics did not address the ex-ternal world but, rather, the image of the external world. Enemy perception of events was filtered through a prism of beliefs and psychological mechanisms that more or less preordained their diagnosis and subsequent behavioral modes. An understanding of such mechanisms would, he argued, allow American negotiators to pierce the enemy's operational code, the series of convictions and rules that dictated their reaction to contemporary circumstances.

The concept of the operational code—the attribution of common characteristics of political behavior—was intimately linked to the veritable flood of elite studies emanating from various branches of the social and behavioral sciences. Beginning in the 1940s, in both purely academic settings and government-ordained projects, behavioral scientists cranked out retrospective and predictive studies of totalitarian elites. At the theoretical level, these studies sought explanations for what was seen as one of the great political contradictions of the twentieth century. Contrary to expectations, sociologist Morris Janowitz explained, "the democratization of the social origins and social recruitment of political elites, world-wide, had not been accompanied by a democratization of elite attitude and behavior."[6] If anything, the rise of the common man to positions of leadership had produced a sharp curtailment of political freedom and an alarming rise in the use of violent, repressive measures in the political arena.

Most attempts to decipher this puzzling development were linked in one way or another to Harold Lasswell. His influential work was based on a number of central assumptions, in particular the sweeping dictum that "the study of politics was in essence the study of elites." All societies, including Western democracies, were governed by a small, well-defined ruling class. Paraphrasing Lord James Bryce, Lasswell argued that "government is always government by the few, whether in the name of the few, the one, or the many." Under these circumstances, one need not waste precious time on conventional political analysis of the masses. The key to understanding political trends was not complex cultural or institutional analysis but, rather, the study of any given society's ruling elite. The elite represented the social sciences' equivalent of the atom, a seemingly irreducible and independent unit upon which a quantitative, predictive science of politics could be built.[7]

The key to splitting the behavioral atom was, according to Lasswell, psychopolitics. In his *Psychopathology and Politics* (1930), a study based on the clinical analysis of political leaders, Lasswell described the democratic politician as the creation of families in which there had been an unusual degree of both freedom and affection. Conversely, he argued that the authoritarian political leader had experienced a repressive and harsh childhood.[8] Lasswell defended his use of records of the mentally ill in defining universal principles of political behavior, claiming that the popular belief that the " 'insane' are a degenerate species quite apart from the 'normal' " was naive. "The frontier between what, in a given culture is supposed to be 'normal' and what is supposed to 'abnormal' is not a cliff but a slope. . . . (T)here is little need to fear that case studies taken from the sick are likely to differ too profoundly from the case histories taken from the well."[9]

Lasswell's theories coincided with a series of wartime anthropological studies on the political-childhood nexus. These studies assumed that reactions to emotionally important, familial situations carried over into adulthood. In other words, adults tend to repeat childhood behavioral patterns when confronted by structurally analogous situations in later life.

This widely accepted hypothesis generated invariably self-congratulatory studies of American society. The eminent Harvard team, Clyde and Florence Kluckhohn, traced the predominant trait of "effort and optimism" in American political behavior to the nurturing practices of American families. The American mother, they explained, provides love for her child on condition that the infant achieves certain performance tasks, none of which are unreachable.[10] Margaret Mead, the dean of American anthropology, offered a similar assessment of the American character, albeit in more critical tones. Mead argued that American parents approach their offspring from infancy as engaged in a perpetual competitive struggle to outscore others and impress their immediate surroundings. Mead claimed that the "American sibling position is one of competition, not for the mother's person, for her breast, and her soft arms, but rivalry for her approval, and her approval has to be got by one's achievements."[11] Such competitiveness, as well as the nagging desire for the approval of others that was inculcated from infancy, affected all facets of American adult behavior.

As for investigations of other cultures, such psychocultural explanations were mostly negative. American anthropologists identified lack of ambition and fatalism in the political behavior of foreign nations and traced their origins to childhood nurturing traditions. Ruth Benedict linked the absence of "the will to achieve" in Romanian political culture to the fact that "the Rumanian child did not have to earn . . . his mother's unconditional pleasure in him. . . . Rewards, either from the mother or from other persons, were not given for specific approved acts or for achievements. . . . The child did not know what he could do to earn approval."[12]

Benedict and Geoffrey Gorer traced political rigidness and submissive attitudes toward authority in Japan to certain dysfunctional practices in childhood. Japanese children abided by extremely rigid prescriptions of boundaries within the house. The rules concerning where and when a child could move about the house were enforced rigidly. As such, Benedict and Gorer speculated that such childhood practices accounted for a lack of spontaneity and disorientation when adult Japanese confronted an unknown environment or social predicament.[13]

Predictably, psychoculturalists had a field day with German culture. In a typical study, Roger Money-Kyrle suggested that the average German Nazi had, as a child, experienced a highly ambivalent relationship with a domineering father. Based on his work in postwar Germany, where the author was responsible for psychiatric evaluations of potential leaders for a new democratic Germany, Money-Kyrle asserted that the reaction to childhood experiences with a domineering father was ambivalent and contained elements of both rebellion and submission. The German responded to these childhood events by identifying with strong, authoritative political figures while, at the same time, denying personal passivity and weakness by despising these traits in others.[14]

Psychiatrist Henry Dicks, who had achieved notoriety for his psychiatric analysis of Rudolph Hess, claimed that "Nazis or near Nazis," approximately 35 percent of the German nation, "were likely to be men of a markedly pregenital or immature personality structure" caused by "a repression of the tender tie with the mother" and a powerful love-hate relationship with an "extra-punitive father figure." Thus, Dicks argued, the rehabilitation of the German nation would entail first and foremost a fundamental transformation of parent-child relations.[15]

The Cold War and its creeping influence on the academic agenda shifted attention from psychocultural studies of German culture toward a preoccupation with Russian society and communism. By 1950, Henry Dicks had moved from studies of Germans to similar psychocultural analyses of Russian political behavior. In a study funded by the usual suspects—Rand, Harvard's Russian Research Center, and the air force's HRRI—Dicks claimed that Russians were distinguished by a compulsive need to be submissive to authority, and that this need could be traced back to childhood. Dicks observed that one of "the dominant and persistent conflicts in Russian society (both pre-Soviet and especially recent Soviet) is that between the ancient Russian *oral* character structure . . . and an *anal-compulsive* ('puritan') pattern characterizing the elite."[16]

Anthropologist Dinko Tomasic assigned the volatile and often extremely violent trends in Soviet political behavior to two conflicting cultural characteristics of in the Russian family. Tomasic identified the roots of nonaggressive, egalitarian modes in Russian society to the original Slavonic inhabitants of Russia. A conversely violent, autocratic, and destructive trend originated in the culture of the invading Eurasian horsemen. Tomasic explained that the historic coupling of male Eurasian invaders and conquered Slavonic women produced families dominated by authoritarian, arbitrary fathers and supportive, nurturing mothers. Such a mismatch of conflicting personality structures produced an unstable Russian character in which dependence and destructive aggression, guilt and fear, and a variety of other clashing traits spilled over into contemporary Russian politics.[17]

Anthropologist Geoffrey Gorer rocked the academic boat with his controversial "swaddling hypothesis" of Russian political behavior. Gorer argued that pathological aspects of the collective Russian character were linked to pivotal childrearing practices. He focused, in particular, on the harsh swaddling of babies—the tight strapping of both legs and arms during the first nine months of an infant's life. The painful constraints of swaddling, according to Gorer, engendered an "intense destructive rage" and a strong urge to destroy "the constraints and the constrainers which painfully limit action." In later life such rage was translated into an "emotional certainty that an enemy or enemies who want to constrain and destroy . . . exist. Because the exact enemy is unknown, the typical reaction is to see the enemy everywhere." Thus, Gorer went on to explain, Russian authorities had perfected a technique for diverting such "free-floating" rage and urge to destroy to a variety of interchangeable enemies, from Jews to capitalists.[18]

The transferal of scholarly interest from fascist and Nazi political behavior to Soviet society was accompanied by the eradication of all but semantic differences between the pathologies of fascism and communism. Thus, sociologist Edward Shils questioned the "obsolete belief" that the radical right and left were two diametrically different political cultures. Shils argued that "Fascism and Bolshevism, only a few decades ago thought of as worlds apart," were actually identical in many crucial aspects.

> Their common hostility towards civil liberties, political democracy, their common antipathy for parliamentary institutions, individualism, private enterprise, their image of the political world as a struggle between morally irreconcilable forces, their belief that all their opponents are secretly leagued against them and their own predilection for secrecy, their conviction that all forms of power are in a hostile world concentrated in a few hands and their own aspirations for concentrated and total power—all of these showed that the two extremes had much in common.[19]

Shils, who is credited with coining the phrase "the end of ideology,"[20] implied that political rhetoric was of little significance. Echoing the predominant strain in Cold War behavioral sciences, he rejected the possibility of cognition among those who held extreme political positions on either side of the political spectrum. Objective social processes were reduced to individual psychological problems that one could unmask by means of Freudian apparati, such as repression, displacement, and projection.

This tracing of psychocultural links between childhood and political pathology was, in part, a reaction of democratically minded scholars to the deterministic, biologically based theories of human behavior of the 1930s and 1940s. According to social psychologist Raymond Bauer, the new wave of psychocultural studies sought first and foremost to refute the link between biology and behavior. Psychoculturists asserted that "differences were due to social instead of biological factors."[21] The psychocultural approach placed emphasis on life experiences rather than on hereditary traits. As such, these studies implicitly suggested that pathological political behavior was rectifiable.

Given the right conditions, in particular the inculcation of new patterns of childrearing, even the most pathological society could adopt structural changes that would, in the long run, affect its political texture. Most psychoculturists did not imply that intimate childhood events exclusively determined adult behavior. Projection of childhood traumas was usually invoked when observed political behavior appeared to be "irrational," by which was meant different from the American norm.

The Operational Code

The most conspicuous attempt to fuse psychoculture and elite studies during the early Cold War years was associated with Rand Corporation's Nathan Leites. A former student of Harold Lasswell at the University of Chicago in the 1930s, Leites joined the Rand Corporation in 1949 following an impressive career as an academic advisor to numerous government wartime projects. He had served on the research staff of the Office of War Information (OWI). Following that, he had worked for Harold Lasswell at his Wartime Communication Division. Prior to joining Rand, Leites had also served as a senior researcher in the Russian Section of Columbia University's Project of Research in Contemporary Cultures, where he participated in work for the ONR.[22] At Rand, he joined the social science division, where he held the title of chief Kremlinologist.[23]

Under the tutelage of the division's director, Hans Speier, Leites participated in the production of a working document aimed at codifying the behavior of modern political elites. By 1948, the division had produced an internal file comparing the behavior of Nazi, Soviet, and American elites. This project, known as the "Western Elite Studies," identified fundamental differences between Anglo-American "negotiatory behavior" and the political behavior of totalitarian adversaries by analyzing actual case studies. The underlying premise of these case studies was that Western elites were ill-prepared for the battle of wits around the negotiation table. Americans, in particular, seemed to miss the point that negotiations were merely the continuation of war by other means.

The fact that the Western case studies was an internal document encouraged its authors to be unusually frank. Thus, Hans Speier allowed himself to entitle his case study of Harry Hopkins's last mission to Moscow, in late May 1945, as "Appeasement."[24] Speier argued that Hopkins's efforts to dissuade Stalin from his Polish designs were even more pernicious than Chamberlain's ill-fated mission to Munich. U.S. negotiatory behavior was not merely appeasement; it was "irrational appeasement." American diplomats squandered opportunities and handed out concessions in order to produce a congenial, pleasant atmosphere. The country's adversaries, by contrast, pursued their goals with ruthlessness, exploiting the irrational American need to be liked in order to drag out further concessions. Speier wrote that American policy toward the Soviet Union was hampered by a historic attraction to isolationism, a compulsive need to appease or to be admired by others, and a nagging irresolution in the pursuit of vital interests. By contrast, the Soviets, who "*always* regarded" other powers as enemies, capitalized on American weaknesses in their pursuit of total victory and annihilation of adversaries. Compromise did not exist in the Soviet lexicon.[25]

These working assumptions of the Western elite file provided the basis for Nathan Leites's extended study of the political conduct of Soviet elites. First published as *The Operational Code of the Politburo* (1951), Leites's theory was later elaborated in *A Study of Bolshevism* (1955). In typical Lasswellian fashion, he viewed politics as the displacement of private motives. Communism, according to Leites, was not the result of ideational or institutional processes, but a characterological problem, a mission for the psychoanalyst. Ideology was of little importance. The key to undermining communism, according to this influential theory, was through the pinpointing of psychological vulnerabilities in the "Bolshevik" mind.

Leites's strategy for extracting a communist behavioral code bore striking resemblance to a previous elite study from 1945. As members of Harold Lasswell's Division for the Study of Wartime Communication, Leites and his colleague Paul Kecskemeti had compiled a report entitled "Some Psychological Hypotheses of Nazi Germany." Based on a content analysis of German press and radio broadcasts, Leites and Kecskemeti claimed that "the Nazi variant of German culture approximates or falls under the 'compulsive character' of psychoanalytic theory," most probably caused by collective "infantile events." These two Rand researchers defined motivations for the typical behavior of Germans as residing in unconscious "libidinal oedipal tendencies of the male child towards his mother" as well as unconscious "passive homosexual tendencies towards the father."[26]

In both this study of National Socialism and his subsequent analysis of Bolshevism, Leites rejected cognitive theory for deciphering the behavior of his "patients." Moreover, he dismissed conscious articulations of political actions as unreliable data. Instead, he sought to uncover the psychological motivating forces operating out of his subjects' collective past. The key to uncovering the unconscious was through a careful reading of texts, the equivalent of a psychoanalytical session.

In employing this unusual manner of research, Leites suggested that elites in general and the Soviets in particular did not formulate policies on the basis of an analytical assessment of actual events. Instead of addressing themselves to the external world, they focused on constructed images of reality. Following in the footsteps of his mentor, Harold Lasswell, Leites approached political behavior as the superstructure of private emotional needs, especially those derived from early formative experiences. His work echoed Lasswell's grim assumption that fundamental political beliefs were molded in early childhood years and were resistant to change.

A conspicuous novelty in Leites's studies of communism was his extensive use of Russian literature to flesh out his speculative readings of Bolshevik political behavior. Bolshevism arose in "the Russian stratum known as the intelligentsia," he observed. Consequently, a careful reading of the exemplary literature of the intelligentsia revealed "what the Bolshevik ones contain in unexpressed form."[27] Instead of seeking overt expressions of political faith, Leites preferred the analysis of "clues," chance gestures of speech that might uncover the real—mostly unconscious, psychopathological—motivation of the Bolshevik character. Indeed, Leites claimed that many of the rules of Bolshevik conduct were adhered to unconsciously and, as such, "might not be recognized easily by them [the Communists R.R.]."[28]

Leites's concept of an operational code dismissed entirely the notion of communist improvisation. He explained that communist elites were orthodox followers of a "secular religion."[29] As faithful devotees they adhered rigidly to dogma. Leites argued that, like most religions, Bolshevism espoused a teleological concept of history. Its canon was self-confirming; every historical event was explicable in its terms. "(T)he present Politburo still believes a contemporary situation in international affairs to be explainable when its prototype can be found in Russian, or Party, history. . . . Since the Revolution, they have continued to see themselves in the same position in relation to the outside world as they were in relation to the tsarist government, i.e., out of power and in a dangerous position. Thus, the . . . aims of the Bolsheviks tend to preserve the importance of the lessons they learned in their earlier struggle."[30] Setbacks meant nothing to the faithful because victory—in this case, worldwide revolution—was inevitable.

Leites's Bolshevik elite appeared as a ruthless, fanatical cohesive subculture, unwilling to compromise except for tactical and temporary purposes. The motto of Bolshevism, he explained, was "Who-Whom?" or, who will destroy whom? Here Leites explained that in the eyes of Bolsheviks, "the only safe enemy is one whose power has been completely destroyed." A weak party was in constant danger of being annihilated, and, as such, should always strive to annihilate its adversaries.[31] He speculated that the "Bolshevik belief that they were surrounded by enemies with "annihilatory designs" was a "classical paranoid defense against latent homosexuality," rather than some calculated move to fend off danger.[32]

The Bolshevik insistence on, in effect, killing enemies and being killed by them is . . . an effort to ward off fear-laden and guilty wishes to embrace men and be embraced by them. This hypothesis is consistent with the existence of certain pervasive Bolshevik trends described in this study:

the fear of being passive . . . the fear of being controlled and used . . . the fear of wanting to submit to an attack.[33]

While nominally dealing with Russian communism, Leites argued that his operational code provided an analytical framework for deciphering all major strains of communist elites, including the Asian varieties. Chinese Communists and their offspring were replicas of the Russian original. Leites claimed that "the Chinese Communists followed without hesitation or qualification the jerky and profound changes of line decreed by the Soviet Union and the Comintern . . . also in affairs affecting it [China] directly—and negatively." He dismissed any notion of "Chinese Titoism." In fact, he preferred the term "Soviet China" rather than the more popular "Communist China," because it underscored the subservience of the Asian version of communism.[34]

The Operational Code in Korea

The spirit of Nathan Leites arrived in Korea courtesy of his colleague, Herbert Goldhamer. Upon joining the team of armistice negotiators, Goldhamer distributed copies of The Operational Code. During the course of the armistice negotiations, Leites's slim volume was the primary, if not only written guide used by American negotiators in their efforts to decipher their enemy counterparts.[35]

Goldhamer's decision to distribute Leites's work was not some esoteric gesture of collegiality. Leites's books had garnered an immediate, mostly favorable, reaction in American academia. In summarizing the reaction to the operational code, an admiring Daniel Bell compared Leites with the pathbreakers of modern social thought. "Like Max Weber who drew his 'Protestant Ethic' from the writings of Luther, Calvin, Baxter, and others, Leites scans the writings of Lenin and Stalin" for a codex of "habitual" norms "from which, in his view, we should be able to predict typical Bolshevik responses to typical situations."[36]

Bell offered special praise for The Operational Code, because it had reduced many complex arguments to a terse set of rules much like a "manual on bridge strategy." The major function of the manual was to provide standard procedures to questions such as "If the Communists make a concession on procedure, should we in turn make a concession, or is this only a bluff to test our trumps?"[37] A more likely analogy for The Operational Code would be that of a guidebook for a poker game from hell. The stakes were high and uncompromising, and the adversary displayed none of the genteel trappings associated with the cerebral pastime of bridge.

The format of The Operational Code was, indeed, designed for the uninitiated. In the interest of those who preferred to use the text as a manual without bothering to follow the intellectual argument, Leites organized the pages in an easy-to-read format. "For the sake of clarity, the *general rules* of Bolshevik conduct are given in full-width text, and the *examples* illustrating them, in indented text."[38] This recourse to text widths and italics suggests that Leites had no illusions about his audience. A catchy set of rules rather than a thick description was his primary concern.

In addition, an easy-to-use index underscored Leites's main points. "Compromise" did not appear in the index; anyone seeking to comprehend sudden, and deceivingly friendly, changes in the adversary's behavior would find, instead, the terms "vacillation" and "zigzags." The notion of compromise appeared, then, as a mirage, a misreading of events by gullible Westerners and unworthy of a separate index entry. A related index entry, "simulated friendliness," dispelled any illusion of concession or willingness to compromise.

All in all, Leites's *Operational Code* provided twenty simplified rules of conduct as the basis for his operational code. The majority of these rules harped on several recurring themes: Communists were beset by fears of liquidation and annihilation; their suspicion of everyone, friend or foe, bordered on paranoia; fixation on discipline, action, and order was compulsive.

Herbert Goldhamer, the Alden Pyle of the Korean War, planned to use Leites's work as the basis for negotiationary strategies for the embattled American team at the armistice talks. The senior staff received copies of the manual, and Goldhamer fleshed out its terse text in a series of briefings, most of which he later described in his memoirs.

Based on his understanding of the operational code, Goldhamer dispelled any semblance of cultural idiosyncrasies among Korean and Chinese adversaries. They were communist clones of their Russian Bolshevik benefactors. As such, their behavior adhered to Bolshevik norms. He dismissed the protestations of American negotiators when, every now and again, they interpreted the moves of their adversaries as adhering to some sort of "oriental" mentality, such as "loss of face" or the mentality of the bazaar.[39] Communist strategy, he argued, was neither determined by a realistic assessment of circumstances, nor by some distant, historical cultural code. Their strategy was derived exclusively from a canon of political writings and inflexible behavioral modes.

Goldhamer emphasized that good-faith bargaining was a nonexistent term in the Bolshevik lexicon. Their concept of the world was that of the zero-sum game, allowing for no "intermediate position between being annihilated or achieving world hegemony."[40] Any attempt to offer concessions was doomed to fail.

Goldhamer did acknowledge that Leites's *Operational Code* allowed for some communist flexibility even when adhering to a very intransigent behavioral code. When faced with inevitable defeat, the communist operational code sanctioned temporary retreat. Communists were quite adamant about striving for a predetermined triumph, but at the same time they were wary of "adventure." Leites defined communist action for the delegates as a strategy of pushing an opponent to the limit, but recognizing the need to make tactical concessions when faced with overwhelming odds. The only manner to achieve such communist concessions, however disingenuous or ephemeral, was to be uncompromising and aggressive, both on the fighting front and in the truce tent.

Based on Leites's golden rules, Goldhamer urged American negotiators never to concede on seemingly irrelevant issues. Communist adversaries were, he explained, great believers in the value of symbolic triumphs. By allowing Communists to get away with trivial matters, such as the size of the delegates' chairs, the placement of flags, personal insults, or even arbitrary changes in the lunch schedule, the enemy sensed weakness. Goldhamer counseled prompt and harsh reactions to minor slights, thereby signaling "the Communist delegation a greater sense of the ultimate intransigence of the U.N. position."[41]

Goldhamer rejected the "naive" belief that displays of friendliness, gestures of military camaraderie, or any other courtesies might induce a measure of flexibility in the enemy's operational code. The communist delegates interpreted all events in light of the "sacred texts of Bolshevism" and induced fail-safe mechanisms to guard against personal judgment or arbitrary change. Thus, the enemy never offered an immediate response to even the minutest point of debates. Every issue, great or small, was referred back to superiors or measured against the canon before offering a response.

The Operational Code of the American Elite

While ostensibly preoccupied with the operational code of the enemy, Gold-hamer could not resist the temptation to produce a similar codex of American behavior. Even though he admired some of the members of the delegation, Goldhamer's overall evaluation of the American mission to the armistice talks was harsh. This Canadian-born, naturalized American citizen described the senior staff—supposedly the cream of the American military establishment—as indecisive, driven by an anachronistic moral code, obsessed with their public image, prejudiced, and constrained by poor intellectual skills. The archetype of the American delegation was Major General Howard Turner, the air force's senior delegate, who reminded Goldhamer of the proverbial overgrown, yet dim-witted boy, always outmaneuvered by his more agile schoolmates. Turner demonstrated a "considerable incapacity to grasp matters that were even rudimentary to many of the people in the camp who were themselves by no means overly astute."[42]

In addition to such intellectual mediocrity, the American military elite, as represented at the armistice talks, were a peculiar montage of David Riesman's inner-directed and other-directed persons. On the one hand, American negotiators appeared to be motivated by a set of inner values: truth, responsibility, and a strong conviction that one should only pursue "those things which were ethically justified." Whenever called upon to transgress such principles in order to outwit their adversaries, they consistently failed. American delegates were unable to "escape entirely from the ethical demands for truthfulness" or the sentiment that "bluff was an immoral or humiliating tactic to pursue." They were, Goldhamer noted, continuously beset by "guilt" and a "disturbed conscience" that undermined most of their negotiatory tactics. When forced to present an aggressive stance at the bargaining table, American negotiators usually bungled such tactics. They were overcome with a "moral inability . . . to tolerate their own aggressiveness."[43]

The American delegates had "no capacity for bluffs" because they believed that "bluff was an immoral or humiliating tactic to pursue." These supposedly battle-hardened individuals who, "among their many manly virtues, considered themselves poker players par excellence, were unable to bring to bear on the negotiation problems the most elementary principles of 'bargaining' as it is exemplified in a poker game." Consistently, they manifested a "marked sense of guilt and almost outright shame at the demands they were making on the Communists."[44] In the detached tone of the psychoanalyst, Goldhamer observed that "it is of psychological interest to note that . . . the occurrence of actual U.N. violations was reacted to with an emotional intensity more fitting for persons who had deliberately created a violation and had been caught at it or had been bothered by their own conscience."[45]

But perhaps the most dominant characteristic of American negotiators was their insatiable craving to be liked by both friend and foe. All delegates worked hard to make sure that Goldhamer, the outsider, had "a good opinion of their activities." The ultimate other-directed type in Goldhamer's memoirs was the delegation chief, Vice Admiral C. Turner Joy, who obsessively scanned "every sign of public reaction almost as a farmer watches the weather."[46] The "bungling, oldish, and indecisive" Joy was mainly preoccupied with accumulating evidence on how others judged him. During the course of the day, while his staff was engaged in the actual negotiations, Joy sat in his tent poring over letters sent by private citizens and scanning newspapers in a relentless hunt for positive assessments of his character, behavior, and achievements at the armistice talks. A favorable letter would send an overjoyed Joy in search of Goldhamer. Critical responses, in particular those from the families of American POWs, induced depression and a series of painful maneuvers to hid these bad tidings from his colleagues.[47]

Joy and his staff craved favorable opinions from their communist adversaries as well. Personal insults caused major disconcertion in the camp; by contrast, the slightest gesture of collegiality was the subject of elated conversation. Unclear signals, those that could not be easily categorized as either positive or negative, sent delegates into a spiral of manic-depressive behavioral manifestations.

In addition to these characterological flaws, Goldhamer described at length the delegates' poor intellectual skills and sloppy approach to the negotiations. He was particularly concerned with their careless attitude toward language. The intellectually limited UN delegates were unable to differentiate between glaringly obvious nuances in communist communiques. "The fact that a certain U.S. proposal is only 'opposed,' whereas the other proposal 'cannot possibly be tolerated' was not of particular significance to the UN delegates," he observed.[48]

Goldhamer claimed that his American clients had no meaningful knowledge of the bargaining process. They suffered from psychological "weakness and negotiatory incompetence."[49] They misunderstood the difference between debating as a process of logical persuasion and negotiating, which he described as the ruthless extraction of concessions from an adversary. In the patient tone of an adult clarifying a simple issue for a dull child, Goldhamer explained that the "conception of negotiations as a process of having a better debating point" or a well- crafted rational defense of one's demands was superfluous, if not outright damaging. "Recourse to a very deliberate logical argument had . . . in some circumstances, the effect of suggesting that one's mind was not conclusively made up."[50] Stubborn insistence, without bothering to persuade, was a much more effective manner of convincing the enemy that certain issues were irrevocable. The enemy, he pointed out, used such tactics, very effectively.

Fancying himself as a modern-day Machiavellian, Goldhamer took delight in shocking the staff with what he called his "a-moralism."[51] Measuring one's demands against a code of moral values, he explained, was a luxury that the U.S. delegates could ill-afford. Goldhamer explained that instead of focusing on the immorality of communism, American delegates were preoccupied by the morality of their own tactical moves at the negotiating table. He described the petty moral preoccupations of UN delegates as the result of a nagging inability "to see the significance of the armistice conference in sufficiently broad political and historical terms to provide them with a sense of moral justification for exercising the maximum pressure against the Communists and securing the maximum gains."[52]

Goldhamer complained, as well, that American delegates expressed great distaste for the actual process of bargaining. They "could not bring themselves to be enthusiastic about anything other than the minimum position itself." Feeling uncomfortable about retreating from any given bargaining point, American delegates left themselves with little leeway at the bargaining table, preferring to shower the enemy with "concessions instead of making bargains." Hoping to improve the atmosphere at the talks, these soldier-negotiators offered concessions without ever demanding any form of reciprocity.

Motivated by a faulty game plan, Americans would propose "a concession in the expectation that then the communists on the next point would give one to them, instead of securing a simultaneous swapping of concessions."[53] At the same time, the American delegates were enamored with the seemingly contradictory device of ultimatums. Goldhamer speculated that both the ultimatum and the insistence on the minimum position represented a misguided "search for security by avoiding the difficulties of more intricate and complex maneuvers."[54]

Goldhamer was particularly appalled by American reactions to the few instances of enemy failures. The American negotiators exhibited an "immensely strong impulse to treat signs of Communist weakness as a basis for" a reciprocal "weak move" or counterconcession. When confronted by Goldhamer's objections, the American generals defended their moves on the grounds that "this is how Orientals bargained . . . when you buy something in a Chinese market that is exactly the procedure that one follows."[55] Goldhamer thought differently. He explained this poor manner of handling negotiations as being unconsciously motivated by a zero tolerance for uncomfortable, tense atmospheres, and by a compulsive "desire to be liked by the Communists."

The One-Dimensional Enemy

A cursory glance at Admiral C. Turner Joy's armistice diary reveals that, despite these poor assessments of his students' ability to handle their task, Goldhamer had made a major impression at Panmunjon. In this diary, devoted almost entirely to abstracts of communiques, Joy signaled his admiration for Goldhamer by recording ephemeral matters, such as dinner dates with the Rand advisor, as well as his efforts to dissuade General Ridgway from terminating Goldhamer's Korean mission.[56] When recording internal discussions among the delegates, Joy rarely presented individual positions, preferring instead to discuss in general terms the various views without mentioning specific delegates. In the case of Goldhamer, Joy made a point of mentioning him by name whenever he voiced specific opinions on the actual bargaining process or the phrasing of difficult exchanges between Panmunjon and Tokyo.[57]

The Joy diary, as well as the transcripts of the negotiations, suggest that Goldhamer had done much to dispel confusion from the minds of his students. The first portion of the diary, devoted to negotiations surrounding the initial sparring with the communist delegation and the bargaining surrounding the establishment of an agenda for the talks, shows much hesitancy concerning the behavior and objectives of the enemy. Following Goldhamer's brief sojourn this uncertainty disappeared. Goldhamer had managed to construct a comprehensible version of the enemy's motives and tactics. At times Joy emphasized certain sections of his diary that appeared almost as a homage to Goldhamer. "Commies employed such adjectives as absurd, unreasonable, useless & ridiculous in discussing UNC proposal, and asserted they cannot & absolutely will not agree to it." This underlined passage suggests that Goldhamer's exhortations to pay attention to the enemy's choice of adjectives had, indeed, made their mark.

Upon conclusion of negotiations on item 2—the establishment of the cease-fire line—Goldhamer departed for home, assuming, as did most other Americans, that the remaining items on the armistice agenda were of a technical nature and would be rapidly concluded. His departure was in flesh only. The diary and memoirs of Admiral Joy suggest that subsequent assessments and tactics of the American delegates relied heavily on Goldhamer's presentation of Leites's *Operational Code*. However, without the physical presence of Goldhamer, delegates lacked a clear hierarchy of communist behavioral strategies. The American generals at Panmunjon had to decide among themselves which, if any, of the traits enumerated in the *Operational Code* were of overriding significance.

Given the very tedious nature of the actual negotiations, the choice was quite predictable. Of all the rules of communist behavior, American negotiators appeared to rank what Leites called "the calculus of the general line" as the essence of the code. Leites's dictum that "every line of Bolshevik conduct is either prescribed or forbidden" left no margin for human error.[58] In what appeared to be a process of creeping determinism, Americans attributed exaggerated intention to the enemy's every move. Thus, the diaries, memoirs, and biographies written by American participants presented an image of an unerring enemy. Fundamental human frailties, such as misreading of the events, mistakes, tension, personal differences within the communist delegation, or sheer human folly were ruled out in American assessments of the enemy's conduct. Consequently, the few sketches of enemy negotiators in the writings of Joy and other participants at the talks had a flat, cartoon-like quality to them. The enemy was described at a superficial level as handsome or ugly, fat or thin, well-dressed or poorly clad. The underlying assumption of such descriptions was that any meaningful analysis of the enemy was superfluous. They were, after all, mere messengers. None of the natural inconsistency and human weaknesses that Americans attributed to themselves were assumed to exist on the other side. The enemy was infallible.

As the negotiations wore on, another no less important reputed trait dominated American perceptions of the enemy. Leites's firm conviction that the enemy had no intention of actually reaching a firm agreement to end their protracted conflict with the capitalist nations appeared with growing frequency in American impressions. Leites had stated that all agreements were nothing else but tactical steps; the ultimate objective—the triumph of world-wide communism—remained constant. "Any agreement between the Party and outside groups must be regarded as aiding the future liquidation of these groups. . . . Therefore there is no essential difference between coming to an ostensible amicable agreement with an outside group or using violence against it; they are both tactics in an over-all strategy of attack." Leites warned, Goldhamer taught, and American negotiators agreed that enemy gestures of flexibility—in this case, engaging in negotiations ostensibly aimed at ending the war—should never be read as an abandonment of the ultimate goal of destroying the enemies of communism. "A 'settlement' with Western powers . . . is inconceivable . . . although arrangements with them, codifying the momentary relationship of forces, are always considered."[59]

This image of the one-dimensional enemy came to dominate the negotiations, and accounted, at least in part, for diminishing results, hardening positions, and protracted negotiations. "Never concede anything to the Communists for nothing merely to make progress," Admiral Joy wrote in his recollections of the armistice talks. "Avoid a 'hurry-up' attitude for such an attitude tends to invoke a Communist conclusion that you are pressed for time."[60] In these very obvious allusions to the coaching of Herbert Goldhamer, Joy illuminated at least one of the reasons for protracted negotiations. Every issue, from the most trivial to the most pivotal, resulted in endless verbal scraps and demands for mutual concession.

Joy's recollections reveal, as well, Goldhamer's impact on the hardening of communications among the sparring delegations Following Goldhamer's departure, the American negotiators lived by the Rand expert's dictum on the futility of logical persuasion. In what was an almost verbatim transcript of Goldhamer's analysis of the art of hard bargaining, Joy stated:

> When a firm position has been taken, from which you do not intend to withdraw, do not thereafter engage in long-winded and repeated statements supporting your position. Having put forth your final proposal, simply be quiet. . . . Defense of your final proposal in response to Communist verbal attacks only offers grist for the Communist mill. The more you talk, the more you offer targets for the Communists' insidious propaganda. On the other hand, Communist negotiators are nonplused by, and fearful of, an unresponsive opponent because such tactics are contrary to their teachings.[61]

The carrying out of Goldhamer's advice ad absurdum occurred on April 28, 1952, when American delegates offered their adversaries a final and nonnegotiable package proposal, ostensibly resolving all outstanding issues. The package proposal recognized the enemy's right to rehabilitate its airfields in the north and accepted the inclusion of communist nations on the proposed neutral nation cease-fire supervisory board. These two concessions were counterpoised by an adamant stand on the "voluntary repatriation" of POWs. Of the approximately 183,000 enemy POWs in American hands, only 83,000 allegedly agreed to repatriation, the rest supposedly choosing voluntarily to remain in South Korea and Taiwan.[62] By insisting on voluntary repatriation, American negotiators believed that they could extract a symbolic victory from what was, in essence, an embarrassing stalemate. Consequently, the American delegation responded to the communist rejection of the voluntary repatriation clause by suspending the talks on October 8, 1952.

Goldhamer's analysis of American negotiators raises the suspicion that suspension-by-package-deal was at least partially aimed at easing the agony of debate, as well as abating American fears that they would be drawn/tricked into a demeaning compromise on the POW question. Moreover, Goldhamer's own memoirs suggest that such abrupt behavior represented a misreading of his advice, as well as a confirmation of his own negative assessment of American advisors. Goldhamer had, indeed, counseled against the use of logical persuasion, but at the same time he feared that his American students fell back on ultimatums in order to compensate for poor bargaining skills and a host of psychological flaws.

This curious format of negotiations, in which certain issues were conceded to the enemy without drawing out counter concessions and ultimatums were posed with no meaningful leeway for compromise, did not achieve the much awaited propaganda victory. In the long run, as historian Rosemary Foot notes, public opinion in the West paid negligible attention to the greatest symbolic victory of the Korean armistice talks: the 83,000 enemy prisoners who refused repatriation. The public focused, instead, on the twenty-one American POWs who chose to remain behind communist lines.

The accounts of delegate members, written after the fact and for posterity, tend to blame superiors in Washington and Tokyo for American errors in general and the bungled attempt to achieve a victory by points at Panmunjon. Nevertheless, Rosemary Foot notes, the actual dynamics of the negotiation process were the creation of the delegates in the field, whose attitudes, image of the enemy, and personalities had an overwhelming effect on armistice talks, its momentum, and its results.

As negotiations dragged on and the American delegation proudly noted the scoring of points, a vicious war continued unabated along the cease-fire line. Fully 45 percent of all battle casualties occurred during the two years of negotiations. During the fifteen months of haggling over the issue of POW repatriation UN forces suffered 125,000 casualties and thousands of American POWs endured tragic hardships.[63]

A firm belief in the enemy's unerring implementation of an operational code was, in many ways, a self-fulfilling prophecy. Having decided that the enemy could only react in a certain fashion, every move was interpreted as a fulfillment of a predetermined modus operandi. Based on their selective understanding of enemy motives and behavior, the American delegation had hoped to extract a symbolic victory from the Korean stalemate by virtue of ultimatums. This was not to be. The May 1952 uprising of enemy prisoners at the Koje Island prison stockades, the kidnapping of the American POW commandant during the course of these disturbances, and persistent rumors of the ideological conversion of American POWs turned the doubtful triumphs of Panmunjon into a pyrrhic victory.

7.

Collective Behavior in
Totalitarian Societies
The Analysis of Enemy POWs in Korea

Koje Do

The most immediate sensation experienced by newcomers to Koje Island was the stench of excrement. The pungent odor enveloping the entire island was the product of about 170,000 enemy prisoners, a few thousand custodial personnel, the island's 118,000 natives, and the 100,000 refugees and camp followers who had turned this once sparsely inhabited island into a gargantuan and surrealistic prison city.[1]

The Koje prison complex was a study in contrasts. The island had many of the customary symbols of strict authority and repression, ranging from looming guard towers to incessant roll calls and heavily guarded work details. Such trappings of a rigorous military prison regime did not, however, conceal ominous signs of neglect and confusion. Compound perimeters were often nothing more than the odd strands of rusting barbed wire. Some compounds were within fifteen feet of each other, thereby allowing almost unhindered communication between the nominally segregated enclosures. These porous barriers provided opportunities for a thriving trade between camp followers and prisoners bartering army rations, various military items, and sexual favors. Disarray, rather than order and rigor, characterized life on Koje Do.

The supervising American personnel on the island were a dispirited crew. While officially charged with running the camp in accordance with customary military discipline and the 1949 Geneva Convention, the American personnel were unable or unwilling to carry out this task. Language barriers and lack of pertinent training aggravated an already chaotic situation. The exact names, true identities, and even precise numbers of POWs posed a mystery to the series of Koje camp commanders — 14 different officers commanded Koje during the first twelve months of its existence. "There must have been 3,000 Kim Il Somebody-or-others" in the camp, one of the itinerant American commanders explained. Only forty of the two thousand American soldiers on Koje Island had any meaningful qualifications for custodial or police duties. The vast majority of Americans were castoffs from other units. Koje, a former commanding officer recalled, was considered the "Siberia" of American fighting forces in the Far East.

Faced with such insurmountable obstacles, the overworked and underqualified custodial personnel conceded internal control of the compounds. With little apparent protest on the part of the American guardians, the prisoners instituted a regime of "home rule"—the management of their own internal affairs. Home rule did not, however, produce the expected results. American custodians had presumed that a certain degree of inmate autonomy would reduce tensions in the overcrowded and poorly equipped compounds. In actual fact, daily life in the Koje prison city was permeated by internal turmoil. Each compound was ruled by an individual leader or a coalition of warlords, supported by legions of peons whose task it was to squash signs of dissension and wage war with rival compounds. Beatings, torture, and executions were employed routinely to suppress even the slightest signs of dissension. Stone throwing between rival compounds, clashes between work details from warring factions, and periodic confrontations with custodians occurred with ever-growing frequency.

The official American interpretation of the Korean War as a struggle between democracy and totalitarianism imparted to these clashes their public character. Compound leaders declared themselves as pro-democratic or pro-communist, definitions that appealed to American custodians but, in actual fact, did little to clarify the meaning of the struggle. The compound war was significantly more byzantine than ideological, with sudden changes of leadership and loyalties, and even occasional clashes between compounds that ostensibly espoused the same views. American officials noted, for example, that the nominally anticommunist Chinese compounds were ruled by two mutually antagonistic pro-nationalist groups, both of which were challenged occasionally by a secret society of Szechwan natives. Western definitions of ideology in these compounds were hardly an issue.[2] In deference to the custodians, these prison wars were invariably translated into the familiar terms of democracy and communism; Americans tended to disregard issues that fell outside this discursive framework.

In actual fact, a confusion of cultures and politics, far more complex than this familiar ideological divide, engulfed daily life on Koje Do. The Koje prisoners were the scarred veterans of two turbulent and partially intertwined civil wars; their loyalties and backgrounds were untidy and had gone through numerous mutations during the course of their respective nations' internal conflicts. At its height, in early 1952, the island accommodated over 170,000 POWs. The Chinese numbered about 21,000, the rest were Koreans.

The political, cultural, and demographic maps of the Korean POW compounds were confusing to the point of being indecipherable. Under the sweeping rubric of North Korean captives, American investigators discovered chaotic clusterings of Koreans from all parts of the country. The misfortune of falling into the hands of either of the Korean armies during the course of swift advances and hasty withdrawals had placed young Koreans randomly in opposing camps. At least fifty thousand of the nominally North Korean captives were from the south, and about forty thousand were civilians who had been impressed into labor battalions or arrested on suspicion of belonging to enemy forces. Three thousand of the prisoners were children. "There were several only six years old," an American officer recalled. "These children had to be taken prisoners along with the adults, as they were used as messengers and frequently carried grenades in their pockets."[3]

American attempts to decipher the Koreans' social and political allegiances were limited by the captors' ignorance. None of the exhaustive reports on POW loyalties and beliefs acknowledged the residuals of the traditional division of Korean society into the four castelike divisions of Wangjok, Yangban, Sangmin, and Chunin. Social divisions, class, and religious tensions among the prisoners were ignored as well.[4] American officials relied, instead, on familiar Western categories of social stratification. Education level and division by occupation—both poor analytical categories given the preponderance of illiterate peasants—served as the major descriptors of Korean captives.[5]

Multiple identities were conspicuous among Chinese inmates as well. The cultural and linguistic differences between north and south, educated and illiterate, hampered any type of generalization: 35.9 percent hailed from the southwest; 30.7 percent were from North China; 11 percent were from Manchuria; an additional 29 percent were natives of Szechwan province, most of whom had served in the National Chinese army during the course of the Chinese civil war. More than half the captive Chinese officers—53.8 percent—were northerners, most of whom had served previously in the ranks of the Nationalist opposition.[6]

Forty-nine percent of the Chinese were illiterates; over 81 percent had less than three years of schooling. Even among the officers, illiteracy rates were high; 23.4 percent could neither read nor write. Thirty-one percent claimed to have been "farmers" (American authorities apparently avoided the use of the non-American term *peasants*). More than half of all Chinese POWs claimed the trade of professional soldier, although about the same number had served in the army of the People's Liberation Army (PLA) for less than a year. According to American analysts, these professional soldiers had acquired their trade prior to their induction into the PLA, as members of the 95th Nationalist Army.[7] Neither educational level, geographic origins, nor even former service in the Nationalist army were clear criteria for joining one camp or the other. The reasons behind individual decisions to either endorse or oppose communism remained a mystery.

The Prison Studies of Enemy Society

For obvious reasons the crowded prison compounds attracted the attention of military think tanks. All three of the major military-sponsored research institutions—Rand, ORO, and HumRRO—sent teams to Koje. The many surveys and studies generated by these consultants did little to rectify the confusion. Even though the various academic advisors employed similar methodological tools and based their studies on the same population of informants, their results were often contradictory.

The major focus of all reports was on the prisoners' political convictions. The HumRRO team, led by University of Chicago political scientist Samuel Meyers and sociologist William Bradbury, described the politics of warring factions on Koje Island in decidedly nonideological terms.[8] As advocates of a realist approach to politics, Meyers and Bradbury argued that the power struggle between ostensibly democratic and communist factions was mainly a battle for the acquisition of basic objectives: territory, food, and shelter. The HumRRO team approached conflict, whether on Koje Do, between nations, or anywhere else, as a natural state of affairs rather than a consequence of immediate ideological or historical circumstances. The structural anarchy on Koje Island, caused by the weak custodial presence, merely exaccerbated a natural state of conflict and struggle for preeminence. Much like warring nations, "each competing faction" on Koje Do sought first and foremost territorial gains—control of compounds based on "power in the form of punitive force sufficient to compel obedience."[9] Whether a faction's approach was primarily "coercive, democratic, or authoritarian" was, as far as the HumRRO team was concerned, a nonissue. Success was measured by the ability of the ruling faction to control nodes of power and spread the spoils of victory among

its supporters. The marshaling of an army of ideologically convinced supporters was, according to HumRRO, irrelevant.

In support of this position the HumRRO team produced statistical indications of political innocence among enemy captives. HumRRO surveys suggested that prisoners of all ranks and backgrounds displayed an "ignorance
about the nature of the struggle raking China," by which they presumably
meant that Chinese prisoners did not share their American custodians' interpretation of the Chinese civil war. A typical interview with an inmate stated
that the ostensible political clashes within and among compounds were in
actual fact struggles against "the others in order to gain hegemony . . . and
thus to enjoy power, sufficient food, and relatively better living, even within
the much restricted compound life."[10] By contrast, "the much-talked-of war
for men's minds seems to have had much less impact upon their attitudes
than we are want to suppose," the HumRRO team argued.[11] "The behavior
of the bulk of the PWs was influenced much more by certain traditional
modes of response to authority and new situations than by attitudes toward
specific political movements and values."[12]

ORO studies of POWs on Koje Island produced similar findings. The ORO
claimed that Chinese captives demonstrated only a cursory understanding of
any of the great issues of the day. Over 30 percent of Chinese prisoners "had
heard nothing at all from their officers about either South or North Korea."[13]
These same surveys disclosed that "most Chinese prisoners had no opinion as
to how the [Korean] war had started." Moreover, Chinese prisoners were at a
loss to point out any benefits that they or their families had accrued under the
communist regime. "Few Chinese prisoners had knowledge of how the land
reform had affected them or their families; of those who knew, only a minority
had received land and no significant difference was discernable between their
capture-surrender behavior and that of prisoners whose families had suffered
under the program."[14]

ORO surveys declared that the political divide between democracy and
communism had not affected the Korean rank and file either. As was the case
among Chinese POWs, ideology had little to do with performance on the
battlefield. Although about 30 percent of Korean POWs claimed to have lost
land during the course of communist-inspired land reform programs, "capture-surrender behavior was not affected to any great degree by whether a
prisoner had lost or acquired land under the reform."[15]

Abstract ideological concepts appeared to be a minor factor, even among
the overtly anti-American North Korean prisoners. Instead, their comments
"reflected the hostility of a small nation afraid of being overrun by an enemy,"
rather than some articulate ideological worldview. A frequent criticism of the
United States among hostile Korean POWs was that America had turned a
local dispute into an incomprehensible global battle. The Korean War was
viewed as "merely a civil war."[16] Only 3 percent of North Korean captives

believed that the war had been "engendered by opposing political ideologies."[17] Almost half of the North Korean prisoners described North Korean motives in terms of real-politik; in answer to the question "Why is the People's Democratic Republic of Korea fighting?" about half of the Korean prisoners replied that the primary motive was to "remove the frontier at 38th parallel." Less than a third used doctrinal answers such as the liberation of "oppressed South Koreans" or the destruction of the "puppet regime of Syngman Rhee."[18]

Given such political ignorance, clashing backgrounds, and internecine tensions, how had Communists managed to form cohesive and disciplined armies? The HumRRO reports identified certain "oriental" traits as the main reason for cohesiveness. According to HumRRO consultants, "orientals," whether Chinese or Korean, shared certain traditional habits. Derived from the work of Lucien Pye, America's foremost orientalist of the period, HumRRO consultants enumerated certain common and unchanging behavioral traits of "orientals":

Authoritarian Order: In the first place, the Korean and Chinese soldiers were thoroughly habituated to a system in which authority has traditionally been exercised without regular accountability to the ruled. . . .
Adaptation to Circumstances: The traditional Chinese view, shared in large part by the Koreans, is that the individual cannot hope to influence the pattern of authority; he can only hope to improve his own situation by adapting to it. . . .
Short-Range Calculations: This orientation to power or authority gives rise to a tendency to act in an expeditious way, to calculate the consequences of an act so as to ensure maximum personal benefits. In addition, most Chinese and Koreans tend to think and act in terms of the immediate situation, rather than to consider the possible long-range effects. This is partly a function of . . . fatalism. . . .
Personal Bargaining: . . . The oriental assumes that he can make bargains with the representatives of power, trading his active assistance for personal security and small privileges.[19]

These "ingrained modes of response" of "orientals" explained away the perplexing behavior of both Korean and Chinese prisoners. The "traditional orientation toward authority" rationalized the outstanding performance of former South Koreans and former Nationalist troops in the armies of their nemesis; "short range calculation" explained how and why prisoners moved from one faction to another in the internal Koje clashes. All other actions could be resolved by leaning on comfortably broad explanations of "oriental" docility and fatalism.

In contrast to this essentialist approach to enemy societies, the reports of the Rand Corporation offered a straitlaced political explanation for enemy motivation. During the spring of 1951, while most enemy POWs were still in temporary prison stockades in the Pusan area, a Rand team, led by political scientist Alexander George, identified ideological influences on the outstanding battle performance of ill-equipped and poorly trained Chinese troops in Korea.[20] The Rand team focused, in particular, on the high percentage of former Nationalist troops in the ranks of the PLA in the Korean theater. Initial intelligence reports had assumed that the former Nationalist troops were essentially cannon fodder, a ploy by the communist regime to rid itself of the dangerous burden of professional enemy soldiers within their midst by sending them to an almost certain death. Such reasoning did little to explain the tenacious fighting spirit of these individuals. Former Nationalist veterans had demonstrated no obvious signs of fighting against their will, and had performed under difficult circumstances with great determination.

PLA battle performance was all the more puzzling given the command structure and basic training of Chinese troops. Military training ranged from negligible to poor, and the entire network of command was dominated by political rather than professional priorities. Officers wore no insignia, required no outward signs of obedience, and were evaluated by their superiors according to political loyalty rather than professional standards.

PLA discipline and motivation, according to the Rand report, was derived from an intricate network of political officers, from the company level and upward, who indoctrinated the troops, monitored political allegiances, and maintained troop morale. Contrary to the American system, where indoctrination was allegedly nonexistent and even frowned upon, the PLA placed political commitment and the absorption of communist ideology above basic training. Indoctrination, together with a surveillance system that turned each and every soldier into a potential informer, was, according to George, the main reason for PLA excellence on the battlefield. For the first time in its history, American troops faced an enemy whose motivation and fighting spirit relied on political commitment rather than professionalism.

The Rand team claimed that PLA performance on the battlefield was fueled by an ideological zeal reminiscent of medieval religious orders. No other modern army, not even those of totalitarian regimes, had produced an ideologically motivated fighting force of such threatening dimensions. Both the Wehrmacht and the Soviet army—the most obvious comparisons—were first and foremost professional armies, where, according to Rand, politics played a lowly second fiddle. American military doctrine avoided entirely "ideological symbols and political rituals." In Western armies "more immediate considerations of self-respect, professionalism" were "more powerful factors than 'political heroics.'"[21]

Despite the obviously unsettling confrontation with an enemy motivated by an "irrational" commitment to a cause, Alexander George and his Rand colleagues found little of enduring value in the Chinese model. Ideological motivation, George argued, was no match for technology. Once faced with overwhelming fighting power the entire motivational superstructure of the PLA crumbled. Defeated soldiers, even the "hard-core" communist cadres, raised doubts and lost much of their commitment to the cause when confronted by technologically superior American adversaries. The " 'spiritual' power of the PLA . . . proved inadequate under the stress of military disadvantages."

Cannons, not canons, professionalism rather than blinding zeal, would decide the battles of the future. "As the PLA's military difficulties and casualties mounted, the positive effect of its war indoctrination on the troops quickly wore thin." The reality of combat in Korea clashed with "expectations which the PLA propaganda had aroused within its forces."[22] Stress and loss of confidence in victory disabused even the most hardened Communists. Political convictions could not withstand reality. A well-trained, well-equipped, apolitical army had nothing to fear from the fervor of zealots.

Hailed as a "major contribution not only to our understanding of the PLA . . . but also to the field of military sociology" in general, the Rand report was, in actual fact, a poorly researched, flawed document. Its authoritative generalizations were based on tenuous sampling. The protocols were the result of only eighty-four interviews of Chinese POWs, who, according to an apologetic Alexander George, had been selected "more or less fortuitously from among those available." George admitted that his informants were far from being a representative sample. His prisoners "did not necessarily reflect the characteristics of those Chinese soldiers who had died, those who had deserted to the rear, those who were still members of the PLA."[23]

George's study was hobbled by linguistic obstacles as well. In a "research note" tacked on to the end of his study, George documented a chaotic and garbled mode of translation. Given his personal lack of knowledge of "the Chinese language" — as if the prisoners spoke only one form of Chinese — "all interviews were conducted by Korean civilians who were fluent in Chinese. . . . The interviewers translated and recorded the Chinese respondents' replies into Korean during the interview. Later, a separate group of translators, more skilled in the English language translated these interview protocols from Korean into English."[24]

Even though communist indoctrination was the central premise of the entire study, George apparently had no idea what such ideological instruction entailed. The study's index contained only four references to communism, all of which were decidedly vague. George described "the basic beliefs of communism" as passed on to the indoctrinated troops as "anti-individualism, dedication of self to the interests of the 'people,' acceptance of leadership of the party."[25] In fact, when questioned about the actual content of indoctrination sessions, George's informants came up with decidedly nationalist, not communist, aphorisms. Indoctrination sessions explained the war as an effort to thwart American imperialistic ambitions to invade China, through Korean territory, just as its Japanese ally had done in the past.[26]

The Rand report presumably ignored conflicting ORO and HumRRO reports on political ignorance, innocence, and the insignificance of communist indoctrination because such information undermined its main conclusion. George's primary objective was quite simply to sing the praises of technology and professionalism in an age of ideological fanaticism. According to George, all quasi-religious motivational factors were of limited value in an age of mechanized warfare. If anything, the ideological indoctrination of troops proved to be counterproductive.

> The morale doctrine implicit in the PLA's approach . . . recognized no limits to what a communist could accomplish if his political ideology was strong enough. The result was a pronounced tendency to demand of the individual, and especially of the Communist cadre, more than seems humanly possible. . . . There was, as we have seen, little sympathy in the PLA with the view taken in Western armies that every man has a breaking point. Rather, PLA authorities acted on the assumption that human failures, even under the most difficult combat conditions, were always due to personal deficiencies of a political character. If one's political ideology was firm enough, one would never flinch from a task, no matter how dangerous and hopeless it might seem.[27]

This stubborn insistence on the ability of committed troops to snatch victory from hopeless situations led to an accruing number of disasters. PLA officers, even among the "hard core cadre members," were accused of political shortcomings for failing to accomplish miracles, and they, in turn, lost their identification with the cause. The Rand report "proved" that "Mao's dictum that 'man' can triumph over 'weapons' " was empty rhetoric. In contrast to the alleged Chinese debacle, American troops had supposedly triumphed in Korea once the presence of a constraining, ideologically motivated commander was removed. Following the departure of General Douglas MacArthur, U.S. commanders avoided the ideological sinkhole that, the Rand report implied, had been responsible for American defeats during the latter portion of MacArthur's Korean command.

> Thus, for example, when General Matthew Ridgway assumed command of the Eighth Army in Korea in December 1950 after its long retreat occasioned by the Chinese Communist intervention, he found that attempts were being made to restore morale in some units by giving politi-

cal peptalks. Instead, Ridgway insisted on the restoration of strict barrack-room discipline wherever possible. From that time, the Eighth Army started to become a professional army, fighting not for the United Nations or against communism but fighting because it was ordered to.[28]

The Reeducation Program

As experts quibbled over the significance of enemy politics and ideology, the FEC initiated its own private venture to pursue the war by other means. In early November 1950, officials from the Japanese-based CIE conducted a pilot project with five hundred "carefully selected" North Korean POWs. The program was sanctioned after the fact by the army, and on March 23, 1951, the army chief of staff officially approved the establishment of United Nations Command, Korea (UN COM). Instruction commenced on June 1, 1951.[29] Original objectives were limited to a duplication of World War II orientation projects, in particular the cultivation of a cadre of democratic pro-American prisoners for postwar Korea.[30] Once established, the program swiftly transcended these limited horizons. Instead of the narrow grooming of a select group of prisoners, program architects launched an ambitious initiative to bolster military achievements on the battlefield with a resounding propaganda victory in the prison camps. By June 1951, with the establishment of a permanent reeducation program on Koje Island, the limited grooming of a select group of prisoners was transformed into an determined effort to choreograph a sweeping ideological transformation of the entire POW population, both Chinese and Korean.

The POW reeducation program was hatched in Japan, in MacArthur's FEC. One of the first steps of American occupation forces in postwar Japan was the establishment of the CIE, a grandiose design for democratizing Japanese society through a structural and ideological refurbishing of its education system. MacArthur's design, according to historian Toshio Nishi, was to impose by fiat "into Japanese daily life such foreign ideals and ideas as 'individuality,' 'liberty', 'freedom', and 'equality.' "[31]

Toshio and other historians have produced somewhat jaundiced accounts of the CIE's attempts to uplift Japanese society. They have argued that the Japanese education establishment maintained its fundamentally conservative structure, and never really internalized anything beyond superficial democratization and Americanization. In MacArthur's eyes, however, the CIE could do no wrong. As far as he was concerned, the CIE had played a major part in the transformation of Japanese society from fascism to democracy. Thus, the move beyond Japan to Korea, the site of what appeared to be the first major clash between the United States and its communist adversaries, was a natural step.

The Korean CIE program was managed from the Tokyo-based director's office. The operation's nerve center, the materials production division, was based in Tokyo as well. This division, which produced all the program's instructional material, was divided into a Korean-language material branch, comprised of three American officials and thirty Korean personnel, and a Chinese-language branch with approximately the same ratio of Chinese and Americans. The third major component of the CIE UN COM, and the only division of the program based in Korea, was the Field Operation Division (FOD). The major branch of this division was the instructional programs branch, comprised of the actual educators and disseminators of reeducation material. Lacking adequately trained personnel of its own, the FOD relied on politically "safe" POWs, teachers provided by the South Korean government, and staff members recruited in Taiwan and Hong Kong. The FOD had no officers claiming the necessary language skills to monitor the politics or performance of these indigenous staff members. The only mechanism available for gauging the program was the FOD's evaluation branch. This branch conducted periodic oral and written tests "to measure the progress of POWs toward the aims on which the instructional program is based, and to identify weaknesses."[32] Here, too, operations were dominated by indigenous personnel whose loyalties lay elsewhere.

CIE UN COM was intimately tied to the Japanese mother-program. Its director reported to the chief CIE, Far East Command, who, for all practical purposes, appeared to be the sole source of major policy decisions; input from Washington was all but nonexistent. CIE staff members, in both Japan and Korea, claimed no specific academic background for their ambitious task. Lieutenant Colonel Donald Nugent, the chief of CIE, Far East Command, was a reserve Marine Corp high school principal. His staff, both those in Korea and in Japan, had about the same level of background and experience. Monta Osborne, the UN COM director of CIE Korean operations, was a civilian and former marine officer too. Prior to his Korean assignment, he had served as the CIE's secondary school education officer for Japan. Osborne would later become the coordinator of psychological warfare in Vietnam.

Ambivalent politics and blurred identities in the prison stockades did not leave much of an impression on Korea's CIE educators. They were, of course, intelligent individuals; presumably they were aware of the competing forms of culture and historical circumstance among their prisoner-students. However, they demonstrated little interest in investigating the significance of these factors. As products of the American educational establishment, the confrontation with cultural and social confusion was nothing new to them; it was, however, irrelevant. In a manner reminiscent of early-twentieth-century American school educators, who had hoped that schools "would substitute American forms for the cacophony of alien cultural modes" jostling for recognition in their schoolyards, these American schoolteachers in uniform anticipated that their presentation of American democracy would eclipse, rather than accommodate, competing forms of social or political identity.[33]

CIE goals were strikingly reminiscent of the social studies program in an American school. Korean-based reeducation officials aimed for an aggressive assimilation of a "democratic," predefined, American form of politics and culture that was derived from the civics textbooks of the schools they had left back home. The American public school system, with its emphasis on unquestioning acceptance of American values by the untutored individuals of alien cultures, represented the primary tool for altering the worldview of their prisoner-students.

The main units of the formal reeducation program were "the history of Korea and China; Korea under U.S. occupation; the United Nations." The themes in all units focused on the "contrast between democracy and totalitarianism. . . and problems of reconstruction in Korea and China."[34] The material was never as abstract as the titles of the study units suggest. Aware of the disparate educational and cultural backgrounds of their students, CIE lessons on the contrast between democracy and communism showed equal preoccupation with the metaphysical and the trivial.

Democracy, according to the instructional unit on this subject, guaranteed the sacred freedom of speech and the equally prized profane right to purchase a new car every few years.[35] The Korean units on democracy taught that in communist societies, land was owned by the government, while "large corporations in the United States are owned by thousands and sometimes hundreds of thousands of people." Perhaps fearing that the concept of shareholding would not impress the average Korean soldier, this same study unit offered, as well, simpler examples. While citizens of communist countries were deprived of personal property, "more than half of all American city families have electrical washing machines."[36] Descriptions of democracy as a land of household appliances and motor vehicles—how many landless peasants dreamt of such devices in their more optimistic moments?—were due to the fact that these study units were mostly translations of material prepared for Japan, which, in turn, was based on didactic units imported from the United States.

"Nothing less than education is powerful enough to save the child," wrote the progressive educator, Robert Hunter, at the turn of the century. "And, 'to prepare for complete living' is the function education has to discharge."[37] It was with thoughts like these in mind that the CIE included vocational education in what was originally planned as a purely classroom exercise. Trade skills and literacy programs were offered as an antidote for both subversive, futuristic communism and regressive, traditional oriental cultures. Thus, the CIE developed a strong vocational element, in what they called, in typical progressive fashion, an "over-all education program." Teaching landless peasants the rudimentary trades of modern living promised to provide a sense of material security and an appreciation for capitalism. "Economic security," the CIE's first interim report stated, was the most fundamental "antidote to communism."[38]

Up until May 1952, CIE Korea did not seek the counsel of behavioral scientists. Advisors from ORO and Rand were unwelcome. When CIE began its pilot program for reeducation in Korea, they found themselves burdened by the presence of ORO advisors attempting to define and dictate the didactical content of reeducation. Through a skillful process of political maneuvering, CIE managed to distance ORO officials from all positions of influence in the program. ORO acknowledged defeat and withdrew entirely, leaving the program exclusively in the hands of the CIE.[39]

A variety of reasons accounted for the CIE suspicion of the ORO and its clones. To begin with, it did not take a grand expert to see that the think tank investigations of the enemy were no less capricious than CIE efforts. Language barriers kept Rand, HumRRO, and ORO investigators from direct contact with their informants. They relied entirely on the services of native personnel whose translations were suspect for both political and technical reasons. Moreover, CIE officials were straitlaced anti-communists; they were unwilling to entertain anything besides political and ideological explanations of POW behavior.

The world of the CIE was a reflection of the politics of the FEC. The civilian and military educational officials who were sent to Korea were all products of General Douglas MacArthur's CIE program in Japan. Much like their patron, these reeducation officials espoused a far-flung understanding of their mission. Their attempt to reeducate was not a narrow propaganda task, but part of a crusade against communism. Eulogies on the end of ideology had not penetrated the CIE. In the Japanese headquarters of MacArthur's FEC ideas still had consequences.

The coordinator of this anticommunist crusade was Major General Charles A. Willoughby, MacArthur's longtime chief of intelligence operations. Historians have cast Willoughby in an extremely negative light. Bruce Cumings has described him as a borderline psychotic. According to Cumings, "Willoughby was a profound racist and anti-semite who saw the Soviet bloc as 'the historical continuity of Mongoloid-PanSlavism.'"[40]

There is no doubt that Willoughby had an unpleasant habit of seeing red just about everywhere, including within the ranks of his own staff.[41] He was, then, meticulous in his choice of staff members for the establishment of the CIE. His emissaries shared his militant views on global divisions, including the Korean microcosm, into Communists and democrats. With the passage of time, CIE Japan spent growing proportions of its resources on combating real and delusionary communist influences on the Japanese educational system. "Under MacArthur's auspices," Japanese historian Toshio Nishi notes, "American cold war attitudes were immediately translated into a repressive official policy of the Japanese government, commonly called the 'Red Purge.' "[42] As early as 1948, the CIE forced about 1,200 teachers to resign because of their allegedly pro-communist leanings. Such administrative steps were followed by the publication of compulsory anticommunist textbooks and growing scrutiny of university staff and students, where communism was allegedly rampant. The officials of CIE Korea had survived the internal and external purges in Japan prior to their new assignment in the UN COM.

The Japanese reeducation program and, subsequently, the Korean offspring, espoused strong ties between Christianity and democracy. Indeed, historian D. Clayton James has observed that MacArthur was obsessed with christianizing Japan, believing that "so long as no religion or occupation was oppressed, the Occupation had every right to propagate Christianity." MacArthur claimed that through the embracement of the Christian faith, millions of "backward," fatalistic, and "therefore warlike" Asians "might achieve a new spiritual strength through which they would develop the opposite attributes."[43] In addition, he saw Christianity and communism as the two mutually exclusive faiths of the modern world. Asia, in his eyes, was "a spiritual vacuum. . . . If you do not fill it with Christianity, it will be filled with communism."[44]

CIE Korea used conversion to Christianity as a measure of its success. In his assessment of the CIE's pilot program, in which five hundred POWs were chosen as trailblazers for the future mass program of conversion, CIE official Colonel Kenneth Hansen resorted to decidedly evangelical terms. His listings of accomplishments of the early pilot program noted that

> At the end of the first day's sessions, the five hundred were asked if they desired religious services. None wanted Buddhist services, quite a few asked for Catholic services, and a surprising number asked for Protestant services. The first service, attended by 120 of the men, was non-denominational; the following Sunday, 45 men attended a Catholic service and 165 a Protestant service.[45]

Upon the establishment of the regular CIE program, Hansen methodically measured progress by counting church attendance, with special emphasis on the growing number of POWs at Protestant events and regular services. Even though he expressed awareness of the "Oriental . . . tendency to ingratiate," Hansen argued that acceptance of the gospel was the ultimate sign of the successful "rehabilitation" of the spiritually blind and politically ignorant.[46]

The most forceful advocate of this missionary faith in CIE Korea was Lieutenant Colonel Robert E. O'Brien, the chief of the CIE's FOD. O'Brien, the only senior official of Korea's CIE program residing permanently on Koje Island, had plans to develop a program extolling the symbiotic relationship between democracy and Christianity. He argued that the "moral and ethical" underpinnings of democracy were intertwined with a belief in Christianity and God.[47]

O'Brien's superiors in the Tokyo-based office of the CIE Korean mission differed sharply on this issue. His commanding officer, Lieutenant Colonel Donald R. Nugent, argued that "religion has no place whatsoever in the CIE program." Nugent claimed that "the Koreans are largely an irreligious people" and that the introduction into the CIE program of "any new concept involving the relationship of man to God could lead only to confusion and controversy."[48]

Such cautionary advice fell on deaf ears. Under the guidance of O'Brien, conversion to Christianity became the dividing line for distinguishing between POW factions. Declarations of religious faith, in the face of "persecution," was by far the most common form of expressing anticommunism and pro-democratic leanings before American overseers.[49] In fact, it became the most common method for interpreting the growing number of internecine conflicts among the POWs prior to the spring of 1952. By the Americans' own admission, any other attempt to describe the warring factions in the camp was problematic.

The Koje Riots

As this attitude toward spiritual conversion suggests, CIE officials in Korea were unwilling to limit themselves to purely intellectual activities. Accepting democracy entailed a dramatic act of faith. With little apparent attempt to inform their superiors, the CIE moved beyond Christianity as the barometer of success and sought more politically tangible measurements. By late 1951, as the armistice talks reached a crucial stage, CIE officials in Korea aggressively encouraged prisoners to declare their unwillingness to accept repatriation to the communist camp. Prisoner petitions and other forms of refusals of repatriation became the ultimate test of success.

These mostly independent efforts of CIE field officials eventually clashed with official policy when, in April 1952, and as part of the effort to resuscitate the armistice talks, American officials initiated a major screening process of POWs. The Panmunjom negotiations had reached an impasse on the mutual repatriation of POWs. Intent on scoring at least a technical victory in Korea, American officials refused categorically to abide by an "all-for-all" exchange of POWs. Guided by policy defined by President Truman, American negotiators insisted on the principle of "voluntary repatriation," the assumption being that prisoners should not be forced to return to invidious, communist-dominated countries.[50]

The United States had adopted this conscious violation of the 1949 Geneva Convention, assuming that the actual number of POWs refusing repatriation would not affect the final outcome of the talks. General Hickey, UN COM chief of staff, estimated that of the 132,000 POWs on Koje Do in February 1952, "about 28,000 would prefer not to go home, but probably only 16,000 would resist repatriation."[51] Based on this unsubstantiated estimation General Matthew Ridgway somewhat hastily informed the president that "only 5000 North Korean POWs and 11,500 CCF [Chinese Communist Forces] POWs could be expected violently to resist repatriation."[52] Given these comparatively modest figures, Ridgway assumed that communist adversaries might reluctantly accept this blow to their prestige in return for American concessions on other outstanding differences at Panmunjom.

In early April, following a detection of Chinese willingness to probe, however cautiously, the principle of nonforcible repatriation, the Eighth Army began screening POWs. The screening process was a mismanaged affair, characterized by violence, political intervention of Taiwanese, South Korean, and communist agitators, and counterproductive CIE efforts to raise the numbers of repatriation refusals. CIE officials, according to POW debriefings, aggressively encouraged nonrepatriation and basically marched to the tune of their own private drummer. Contrary to the official policy of limiting defection, CIE officials and their indigenous staff sought massive repatriation refusals, mostly in order to vindicate their program.[53]

Upon completion of the rescreening process, a shaken Ridgway learned that the numbers of prisoners ostensibly refusing repatriation was far from symbolic and bore no resemblance to his initial estimate. Despite all sorts of attempts to manipulate the final figures, only 70,000 of the 170,000 POWs were willing to accept repatriation. The bungled screening had transformed the item of POW repatriation from a symbolic to a substantive issue. The plan to declare symbolic victory in Korea by persuading a limited number of enemy POWs to defect had spun out of control. In due course, repatriation became the only unresolvable issue of the Korean armistice talks. Both sides dug into intransigent positions and the armistice talks reached an irresolvable impasse. The United States unilaterally suspended talks on October 8, 1952. Following months of bloody trench-war fighting and the enemy's acceptance of the American position on repatriation, the warring sides eventually signed an armistice agreement on July 27, 1953.[54]

As for life on Koje Do, the 1952 spring screenings initiated a new phase of violence and turmoil. Unrest reached a boiling point on May 7, 1952, when prisoners from one of the most defiant compounds managed to kidnap the camp commander, Brigadier General Francis T. Dodd. During the course of a conversation with POW leaders at the gateway to one of the communist-controlled compounds, an unarmed and unprotected Dodd was swept into the bowels of this enemy stronghold by a returning work duty.

Unlike American POWs languishing in enemy prisons while their superiors haggled over more or less symbolic issues, Dodd endured only a brief incarceration. On the evening of May 10, Dodd was released following the transmittal of a signed statement by Brigadier General Colson, Dodd's replacement. His hastily worded statement admitted "instances of bloodshed where many PW have been killed or wounded by UN forces," promised more humane treatment, and indirectly acknowledged that the repatriation screenings had been "forcible." Colson, who claimed to have received permission from his superiors to sign this incriminating statement, was indicted for breach of duty. Together with Dodd he was demoted and removed with alacrity from the Korean theater.[55]

Whether Colson had acted on his own initiative or not was, of course, a moot point. His damaging statement turned the entire issue of nonforcible repatriation into a Pyrrhic victory. A cloud of doubt dispelled what advantages the United States had hoped to gain from the mass defection of enemy captives.

The CIE program, accused of inflammatory actions prior to the Dodd incident, was another victim of the kidnapping debacle. Colonel Robert O'Brien, the militant anticommunist CIE representative, was summarily dismissed on June 6, 1952, prior to the resumption of revised, and significantly tepid, CIE activities.[56]

Revised CIE guidelines prohibited attempts to induce any form of ideological conversion. Acting under orders from the Department of the Army, CIE UN COM flooded its field staff with sociologists and social psychologists. The Korean reports hummed with the buzz words of the behavioral sciences. Detached discussions of projective tests, social stratification, and behavior modification replaced the ideological terminology of previous reports.

Prisoners' stances on repatriation were no longer analyzed as part of a struggle against communism. Following the Dodd kidnapping, the reorganized CIE, now controlled by behavioral scientists, dismissed all interpretations of prisoner unrest in anything but behavioral terms. According to the CIE internal audits, professions of "strong anti-communist feeling" did "not imply that the PWs identify themselves with the UN and democracy." CIE officials explained that "the adjective 'democratic' . . . in Chinese is very vague," and that declarations of political loyalties were apparently motivated by a series of inscrutable reasons that had little to do with the familiar divide of communism and democratic inclinations.[57] The CIE's new interpreters of POW behavior argued that POWs who espoused the most "extreme political views" suddenly changed their views with little apparent compunction. The sudden move from one extreme political position to another occurred when individual prisoners were under pressure from "an organized PW political group" or as a result of sudden changes in their group leader's attitude.[58] On the sensitive issue of repatriation, the post-Dodd CIE claimed that ideological convictions had little to do with these decisions. "Evaluation supports the hypothesis that group pressures were the fundamental key to the decision of those who chose not to return home."[59]

The recommendations of the behavioral phase of CIE reports, complete with statistical apparatus, challenged ideological interpretations of prisoner behavior. The CIE of late 1952 argued that scientific "attitude tests failed to show the cumulative effect of the CIE program upon the political attitude of PWs." Manifestations of anticommunism were caused by "alien factors such as mass psychological pressure."[60] The most reliable indicator of internal trends among the rank and file was the political stance of compound leaders. "The majority are taking the expedient course of simply following their leaders." As far as these leaders were concerned, CIE reports argued that "it is not likely that the anti-communist leaders' attitudes were based upon an allegiance with democracy and democratic methods."[61] Declarations of faith in democracy were mere rhetoric.

Such provocative findings offered military officials a window of opportunity to resort to forcible repatriation. If, after all, repatriation refusals were not motivated by true ideological convictions, there appeared to be no compelling reason to ignore the plight of allied POWs for the sake of superficial opposition to communism. By the summer of 1952, with presidential elections in the offing, such backtracking was, however, impossible.

Whatever benefits American officials had hoped to reap from enemy defections were, in sum, shortlived. News trickling in from the enemy camp suggested that American soldiers, too, had shown distinct signs of political conversion. The repudiation of communism by the masses of Chinese and Korean POWs was overshadowed and almost forgotten by an astonished American public. With attention now focused on rumors of defections among American POWs, the symbolic significance of mass communist defections lost most of its resonance.

8.

Prison Camps and Culture Wars
The Korean Brainwashing Controversy

In late June 1953, as the last of America's POWs returned home to a lackluster welcome, the American public learned that twenty-one Americans had refused repatriation. Over the course of the next decade, a disturbing debate on POW conduct in Korea dominated the public memory of the war. Prominent journalists provided an unsettling picture of undisciplined prisoners, lacking in camaraderie and indifferent to the military code of honor. As many as a third of the prisoners were accused of having collaborated in some form with the enemy. None had apparently tried to escape. Twenty-three airmen, including a marine pilot, Colonel Frank H. Schwable, had made highly publicized public confessions of war crimes that included detailed statements of germ warfare bombing raids. The Hollywood image of defiant Americans behind barbed wire had failed to materialize.

The primary purveyors of this dismal picture attributed such behavior to faults in the American character, born out of excessive abundance and lapsed values. The POWs were damned as the products of an education system riddled with relativism and lacking in moral standards. As the representatives of an effete society, they had proven to be a poor match when faced with ideologically dedicated adversaries. Journalist Eugene Kinkead, the most prominent critic of POW conduct, claimed that such manifestations of weakness were not a purely military issue. The POW debacle was an ominous sign of malfunction in "diverse aspects of our culture—home training of children, education, physical fitness, religious adherence," and the result of complacency born out "of existing under the highest standard of living in the world."[1]

Other commentators preferred blaming the enemy for the allegedly dishonorable conduct of POWs. Rumors and leaks from the debriefing sessions raised the suspicion that Americans behind barbed wire had indeed capitulated, but not due to any personal or collective defects. They were the victims of brainwashing, a powerful, manipulative psychological weapon that could break even the most hardened soldier.[2]

These grim representations of psychological manipulation, poor military performance in the face of adversity, and/or fundamental characterological flaws contrasted sharply with government-ordained reports and studies. The official teams of behavioral scientists employed by the military produced a significantly benign profile of America's POWs. According to reports issued by both army and air force research centers, the damning of American POWs as either weak collaborators or helpless victims of brainwashing was patently false. Such alarmist accounts, they argued, were sensationalist, politically motivated exaggerations. The investigators claimed that the behavior of American POWs was no different from that of their peers in previous wars. They stated that deviancies from standard military conduct had occurred less frequently than in previous wars, despite the particularly harsh circumstances of the Korean prison camps. Contrary to those who identified characterological flaws or psychological breakdowns among American POWs, the behavioral experts maintained that the prisoners had withstood unprecedented physical hardships, arbitrary punishments, and constant fear for their lives. As for the idea of brainwashing, the official reports dismissed the concept of menticide as science fiction, preferring, instead, to explain deviant behavioral patterns as statistically marginal, and the result of either coercion or standard psychological manipulative tactics.

Retrospective assessments of the POW controversy invariably described these behavioral scientists as fearless supporters of the truth. By contrast, their adversaries—scheming politicians and unscrupulous journalists—were accused of ulterior, mostly political motives.[3] There is no doubt that both the collaboration narrative and the brainwashing hypothesis were poorly researched and rife with bias. However, the scientific reports were no less politically informed. The behavioral scientists swept aside a host of challenging social and political issues associated with the POW experience. Their reports avoided the racial and ethnic composition of American POWs, and skirted the issue of social stratification in the armed forces and its impact on prison camps and battlefields.

The various interpretations of the American POW experience do not divide easily into false—political—and true—scientific—accounts. In fact, veracity is not the most compelling issue. Whatever its immediate concerns, the POW controversy was a sign of a fundamental cultural struggle in which the POW experience in Korea served as an illustration only. Conflicting interpretations of the American POW experience were derived from a clash between two strong intellectual currents. One was resoundingly technocratic, the bearer of a demystifying secular creed. The second impulse was adamantly ideological, critical of "scientism," the scientific monopolization of moral and philosophic issues, and the extension of scientific methodology and inquiry beyond its "legitimate" scope.

"In Every War But One"

"In every war but one that the United States has fought, the conduct of its servicemen who were captured and held in enemy prison camps presented no unforeseen problems to the armed forces. . . . That war was the Korean War." This opening salvo in Eugene Kinkead's book, *Why They Collaborated?* (1959) reflected widespread frustration concerning the ambivalent outcome of America's first major confrontation with its communist arch-rival.[4]

Critics found no extenuating circumstances for the alleged debacle behind barbed wire. According to army psychologist Major William Mayer, there was no correlation between socioeconomic status and dishonorable conduct, or for that matter any other social variable and the embarrassing behavior of the captive troops. Mayer and others offered, instead, a cultural explanation for the mass capitulation. They described American POWs as emotionally weak, a pampered cross-section of American youth who were unable to withstand any form of physical or mental stress. Compared to American POWs in other wars, no prisoners had tried to escape and they had allegedly died in droves from what unkind critics called the disease of Give-Up-Ititis. Critics claimed that the ephemeral, materialistic values of the average American had produced a dangerously fragile modern army. American soldiers in Korea lacked "the historical American standards of honor, character, loyalty, courage and personal integrity."[5]

Such assessments reflected widespread discontent among career army officers, opponents of post–World War II reforms in the army's disciplinary code and recruitment policy. Based on anonymous army sources, Mayer, Kinkead, and others claimed that at least a third of the American POWs had died in captivity, compared to Turkish troops, who, under identical conditions "survived almost to a man." They attributed the Turkish survival rate to their "strict system of military organization and discipline." By contrast, reforms in military training placed American POWs at a distinct disadvantage. Instead of instilling discipline and toughness, the "new" army was based on getting the recruit "to like us."[6]

Prominent sociologist Ralf Dahrendorf concurred. In his review of David Riesman's *The Lonely Crowd* (1950), Dahrendorf described American POWs as the ultimate example of predominant, other-directed persons, lacking in internal convictions and addicted to the opinions of others. Deprived of the "internal gyroscope" of stable convictions and values, and torn from their social referents, the other-directed American POWs had fallen into a state of existential confusion that made collaboration inevitable. "Is it not conceivable that, in the absence of an internal gyroscope many of" the prisoners "decided to apply their one means of coping with situations—adaptation and conformity?" The Korean situation, Dahrendorf concluded, was an alarming example of the manner in which an other-directed American culture "might display a striking and, perhaps, frightening lack of resistance against new influences and ideologies, totalitarian or otherwise."[7]

Major William Mayer, the primary spokesman of the army critics, preferred a more gender-specific indictment of American society. Claiming to have examined over one thousand of the returning prisoners, Mayer placed special emphasis on what he considered to be the pathological adolescent experiences of young Americans, in particular, the phenomenon of underdeveloped masculinity. "A boy who has been brought up largely by his mother alone, a boy who has become what in psychiatry we refer to as a dependent character, something like the result of 'momism' as described by Philip Wylie . . . [could] not withstand the stresses of captivity," he argued.[8]

In her own strange way, feminist Betty Friedan agreed with this sexist interpretation of the American malaise. Young men in American society were, according to Friedan, "helpless, apathetic, incapable of handling freedom." Friedan offered the Korean POW experience as evidence of the inability of the passive male—"arrested at the level of infantile fantasy and passivity"—to cope with stress and maintain values when confronted by adversity. Quoting Kinkead and Mayer, she claimed that the Korean experience was a manifestation of personality disorders, the result of nurturing by mothers "who lived within the limits of the feminine mystique," where the smothering of children became the only avenue for self-fulfillment.[9]

This license to attack the hapless victims of the Korean deadlock was intimately linked to the social composition of American fighting forces in post–World War II America. Contrary to Friedan's critique, the typical army soldier, both on the battlefield and in the prison camp, was not the product of a pampered suburban environment; the privileged had remained at home. Army ground forces—the least prestigious of the services—bore the brunt of this protracted war and suffered the largest proportion of casualties and captives. Out of a total of 7,140 American captives, 6,656 were army personnel. These prisoners in uniform claimed none of the glory of the eloquent and prestigious aircrews of World War II who were the subjects of admiring, some-what unrealistic, and self-serving portrayals of bravery behind barbed wire in Nazi Germany.[10]

In a foreboding of the Vietnam War, army ranks were dominated by the inarticulate lower strata of American society. The low socioeconomic back-ground of army personnel in the aftermath of World War II, and the sweeping draft exemptions for the well-educated and well-connected, produced a fight-ing force dominated by minorities and poor whites.[11] The typical army soldier in Korea was an undereducated, marginal individual.

The background of POWs reflected this state of affairs. Forty-four percent of army POWs had only a grade school education, 51 percent had an IQ below 90. Only 10 percent came from a white-collar background.[12] Korea was also the first integrated war. A disproportionate percentage of both captives and casualties were people of color, this being the first war in which they fought side by side with white comrades in arms. By May 1951, there were over 27,000 African American soldiers—about 13.5 percent of the total U.S. strength in Korea. By the end of the year this figure had risen sharply, particu-larly in combat units where turnover was rapid.[13]

The lowly army troops were easy targets, and tongue-tied defenders of their performance on the battlefields and in the prison camps. Lacking in political power or social status, America's prisoners were the ultimate pawns of the war. The protracted armistice talks, mired down by haggling over POW exchange policy, generated little public protest. In fact, all signs of discontent were rou-tinely squelched. Administration officials were ruthless in their efforts to dis-credit the occasional protests of POW families. Letters, petitions, and direct appeals to the president were viewed suspiciously and were turned over to the FBI and other investigative bodies charged with inquiring into the political credentials and private motives of protesting family members.[14]

In response to infrequent expressions of concern by public officials, the administration made no effort to conceal its priorities. The prisoners, a State Department official informed a protesting U.S. senator, were, unfortunately, but unavoidably, pawns in a battle of cosmic proportions, in which the suffer-ing of the few was of little significance. "After weighing all alternatives," the administration had decided against forcible repatriation of enemy POWs and a speedy release of American captives, so as not to inhibit future waves of mass defection from behind the Iron Curtain. Moreover, forcible repatriation, whatever its benefits for the suffering few, threatened to damage the United States' credibility and status as leader of the free world.[15]

A significant change in administration policy occurred only after the series of uncomfortable public confessions of war crimes, the most momentous of which were the germ-warfare confessions of captive aircrews. Previous radio broadcasts and incriminating articles written by POWs had attracted little public attention. The highly publicized confession of Marine Colonel

Schwable was of particular significance. He could not be dismissed as a symbol of decadent America. He was a marine, a pilot, and a senior officer. In contrast to the typical statements of collaborators, mostly testimonies on the kindness of communist captors and condemnations of Western capitalism, Frank H. Schwable's provided a detailed, allegedly false, description of American biological warfare air raids in Korea.

This confession, as well as a growing number of uncomfortable reports on other forms of collaboration and dissension within the ranks of American POWs, produced an alternative interpretation of American conduct behind barbed wire. Rather than focusing on character weaknesses, another group of commentators raised the specter of brainwashing, an intensive psychiatric program calculated to alter principles and convictions by means of mental manipulation.

Brainwashing

The roots of the brainwashing theory in Korea were derived from a distant European milieu. Based on recurring reports of public confessions of treason by prominent dissenters behind the Iron Curtain, American officials speculated that communist adversaries had developed an insidious form of psychological manipulation, a methodic, scientific mechanism for reprogramming the thoughts, beliefs, and values of defenseless victims. Journalist Edward Hunter supplied the Asian context for the brainwashing hypothesis. In 1951, Hunter published his study of ideological coercion, entitled *Brainwashing in Red China*, thereby popularizing the term, and its more pretentious twin, "menticide," as explanations for the enemy's supposedly mesmerizing hold on captive masses.[16]

Ritual of Liquidation (1954), a Rand Corporation study of public political trials in the Soviet Union of the 1930s, provided the scientific underpinnings for the brainwashing thesis. Written by the ubiquitous Rand Kremlinologist, Nathan Leites, this study argued that physical coercion was not the reason behind public confessions in communist countries. Leites proposed, instead, a variety of complex psychological explanations for the self-incriminating behavior of communist victims. He called attention to the fact that the defendants in most of the purge trials were convinced Bolsheviks. He interpreted their self-damning confessions as the faithful's final service to the Party. Physical coercion, he claimed, had little to do with the dramatic gesture of self-incrimination. Concerted acts—be they collaboration, participation in propaganda campaigns, or confessions of treason—occurred only after the conversion process. While never mentioning the concept of brainwashing in so many words, the Rand study implied that the act of embracing communism was in itself abnormal, most probably the result of a powerful strategy to overcome the mental defense mechanisms of normal human beings. Psychology and psychiatry were employed in new and frightening ways in the Soviet bloc. Instead of functioning as a therapeutic tool for individuals, psychology and psychiatry had become instruments for manipulating the minds and souls of defenseless citizens.

Distinguished psychiatrists commissioned by the government to explain U.S. POW confessions of war crimes elaborated on the threat of psychiatric weaponry. Although none of these psychiatrists had actually examined the Korean War prisoners, they did not hesitate to diagnose their virtual patients by remote control. Henry Laughlin, president of the Washington Psychiatric Society and a CIA consultant, provided a series of reports for the Psychological Strategy Board explaining the workings, scientific assumptions, and difficulties entailed in combating this "perverse science." Laughlin explained that brain-washing was not the working of a few unscrupulous individuals. It was, instead, a natural outgrowth of Soviet ideology. "Brain-washing," he claimed, "is directly in line with the concepts of dialectic materialism, which are in turn . . . an integral part of psychological thinking in the Soviet Union." In other words, brainwashing was easily accepted in a society "where the end always justifies the means."[17]

Most treatises on brainwashing universally described the technique as "Pavlovian." The Soviets, according to this explanation, had perfected the taming and conditioning of man, using methods of the nineteenth-century Russian pioneer of behaviorism, Ivan Pavlov. The common theme permeating all these studies was that the Soviets had cultivated a procedure used in the conditioning of animals to control the responses of human beings. Joost Meerloo, a Dutch-born Columbia University psychiatrist, described how in "the POW camps in Korea . . . the negative and positive conditioning stimuli were usually hunger and food. The moment the soldier conformed to the party line his food ration was improved: say yes, and I'll give you a piece of candy!"[18] University of Washington professor of neuropsychiatry George Winokur explained that the recitation of enemy propaganda in order to satisfy such primary needs as hunger had far-reaching consequences. "If at first the prisoner did not believe in his statements and actions," he would be overwhelmed by irresolvable conflict between his beliefs and his "motor and speech activities. In order to resolve the internal conflict and escape the concomitant anxiety, the prisoner would have to change his way of thinking to conform with that of his captors."[19]

The menticide explanation received prominent coverage because this tenuous theory reflected contemporary cultural and political anxieties. American society of the 1950s was increasingly fascinated by the threat of a foreign presence within the American body politic. The political, social, and intellectual atmosphere of the period reflected concern for, and fascination with, the enemy within. In a period in which conspiracy was a widely accepted explanation for political developments in the United States, brainwashing seemed altogether plausible. If blue-blooded Anglo-Protestants like Alger Hiss appeared to be fifth columnists, then the uniformed defenders of the American body politic could conceivably be the enemy in disguise. Moreover, popular fears of the enemy were such that any cognitive acceptance of communist doctrine was widely regarded as an act of abnormality, an involuntary act brought about by covert, treacherous techniques.

Such fears of involuntary, subconscious persuasion reflected contemporary apprehensions concerning a decline in personal autonomy and control in modern society. At times, the anxieties focused on communist brainwashing; often fears were directed toward an equally pernicious army of "Hidden Persuaders" who, by use of state-of-the-art motivational research and subliminal stimulation, controlled the minds of an unsuspecting citizenry. "Concepts like 'brainwashing,'" psychologist Edgar Schein noted, "express graphically our loss of confidence in our capacity as individuals to master our world. When things go wrong, it is far less ego-deflating to say that we have been 'brainwashed' than to recognize our own inadequacy in coping with our problems."[20]

The fear of covert threats dominated the American cultural agenda of the 1950s. In addition to the familiar theme of struggles with powerful alien forces, the science fiction and horror movies of the period focused on invasive, invisible, and enslaving powers. Movies of sinister transformations, the takeover of the private by deceptively familiar yet hostile forces, were among the most popular cinematographic products of the period. "The dark secret behind human nature used to be the upsurge of the animal," the beast within, "as in King Kong (1933)," Susan Sontag has observed in her study of film and culture. By contrast, the movies of the 1950s reflected fears of a far more frightening quality: the unwilling transformation of human beings into machines, the seeping in of alien, dehumanizing powers into the psyche. In this genre, surfaces were preserved, but the soul was destroyed. The contrasts between normal and sinister, familiar and foreign, were hard to detect and, therefore, all the more frightening. In America of the 1950s, appearances were deceptive, and subversion seemed to be the norm. Under these circumstances, the undetected presence of an alien entity occupying the souls of deceivingly typical Americans appeared to be a clear and imminent danger.

The Manchurian Candidate (1962), one of the most powerful of Cold War movies, moved beyond generic fears of secretive, foreign invasion and addressed directly the issue of brainwashing in Korea.[21] In this movie, Raymond Shaw, the son of a prominent anticommunist political family and a highly decorated Korean war POW, is the victim of methodic brainwashing. Raymond's mother, an ostensible anticommunist married to a McCarthy-like senator, Raymond's stepfather, is in actual fact a communist operator. She controls her son's actions, who, following intensive brainwashing in a Korean POW camp, has been programmed to become a political assassin. Raymond's ultimate mission is to murder the (Republican?) Party candidate for president of the United States, once his opportunistic, hen-pecked, and unsuspecting stepfather has gained the candidacy for vice president. Aided by his former army mates, Raymond overcomes the brainwashing and eventually kills his mother and stepfather in a desperate attempt to foil their plot. He then commits suicide, thereby destroying the last American link in the communist conspiracy to overtake America.

The film's premise is that communism, by exploiting the frailties of modern American society, had infiltrated the nation's hearth. The enemy in this movie is deep within the American political system and its cultural fiber. "Reds were visibly alien in earlier Red scares; they were the others," historian Michael Rogin reminds us. In the cultural and political discourse of the 1950s and 1960s, they had "moved inside our minds and bodies . . . and one could not tell them from anyone else."[22] Much in line with cultural critics such as Betty Friedan and William Mayer, the movie is a political indictment of childhood nurturing practices. Corrupt parental figures are the instigators of the peril facing the American nation. In failing their children, due to ambition, a false political consciousness, or other reasons, American parents became partners, knowingly or unconsciously, in the brainwashing threat.[23]

The Behavioral Explanation

Brainwashing as an explanation for the Korean story was easy prey for its critics, most of whom were behavioralists. To begin with, the major advocates of the menticide explanation had never examined the returning prisoners. Their expositions were pure speculation. The menticiders never produced a widely acceptable definition of the term, and had no tangible proof of the overwhelming influence of Pavlovian conditioning in Soviet psychiatry. Critics argued that the entire brainwashing premise was flimsily balanced on speculative premises and blind fear.

The most prominent critics emerged from the ranks of the professional teams charged with the actual debriefing of returning POWs. The experts employed by army and airforce research institutes treated the claims of menticide with ill-concealed contempt. They chastised the psychiatric diagnosis of brainwashing for its lack of scientific rigor, in particular, the total absence of verifiable data. They ridiculed the implicit assumption among brainwashing advocates that it was inconceivable for even a single soldier to collaborate with the enemy without having been exposed to psychological demonology. They maintained that uninformed psychiatrists had persuaded a gullible public that "nothing less than a combination of the theories of Dr. I. P. Pavlov and the wiles of Dr. Fu Manchu could produce such results."[24]

The cultural critique of the POW received an equally hostile reaction within academic circles. In a prominent indictment published by the *Harvard Business Review*, a coterie of leading figures in the social and behavioral sciences argued that scientific evidence proved that American captives had upheld the highest of military standards behind barbed wire. Their actions were ultimate proof that the American character was flawless, and that communist methods of indoctrination had not and could not undermine Western society. The statement rebuked the critics of POW conduct for relying on distorted data in order "to make the case for one view of American society."[25]

These academic reactions were based on reports published by the Air Force Personnel and Training Research Center (PTRC) and by army-funded research centers: the Johns Hopkins-administered ORO, and a collaborative project between the Walter Reed Army Medical Institute and HumRRO associated with George Washington University. All of these major reports were later summarized and published in scholarly journals and monographs.

The ORO team, headed by Edgar Schein, at the time a social psychologist at the Walter Reed graduate school, dismissed the concept of menticide and argued that the methods of coercion employed by Chinese captors did not represent anything out of the ordinary. Schein, who would later chair MIT's School of Industrial Management, stated that the enemy had not employed unusual "Pavlovian" techniques to break the will of the prisoners. Chinese captors had used simple manipulative techniques and harsh physical coercion to induce collaboration; but there was no evidence of successful "brainwashing," a conscious conversion of beliefs rather than a temporary altering of behavior. In fact, the ORO study claimed that only a small proportion of American POWs had actually engaged in collaborative behavior.[26]

The HumRRO study dismissed the explanation of an ideologically vulnerable army. HumRRO team leader Julius Segal underlined his most important conclusion that "the dynamics of collaborative activity must be explained on grounds other than purely ideological ones." His report divided the prisoners into three categories: participators, approximately 15 percent; resisters, about 5 percent; and "middlemen," the remaining 80 percent. Segal and his associates dismissed even the theoretical possibility of significant personality or ideological change whether by brainwashing, physical coercion, or actual intellectual persuasion. The HumRRO investigations discovered no significant physical coercion or psychological manipulation of American POWs. This report claimed that collaborators usually endured fewer hardships, and had collaborated due to an opportunistic personality and other characterological flaws.[27]

The air force team followed suit in downplaying ideological conversion and collaboration within the prison camps. According to Albert Biderman, a Chicago-trained sociologist who had researched both enemy and American POWS, there was no meaningful correlation between a prisoner's political views and his willingness to collaborate. "Prisoners who accepted some of the indoctrination nonetheless responded selectively so that they accepted only material which caused no conflict with pre-existing beliefs and loyalties." Moreover, Biderman claimed that acceptance of communist dogma at the intellectual level did not necessarily elicit collaboration with the enemy.[28]

Having dismissed the link between collaboration and ideological persuasion, the three major reports on POW conduct sought statistical correlations between collaboration and what they considered to be the most meaningful parameters of the POW population: age, education level, occupation, combat experience, geographic origin, and length of internment. Cross-tabulations of such vital statistics served as the main tool for refuting the impressionistic findings of the menticide and cultural explanations of POW behavior. At one very crucial junction, however, these three major studies deviated from this scientific, statistically based formula and employed, instead, the much maligned "essay tradition" of writing. On the issue of race and ethnicity, the different reports wavered between silence and nebulous dismissal.

The Walter Reed study of collaboration and social stratification dispensed with race and ethnicity with a few vague remarks. Even though he was aware that American prisoners "were segregated by race, nationality [ethnicity-R.R.], and rank," Edgar Schein saw such divisions as self-defeating. The propaganda aimed at African Americans "was too extreme"; and as far as the segregation of soldiers of color was concerned, Schien claimed, without offering supporting statistical data, that the "Negroes felt that if they were going to be segregated, they might as well be segregated in the United States— . . . there was nothing new or better about communism in this respect." Even though he could muster no statistical evidence, Schein claimed that "the Chinese might have persuaded more Negroes to collaborate and to embrace communism had they not made the fundamental error of segregation." African Americans, he implied, were not a special social category, and were better understood as an integral and indistinguishable element of lower-class, undereducated America. Some African Americans may have collaborated because of their "low status category," but not because of race.[29]

The HumRRO report was no less adamant in its studious avoidance of race. This report, perhaps the most sophisticated of the three major studies, dedicated less than a sentence to minorities. Among the 78 percent of returning POWs who "named at least one type of prisoner on whom they believed the captor concentrated his indoctrination," 22 percent identified "members of minority groups" as specific targets for indoctrination; 47 percent named "younger PWs," the "more highly educated (22%), the less educated (21%), . . . those showing interest in Communism (11%), those of lower rank (10%), those from lower socioeconomic levels (6%), and emotionally weak prisoners (6%)."[30]

Curiously, the HumRRO report did include observations on the physical appearance of the POWs. Armed with tabulations and statistics, this report offered a lengthy analysis of "the interesting finding" that "the Resister Group was found to be unique in having a higher proportion of heavy men and a lower proportion of slender men than are found among the remaining PWs." The HumRRO researchers argued that there was a strong relationship "between physique (and its personality correlates) and behavior in a prison-of-war setting."[31] Neither Segal, Schein, nor anybody else found anything "interesting" in a no less conspicuous physical attribute of the prisoners: their skin color. The existence of an African American subculture, the effects of discrimination, and racial tensions within the camps and in American society in general were met with silence.

In lieu of statistical data all three major studies coped with race and ethnicity by means of generalizations. Albert Biderman's *March to Calumny* (1963), a meticulous summary of all military research of POW behavior, dedicated a single page to the issue of race. Within the context of this limited scope, Biderman reserved a dozen lines to support the questionable contention that the Chinese captors had been unable to stir racial and ethnic dissension among the prisoners. Although Biderman's monograph had tables and statistics for the most intimate aspects of the POW persona, he offered no statistical analysis of the ethnic composition of POWs in particular or American military personnel in Korea in general. Instead, he used uncharacteristically nebulous phrases. "A great percentage [of POWs] were Negroes; a very large number were Puerto Rican and Spanish-Americans."

In describing the predicament of minority soldiers Biderman and the other researchers discarded statistical analysis in favor of narrative. They related tales of Spanish speaking soldiers feigning a lack of knowledge of the English language. As for the behavior of African Americans, Biderman turned decidedly anecdotal:

> The attitude of the American Negro Soldier in Korea is perhaps well conveyed by a remark attributed to Joe Louis. Upon his induction into the Army in World War II, the champion was asked how he could fight for a country that so oppressed members of his race. He is said to have replied, "There may be a lot of things wrong with the U.S., but there ain't none of them Adolf Hitler can do any good for.[32]

The initial debriefing files of repatriated POWs suggested otherwise. Reports of ethnic strife and the existence of clandestine racist organizations appeared quite frequently in the accounts of returning POWs. An internal HumRRO summary of "Operation Little Switch," the preliminary exchange of sick and wounded prisoners that preceded the general POW armistice agreement, documented violent clashes between Spanish-speaking prisoners and gangs of "reactionary" white prisoners—reactionary being the term used for stubborn resisters. This same report mentioned the existence of racist gangs, known as "the KKK, KTC, and FHA (Faithful Hearts of America)," whose activities appeared to be linked to "preferences of treatment given to minority group Americans."[33] Such material disappeared from the scientific reports of Americans behind barbed wire in Korea.

In a letter to the author, Edgar Schein recalls "no 'big' reason" for ignoring the issue of race. "I think it would not have occurred to us at the time that blacks would be more or less vulnerable."[34] However, in his own writings, Schein has acknowledged that, at least, theoretically, race may have mattered. In his most comprehensive assessment of the POW experience Schein has stated that the prisoner "who was most vulnerable *ideologically* was one who had never enjoyed any kind of secure or rewarding status position either in his home community or in the Army." Among those "whose social reference groups made the attainment of status difficult" Schein singled out African Americans. "Because of the low-status category of most of the Negroes, the positive appeals made to them must have struck responsive chords in some."[35]

Why, then, was race ignored? One may dismiss factors such as low numbers of minorities among the POWs. Without ever mentioning exact figures, Biderman and others acknowledged "a great percentage" of African Americans among the POWs and "large numbers" of Puerto Ricans and other Hispanics.

Incomplete data may have affected a racial analysis. Schein observed that "the accounts of the repatriates were unclear regarding the reactions of members of the various minority groups, especially the Negroes." All the researchers understood that their data were faulty. Their reconstruction of the prison milieu was based on the subjective recollections of the returning prisoners, all of whom had vested interests to explain away their own questionable activities by disparaging others. Understating ethnicity and race may have been the result of good scientific caution.

Reluctance to deal with the uncomfortable racial and ethnic tensions among the prisoners was, perhaps politically prudent as well. Korea was the first war fought by a partially integrated army, and one may presume that these researchers had no desire to bite the hand of military benefactors who were already on the defensive for taking a forceful stand on a socially sensitive issue. While the exact number of African Americans and Hispanics among the prisoners is unclear, all studies acknowledged a substantial minority presence due to the increasing number of integrated frontline units.[36]

Understating the minority issue most probably occurred because a racial analysis did not fit the theoretical paradigms of the researchers and their mentors. In his correspondence to the author, Schein describes himself and his colleagues as products of the "Chicago School of Sociology," a school renowned for what one critic has called "cultural stripping or deracination."[37]

Chicago sociology in the 1950s denied the existence of a uniquely African American subculture, characterized by distant African cultural survivals. As far as the Chicago paradigm was concerned, the assignment of African cultural attributes was essentialist and scientifically false. Thus, as point of departure, the POW inquiries assumed that African Americans, as a distinct group, had no autonomous aspects. To the degree that Blacks exhibited deviant behavior, the source was in social backgrounds common to poor, undereducated Americans irrespective of race. It is within this context that one must understand Schein's statement that "it would not have occurred to us at the time that blacks would be more or less vulnerable."

In an additional, related illustration of the Chicago influence, Schein recalls the presence of eminent sociologist Erving Goffman, "who was also a consultant and probably influenced me most." Goffman urged the young Walter Reed researchers to accept his premise that "our strength resides in our relationships and the social order, not in personality" or any other essentialist attribute.[38] In other words, the main theoretical interest of the POW studies was to dispense of the notion of the internal moral gyroscope as the main motivating factor in opinion formation. The behavioral scientists of the POW experience were unconcerned with personality typologies, or the assignment of some sort of primordial nature to any one subculture. They were far more concerned with reconstructing the social milieu within the camps and its generic effects. Schein explained that "people"—be they Catholics or Jews, black, brown, or white—"tend to rely primarily on the opinion of others for determination of whether they themselves are 'right' or 'wrong'—whether these opinions of others are obtained through the mass media of communication or through personal interaction."

The POW studies did, however, move beyond social dynamics and were willing to examine essentialist issues such as personality when analyzing the "deviants": POWs who had either violently resisted the captors, or conversely, had collaborated openly and willingly with the enemy. Sensing no apparent contradiction, all three major reports labeled both resisters and collaborators as deviants, and therefore worthy of in-depth psychological, rather than social, analysis.

According to Edgar Schein, the similarities between resisters and collaborators were more meaningful than their differences. Having established that there were no significant "background factors" distinguishing either collaborators or resisters from other POWs, Schein and his associates offered the surprising observation that resisters and collaborators were basically indistinguishable personality types. They "always deviated from the neutrals in the same direction." The most meaningful division of prisoners, then, was not on the continuum of "*resistance-collaboration*, but *action-inaction*." Based on the assumption that "ideological change was *not* an important determinant of prison camp behavior" Schein claimed that he could predict whether a certain personality type would take an active role within the camp. However, whether that role would be that of a resister or that of a collaborator was, according to Schein, extremely difficult to predict. Both forms of behavior were the result of the same innate traits: "under-inhibition of impulses" as well as a pathological "disregard for authority." The decision to become a collaborator or resister was often arbitrary, and as far as Schien was concerned, of secondary importance; both forms of behavior were equally extreme, deviant, and, by implication, negative. "Those men who were not able to inhibit impulses when under stress may have been forced by their own acting-out tendencies into taking some action: either collaboration or resistance."[39]

Julius Segal's HumRRO report reached nearly identical conclusions. He too argued that "Resisters and Participators—the minority among POWs— were basically not different from one another, . . . both tended to meet the threat of internment by acting out the conflicts aroused in them." Segal defined both participators and resisters as " 'deviates' in a behavioral sense," claiming that they both "showed little or no regard for the welfare of their fellow prisoners." The two typologies were, from a behavioral point of view, identical because both courted defiance of authority. "Participators *acted* in ways which brought them into conflict with the 'laws' which govern our national security; Resisters *acted* in ways which brought them into conflict with the laws which governed the captor's program of exploitation." By contrast, the vast majority of prisoners, the middlemen who just tried to flow with the course of events, were not worthy of personality studies because their conduct was in accordance with contemporary behavioral theory. Segal explained that "withdrawal and 'anonymity,' the tendency to blend with the crowd, were more natural positions to take than was the case with either Participators or Resisters."[40]

In describing resisters as social misfits who pathologically defied all forms of authority, Segal and the other researchers ruled out patriotism or ideology as motivating factors for this group of ostensible heroes. Although the official army sociological reports begrudgingly admitted that "some" of the resisters were "well integrated," emotionally stable, intelligent persons, most resisters were described as "chronic obstructionists." They had supposedly "demonstrated a life-long pattern of indiscriminate resistance to all forms of authority and had histories of inability to get along in the United Nations Army just as they were unable to get along with the Chinese." Those resisters whose records would not support such harsh statements were described equally disparagingly as "idealists or martyrs of religious and ethical principles." Finally, a third group of resisters appeared in these reports as "anxious, guilt-ridden individuals who could only cope with their strong impulses to collaborate by denying them and over-reacting in other directions."[41] This exercise in tautology implied that resisters were the ultimate villains and the bearers of the most un-American of qualities: the affliction of zealous and at times illogical adherence to principles.

Such explicit value judgments, embedded within an otherwise detached scientific format, suggests that this cohort of behavioralists was not concerned with a mere technical debate. Harsh assessments of resisters reflected what seemed to be a broad, negative approach to firm ideological convictions, of any form or shape. Not only did these persons dismiss the role of will power, strict training, or ingrained patriotism as insurance against collaboration with the enemy. They also made the claim that contempt for all forms of ideology—democratic or totalitarian—was the best possible mechanism for thwarting the relentless ideological campaigns of the enemy.

Biderman's air force report argued that American POWs would have been significantly more vulnerable to enemy indoctrination campaigns "had they had a highly rationalized ideology, as for example did the Nazi troops who as POWs were relatively easy marks for both Western and Soviet political indoctrinators."[42] As far as the Korean chapter was concerned, Biderman praised the "anti-ideology" of the American POW. American captives were not only "apolitical," they were "anti-political." Indoctrination in the camps had failed because prisoners considered it " 'crap' not only because it was Communist, but because it was political." Prisoners regarded all politics and ideology as "a lot of unimportant nonsense," thereby condemning all Chinese indoctrination campaigns to failure. Biderman acknowledged that, at times, prisoners would mouth enemy propaganda because the recitation of politically correct statements was linked "to the satisfaction of most everyday needs and, sometimes, to survival itself." In stark contrast to the brainwashing explanation, he claimed that such perfunctory acceptance of the enemy's demands was not a sign of ideological transformation. Propaganda was "merely 'crap' you had to put up with, for most."[43]

Biderman offered examples of air force prisoners who had actually accepted the ideological principles of communism while stubbornly refusing to engage in collaborative behavior. For example, the pilot, who on most counts was rated as the air force returnee most affected by communist ideological indoctrination, resisted giving a false confession. "Another officer, at a time when he was reacting quite sympathetically to Communist dogma, effected a difficult escape." The explanation offered for such dissonant behavior was "that men who take ideological matters seriously" behaved "in accordance with a patriotic commitment," even when such behavior conflicted with intellectual underpinnings.[44] By arguing that "there can be 'acceptance' of doctrine on the intellectual level without a corresponding emotional identification with that doctrine or any tendency to act in accordance with it," Biderman and his associates turned all previous explanations on their heads. Collaboration now became a sign of inner strength and conviction; public compliance signified private rejection.

These speculative profiles of collaboration and resistance suggest that, despite the mobilization of scientific apparatus and empirical data, the behavioral explanations were no less controversial and politically informed than the alternative narratives of the POW controversy. The glorification of middlemen and, conversely, the equally derogatory assessments of both collaborators and resisters were cultural and not scientific issues.

The Cultural Wars

The cultural meaning of the POW inquiries becomes clear when they are approached as an illustration of the overarching contemporary debate on culture and politics. Behavioral scientists in mid-century America were partisans in a riveting debate on the ostensible clash between ideology and science in modern democracies. It was within the context of episodes such as the Korean POW controversy that behavioral scientists staked their claim for a rational, scientific, public culture as an antidote to a frightening world torn apart by the authority of blood, tradition, and myth. Historian David Hollinger explains that in contrast to the traditional keepers of culture who sanctified timeless "values," social and behavioral scientists pleaded the code of science and rationalism: a society based on verifiable norms and critical "evidence-based, universalistic, antiauthoritarian, and hence 'scientific' conduct."[45]

Hollinger's analysis of academia at mid-century draws attention to the ethnic background of these behavioral scientists. Schein, Segal, Biderman, and most of their associates were Jews. As a cultural group, Jewish academics figured prominently among advocates of secularism within an academic world split between keepers of culture and partisans of science.[46] Excluded throughout most of the century from intellectual enterprises associated with the defining of culture and tradition, Jews were prominent in the production of alternative and more inclusive definitions of the American body politic. In the budding behavioral sciences—where neither tradition nor prejudice had barred them from rapid assent—Jews were numerically prominent, and therefore conspicuous in the promoting of science-as-democracy.[47]

Behavioral scientists in general, Jews and Gentiles, touted "science" as the ultimate symbol of liberal, democratic values while, conversely, rejecting the authority of tradition. Attributing the nation's well-being to such diffuse issues as religious convictions and tradition was anathema to them. They rejected the notion of an enduring cultural essence permeating the American body— a belief that had, according to Hollinger, "barred Jews and other non-Christians from full participation" in American intellectual life.[48] Their faith in rational values validated by scientific inquiry challenged American particularism and the cultural authority of a mostly Protestant cultural heritage. These intellectuals identified the mesmerizing forces of "faith" as the antithesis of a healthy democratic society. Solidarity based on murky ideology or romantic morals was, as far as they were concerned, a poor basis for a thriving and enlightened democratic society. "Cognitive demystification" and "secular inquiry" were of far more importance than devotion to ideology or tradition. Hence, it is not surprising that, within the context of the Korean debate, these predominantly Jewish intellectuals expressed animosity toward the POW patriot—the bearer of a supposedly unthinking adherence to traditional values— while simultaneously praising the skeptical middleman.

A cursory glance at academia in the 1950s and 1960s reveals that leading Jewish academics, writing on subject matters far removed from Korea, were making strikingly similar statements. Perhaps the most prominent common issue was the lavish praise reserved for the anti-ideological, political middleman, and, conversely, the indictment of strong ideological stances. In their pathbreaking study of American political folkways, Paul Lazarsfeld and Bernard Berelson praised the virtues of "political apathy" in democratic societies, by which they meant the indifference of American voters to ideologically based arguments. In their study of the American election campaign of 1948 these two leading members of the professions praised "the apathetic segment of American society" that had "helped to hold the system together and cushioned the shock of disagreement, adjustment and changes."[49]

Suspicion of ideology as a motivating factor in the American context led historian Richard Hofstadter to lump together nineteenth-century populists and McCarthyites of the 1950s as persons motivated by status-anxiety and an assortment of other psychological afflictions. Other academic experts joined Hofstadter in dismissing the ideological dimension of McCarthyism, ostensibly the quintessential example of the dysfunctional nature of true believers. Sociologist Seymour Martin Lipset argued that the status insecurities of ethnic and religious groups—mostly second-generation Catholics—was the major motivating force behind McCarthy supporters.[50] Social historian Will Herberg agreed that McCarthy operated with no ideological framework. "He stands for no cause, no program. He rallies his support by exploiting . . . fears, anxieties, and frustrations." McCarthy's popular brand of anticommunism, according to Herberg, was not derived from an ideological counterconviction. It was, instead, "the surrogate of inner threatening forces on the unconscious level."[51]

These iconoclastic studies, with their skeptical attitudes toward the power of ideas, clashed with the pervasive intellectual celebration of tradition and "values" as ballast against the upheavals of modernity. At issue was the crucial debate over the rise of totalitarianism and the creation of mechanisms for the defense of democracy and the Western way of life. Both sides were preoccupied with the issue of the origins of tyranny: Was it a reaction to "corrosive, skeptical relativism, or militant reaffirmation of traditional absolutes?"[52]

Prominent humanists laid the blame for the mid-century crisis squarely at the door of liberalism and scientism. The enemy of Western civilization, according to conservative commentator Bernard Iddings Bell, was America's secular, antitraditionalist intelligentsia who gaped admiringly at science, scoffed at religion and tradition, and claimed that "mere freedom from standards and restraints" would lay the foundations for a stable democratic society.[53]

Such criticism was not the exclusive domain of conservatives. Harvard University's Howard Mumford Jones, very much a liberal, had similar misgivings. In a sharp defense of tradition in American society, Jones lashed out at the reductive, allegedly anti-intellectual premises of the behavioral and social sciences:

> The clear light of eighteenth century right reason fades into the murk of libido, the inferiority complex, penis envy, incest, sadism, masochism. . . . Personality traits are made the subject of statistical inquiry, as if people had gone to the wrong clothing stores and had to begin sorting out ill-sorted garments. Such phrases as a "disturbed person," the well-adjusted (or badly adjusted) person," the "neurotic personality of our time," a pleasant personality" are the terms in which we now categorize the political heirs of Jefferson and Franklin.[54]

Jones's tongue-lashing suggests that the rift between spiritual values and scientific inquiry resonated beyond the conventional division between conservatives and liberals. It was a sign of two irreconcilable sources of cultural authority. As far as the Korean POW episode was concerned, the assignment of personality flaws to the resisters and the praising of skeptical middlemen was part of a much larger secular construction of American society. By contrast, the discovery of mass collaboration, whether real or a figment of the debate, was a parable for the upholding of tradition and a diatribe against the influence of science and secularism.

The Korean POW episode was, then, embedded in a master-controversy. When placed within this broad context of a significant rift within the American intellectual community, the sharp division of opinion over the meaning of the POW experience, the mixture of fact and speculation, and the simultaneous marshaling of "science" and "values" as respective strategies for understanding the POW predicament begin to make sense.

The POW polemic, like most political controversies, faded away into a compromise that was meant to satisfy all sides in the debate. In 1955, the Secretary of Defense's Advisory Committee on Prisoners of War issued a report that incorporated the conflicting recommendations and findings of all parties. On the one hand, the report declared that the record of American POWs in Korea was honorable, and that these unfortunate men had been tried unjustly by a sensationalist press. In the same breath, the committee issued new, stringent guidelines for POW conduct that implied acceptance of accusations regarding negligible resistance and possible collaboration:

> If I am captured I will continue to resist by all means available. I will make every effort to escape and aid others in escape. I will accept neither parole nor special favors from the enemy. . . . If I become a prisoner of war, I will keep faith with my fellow prisoners. I will give no information or take part in any action, which might be harmful to my comrades.[55]

"Why did some men break, and some refuse to bend?" Given the manifest aim to please as many parties as possible, the report offered multiple answers. Brainwashing, physical coercion, and lack of civic training in the schools all received prominent exposition. The incorporation of the central assumptions of the POW behavioralist investigations was, however, guarded and quite selective. The report rejected the notions of political apathy, or anti-ideology as an inherent strength. The heroes of the government report were resisters who were motivated by strong patriotic sentiments. In the same breath, the report acknowledged that such outbursts of patriotism were rare. The key to resistance was social dynamics. From the broad range of possible strategies for increasing solidarity among soldiers, the report chose to praise the proverbial "buddy system." Prisoner solidarity and resistance "was particularly pronounced where they had belonged to the same unit for years. They stood by one another like that 'band of brothers' inspired by Nelson. . . . They exhibited true fraternal spirit. . . . These soldiers did not let each other down. Nor could the Korean Reds win much cooperation from them."[56]

As a political text the committee report was predictably silent on the socially unbalanced results of selective service in the Korean War. One of the most significant consequences of the Korean POW experience, its indication of the narrow social stratification of America's fighting forces, and the racial and ethnic tensions that no disciplinary action could erase, played no part in this report or any other government assessment of troop performance in Korea. As this document suggests, America turned its back on this final episode of the Korean conflict and marched toward Vietnam with little acknowledgment of the inherent social problems plaguing its armed forces.

PART THREE
CRISIS

9.

Vietnam

From "Hearts and Minds" to

"Rational Choice"

The Counterinsurgency Symposium

In the summer of 1962, the American University in Washington D.C., hosted a conference on "The U.S. Army's Limited War Mission and Social Science Research." The event was sponsored by the Chief of Research and Development in the Department of the Army, and organized by the SORO, a military-academic think tank funded by the army and nominally administered by the American University. Over a hundred prominent academic advisors as well as a battery of army officials and officers, ranging from the secretary of the army to the commandant of West Point, participated in this three-day conference.

The focus of the symposium was the army's counterinsurgency doctrine and its implementation in Vietnam. Counterinsurgency, according to official definitions, was "the entire scope of actions (military, police, political, economic, psychological, etc.) taken by or in conjunction with the existing government of a nation to counteract, contain, or defeat an insurgency."[1] By the time of the 1962 conference most attention focused on the nonmilitary aspects of the doctrine. Given the disappointing results of superior American fire-power on Asian battlefields, the revised national strategy for fighting and win-ning the localized armed struggles of the Cold War assumed that victory hinged upon the allegiance and support of the local population.

Conference organizers explained that, in contrast to previous wars, where "the primary source of enemy strength—e.g., military personnel and equip-ment, major war industries—could be destroyed physically," the war in Viet-nam featured an enemy that derived its strength from nonmilitary sources, in particular, "the people within the nation." Fighting insurgents, therefore, was not a conventional military task of territorial gains or the physical annihilation of the enemy; its requirements were "primarily *nonmaterial* in nature—politi-cal, social, economic, and psychological." Constructive and effective counter-insurgency entailed winning back the people, and halting the erosion of mass support for established institutions. The conflict, therefore, was first and fore-most a political, social, and economic problem.[2]

Lest there be any doubt concerning the administration's endorsement of constructive counterinsurgency, Secretary of the Army Elvis Stahr com-menced his keynote address at the SORO conference by explaining that, as far as the Vietnam War was concerned, the army could not rely on its "mailed fist." Quoting "Che Guevara's observation" that "all the facilities which make life easier are unfavorable for the guerrilla force," Stahr proposed that con-structive measures, rather than destruction, were the primary tools for "striking at the very roots of insurgency and guerilla activity." Hence, he declared, "a major focus of our army's cold war effort" in Asia and elsewhere was not the provision of military force, but the actual participation in civic improvement programs, ranging from the establishment of health clinics to the building of bridges and highways.[3]

Constructive counterinsurgency, was predictably endorsed by other high ranking administration officials. Roger Hilsman, the director of intelligence and research at the State Department and one of the principal architects of constructive counterinsurgency, stated that "in situations such as the South Vietnamese predicament, purely military sweeps against guerrillas will not work." Hilsman reminded his audience that "the military commander is faced with the fact that the more he sweeps out guerrillas at one point, the more they flow in at another." As such, he urged the continuation and expansion of civic action, lest "the struggle be lost."[4]

General Clyde Eddleman, vice chief of staff, United States Army, offered the military establishment's guarded acquiescence. Eddleman maintained that the main task of the army remained the "arrest of Communist expansion" by means of military power. However, given the nature of Cold War regional conflicts, he conceded that such a mission was impossible without vigorous, military-directed fostering of economic growth and other nonmilitary programs. "Our residual feeling that peace is peace and war is war" was no longer operable in the fuzzy multidimensional arena of counterinsurgency. The army had to adjust to an ostensibly civilian, peacetime task of "nation building and civic action" in addition to its traditional military mission.[5] It was for these purposes that the defense establishment had called upon "the types of scientists—anthropologists, psychologists, sociologists, political scientists, economists—whose professional orientation" would help produce a successful strategy for winning the hearts and minds of the indigenous population in Indo-China.[6]

The SORO conference's mixture of military and academic participants produced two distinctly different paper formats. Military participants demonstrated a candid uneasiness with the very concept of constructive counterinsurgency. Their papers were markedly awkward. Brigadier General Richard Stilwell, the commandant of the U.S. military academy at West Point, explained that military apprehension was caused by unexpected changes in the role of modern soldierhood, as well as novel definitions of victory in the age of Cold War. The transition from traditional battle skills to the struggle for the hearts and minds of foreign civilians was a difficult task for an army trained in the use of brutal and efficient force. "It has not been easy . . . to reorient thinking throughout the Army structure as to what we are doing anyhow in environments which are noncombat, nonoperational, in the traditional sense." Somewhat apologetically, Stilwell explained that "we do much better with the hard, concrete issue; we do much better in war."[7]

The awkward tone of military papers at the symposium reflected institutional and doctrinarial uncertainty. American military doctrine, historian Larry Cable has noted, was decidedly Clausewitzian; the ultimate aim of its doctrine was the physical annihilation of the enemy. "Whether dealing with grand strategy or minor tactics, considering the army as a whole or its smallest tactical element, the guiding principle was the destruction of the enemy's military power."[8] Under these circumstances, the introduction of constructive dimensions into army doctrine was a source of confusion. Army participants at the SORO conference did, indeed, acknowledge the importance of psychological warfare and civic actions in the pursuit of antiguerrilla warfare. However, their approach to such matters was circumspect. Throughout the course of the conference they repeatedly expressed an uneasiness with the nonmilitary dimensions of counterinsurgency.

The unsettling nature of the Vietnam conflict compounded the aura of uncertainty among the military participants at the Limited War symposium. Unexpected failures, both tactical and strategic, had cast a cloud over the army's comprehension of the Vietnam War. The military participants at the symposium stumbled and stuttered over definitions of the conflict. Was Vietnam a "war by proxy," Korean-style, or was it a "subversive insurgency" war, or perhaps some lethal combination of both? Despite the seemingly confident assertions that all Vietnam-type conflicts were succored, supported, and inspired by outside forces, the level of ambiguity in this armed struggle was confusing. Incoherence affected, by default, attempts to agree upon a doctrine of counterinsurgency. Lacking a clear understanding of insurgency, the military contributors implied, there was little chance of producing counterstrategies.

In contrast to the military participants, most of the civilian participants produced a significantly crisper comprehension of the Vietnamese struggle and the challenge of insurgency. They dismissed the search for a conventional military strategy for Vietnam as irrelevant and counterproductive. They were near-unanimous in their definition of the war as a sociopsychological task, not to be measured in simple military terms. The weapons of choice, they argued, were civic improvement and effective communications rather than military force.

The point of departure for the civilian advisors was Roger Hilsman's assertion that "it is nonsense to think that regular forces trained for conventional war can handle jungle guerrillas." Hilsman and his colleagues argued that "there is no question that economic development, modernization, and reform are key factors" in defeating insurgency.[9] The civilian advisors sought to convince their military clients that they would have to adopt certain constructive tasks in addition to, and, occasionally, instead of, traditional military activities. The key to a successful execution of the war was the mood of the Vietnamese peasantry. If, by means of propaganda, social works programs, and economic enticements, the peasants would develop a positive attitude toward the legitimate government, they would not be vulnerable to the propaganda of insurgents.

The academic participants argued that the main mechanism for accomplishing this mission was through a reorientation of the traditional role of the military. In addition to combat, these experts urged the employment of the armed forces in civic improvement programs, ranging from health care to the construction of dams and bridges in remote areas. Armies on the modern battlefields of limited warfare would have to adjust to the employment of "nonmaterial" weaponry, "which is not tangible or hardware." Klaus Knorr, the director of the Center of International Studies at Princeton University, explained that "civic action is not just a useful way to hedge one's bets in an internal war situation, not just a useful supplementary technique to counterrevolutionary warfare, but the key to the whole problem."[10] William Lybrand, the conference coordinator and senior SORO staff member, concluded that, given the forms of military challenges faced by the United States in Asia and Latin America, physical coercion was no longer the principal technique for influencing the enemy. All standard definitions of "the counterinsurgency mission, by civilian and military leaders alike, is accompanied by the axiomatic assertion that success . . . is as much dependent on political, social, economic, and psychological factors as upon military factors, and sometimes more so." Victory entailed command and control of the "behavior of people, their interrelationships, their cultural norms, their attitudes and values."[11]

A conspicuous civilian dissenter at the SORO conference was Guy Pauker, professor of political science at the University of California and head of the Asian section at Rand Corporation's social science division. As the representative of a think tank funded by the air force rather than the army, Pauker exhibited little sympathy with the conference's formula for winning the hearts and minds of indigenous populations. He implied that, contrary to conventional wisdom, a series of new Rand research projects questioned the efficacy of psychological, social, and civic action as effective weapons for winning the insurgent brushfires of the Cold War. Pauker claimed that Rand researchers had arrived at these conclusions following painstaking research and the application of objective, scientific criteria. In a jab at advocates of constructive counterinsurgency, Pauker claimed that when studying a "scientific issue," such as the optimal strategy for counterinsurgency, "I leave my political philosophy at home. Outside the United States I am neither for nor against land reform, rapid industrialization, higher education . . . and so forth." War was war, not a popularity contest. As such, the concept of constructive engagement was, perhaps, a soothing solution for the troubled souls of certain military intellectuals. However, from a military standpoint, it was quite futile.[12]

Caught somewhat off guard by these aberrant remarks, subsequent discussants navigated a wide berth around Pauker's presentation, preferring to stick to the common, positive theme offered by conference organizers. For the moment, at least, Pauker's challenge remained unheeded. However, Pauker was not playing devil's advocate. His presentation at the SORO conference was derived from new conceptual frameworks formulated at Rand. The focus on primary groups and psychocultural formats that had characterized much of the work of the behavioral scientists in the United States had reached an impasse at major think tanks. Alternative conceptual tools, derived primarily from economics, would soon replace much of the social and psychological bias of the behavioral sciences in general and its military implementation in particular.

The Rand Alternative: Rational Choice

Beginning in the early 1960s and on, Rand researchers turned a skeptical eye toward constructive measures on the modern, Cold War battlefield. Hans Speier, the director of Rand's social science division and one of the primary revisionists, declared that the insurrections of the post-World War II period revealed that "deterrence of subversion by economic aid is more precarious than is deterrence of subversion by military means." In his treatise on "Revolutionary War" Speier contended that "the political effects of economic aid are as problematic as is the relation between economic misery and political insurgency." Quoting conservative sociologist Edward Banfield, Speier described the theoretical link between economic aid and political stability as consisting "mainly of unverified and unverifiable assertions"; there was "at least as much to be said against it as in favor of it."[13]

Skepticism at Rand was expressed in its most elaborate form in a major study of the National Liberation Front, entitled "The Vietcong Motivation and Morale Project" (M&M). Based on over 2,000 interviews of National Liberation Front (NLF) prisoners, defectors, and refugees, the project produced over thirty different Rand publications documenting the Vietcong's military strengths and weaknesses, as well as enemy strategies for winning over the country's peasant population.[14]

The results of the M&M studies were erratic at best, and reflected two divergent views within Rand. Under the auspices of the project's first director, University of Pittsburgh political scientist Joseph Zasloff, the M&M survey offered a picture of a practically invincible enemy who had captured the hearts and minds of the peasants. Beginning in the spring of 1965, with the appointment of Leon Goure as the project director, M&M studies were aimed primarily at "proving" that the source of enemy strength among peasants was coercion rather than persuasion. Goure claimed, as well, that superior American firepower could defeat the enemy and counter, by force, the Vietcong's organizational advantages. Despite such substantive differences, both approaches agreed that constructive counterinsurgency was a misguided strategy, unlikely to accomplish anything beyond the squandering of funds. Both strains of the M&M studies urged the adaptation of different approaches derived from new conceptual frameworks.

During the course of the Zasloff tenure at M&M, the Rand reports documented the Vietcong's skillful recruitment of peasants as soldiers and collaborators. The enemy's strategy for winning hearts and minds combined an acceptance of local customs, the distribution of material rewards, and the attractive packaging of nationalistic goals. All reports stressed that the key to the Vietcong's hold on the peasant population was not terror or coercion; the enemy appeared to resort to coercive measures only in well-defined marginal cases.[15]

In the most comprehensive of the early M&M studies, senior Rand consultant Nathan Leites declared that the Vietcong had easily won the psychological war for hearts and minds. Leites's admiring account of Vietcong culture and politics was, in essence, an indictment of the South Vietnamese political system. He did not attribute the raging Vietnamese conflict to outside intervention. He rejected, as well, the typical argument of economic deprivation or class tensions as the main cause of the war, arguing that "it would be hard to explain the outbreak of rebellion in Vietnam, rather than in other parts of Southeast Asia, simply on the premise that poverty and inequality are the main cause of every revolt." Other countries in the region were just as poor, if not poorer, and offered even greater class discrepancies. The key to understanding the source of rebellion in Vietnam was cultural. The South Vietnamese government, he argued, had not lived up to Confucian expectations and tradition and, as such, had lost all remnants of popular support.[16]

The Leites study was a litany of "unworthy" behavior of South Vietnamese officials, ranging from capricious cruelty to burdensome taxation. By contrast, he described the Vietcong as catering to the moral and emotional needs of the peasant population, rather than furthering a revolutionary restructuring of peasant society. The Vietcong offered dignity and respect of tradition while scrupulously avoiding or camouflaging the superimposing of a communist master plan on the gentle gradated class structure of the Vietnamese village. The Vietcong garnered support by demonstrating "clean, honest and frugal living" that contrasted sharply with the "debauchery" and "unbridled indulgence" of America's South Vietnamese allies. The accounts of "both loyal and disaffected VC followers suggest that GVN personnel often indulge in seemingly senseless brutality and appear to take pleasure in trampling crops and gratifying personal resentments."[17]

Other studies during the first stage of the M&M project offered similar observations. John Donnell's analysis of Vietcong recruitment policy concluded that an attractive social doctrine, rather than coercion, was responsible for enticing young peasants to join its ranks. Based on interviews with prisoners and defectors, Donnell attributed Vietcong attractiveness to its development of a "language of discontent" and the manner in which they "trained" the peasant to think within this linguistic format. "VC agents dramatize (and often exaggerate) the peasant's hardships, his difficulties with the local authorities, and the alleged futility of obtaining justice. . . . And once discontent has been kindled, the Vietcong itself becomes the organizational vehicle for aggravating and spreading it, tying it to the native blend of Communist theory and nationalist ideals, and then channeling the resultant hostility into insurgent activity."[18]

In summarizing the first phase of the M&M project, a senior Rand official explained that, given the skillful tactics of the Vietcong as well as the unbridgeable gap between peasant and government, good deeds and artful propaganda would have little positive effect on the psyche of peasants. "No amount of skill, organization, indoctrination, coercion, or psychology would have enabled [Vietcong] leaders to design and make work such a variety of well-fitting forces to play upon the young and not-so-young to join, if the situation had not been so propitious. . . . The power of the VC to organize itself is, ultimately, inherent in the situation—with all that implies for the GVN and the United States."[19]

Such candid assessments of Vietcong advantages did not amount to any meaningful questioning of an American presence in Indo-China. Rather than suggesting the folly of the war, these Rand studies questioned the recourse to the policy of constructive counterinsurgency. The distant Vietnamese government, far removed from the folkways of ordinary people, was no match for the enemy's well-organized and highly motivated campaign for the loyalty of the peasants. These studies advocated, in effect, the revision, if not actual jettisoning, of constructive counterinsurgency.

The full-blown rejection of constructive counterinsurgency occurred during the tenure of Zasloff's successor, Leon Goure.[20] In his capacity as director of the M&M project, Goure discontinued the churning out of studies on enemy insight and GVN iniquities. Instead, the second phase of M&M publications identified enemy vulnerabilities, the result of alleged Vietcong fanaticism and disregard for rural customs. Contrary to previous lavish praise of Vietcong respect of local traditions, the new studies claimed that enemy control of peasants was based on "social disruption" — the isolation "of the peasant from his neighbors, friends, and even his family" — and ruthless domination by coercion and occasional terrorism.[21] These reports faulted American constructive counterinsurgency for repeating the mistakes of Vietcong rivals rather than offering alternatives. The well-intentioned, yet misguided transplanting of peasants from their native soil to strategic hamlets and the reliance on socially distant government officials rather than the traditional village social structure was, according to M&M studies, no less alienating than the Vietcong's heavy-handed control of every aspect of village life.

Given the manifest failures of materialistic, economic programs, M&M researchers proposed alternative strategies. R. Michael Pearce's research of the "insurgent environment" advocated the resurrection of tradition rather than indiscriminate economic aid as the most expedient strategy for regaining support in the countryside. "The Vietnamese peasant," Pearce explained, "can be summarized in three words: family, subsistence, and subservience."[22] Respect for the authority of the family, and abstinence from a socially disruptive attempt to modernize a primitive, yet functional agricultural economy, would, he argued, regain support for the government in the countryside.

As for M&M director, Leon Goure, he identified fear rather than economics, ideology, or tradition as the major force for gaining advantages on Vietnamese battlefields. In his study of enemy defectors Goure announced that his informants had been motivated by survival instincts rather than pecuniary gain, political persuasion, or anything else. Most defectors had crossed the lines when confronted by annihilating firepower. By the same token, the major barrier to increasing rates of defection was fear as well. Goure's informants reported fear of reprisal following captivity. Accordingly, Goure's recommendation was to compound fear of annihilation by means of increasing firepower, while allaying fears of maltreatment in captivity by means of propaganda.[23]

Other Rand studies rejected economic aid projects as the most expedient route to the heart of the Vietnamese peasant. Rand economist Edward Mitchell went so far as to suggest that a successful program of good deeds was not only ineffective; it was counterproductive. Mitchell claimed that "the more prosperous the peasants, the more discontented" they were. Inequality and poverty did not produce support for insurgency. In fact, he argued, economic improvement in the Vietnamese countryside increased rather than decreased the likelihood of insurgency.[24]

Mitchell concluded that the Vietcong did not derive its strength from areas of high tenancy and poverty. Based on a somewhat questionable statistical analysis of the distribution of government-controlled hamlets, he argued that provinces characterized by poverty and unequal land distribution were "precisely the areas of greatest security." Mitchell explained his findings as the result of the "docility and low aspirations of poor peasants," the power of landlords in "feudal" provinces, and the "ingrained habit of obeying superiors" in areas that had yet to be exposed to the forces of change. While shying away from explicit recommendations, Mitchell emphasized in bold type that "**greater inequality means greater control.**" Constructive counterinsurgency, he suggested, made no sense. By upsetting customary arrangements, the United States was literally digging its own grave.

> In this and other historical precedents, the behavioral precedent is similar. There exists in the areas of unequal distribution a powerful landlord class exercising firm control over a conservative peasantry, which has thoroughly rationalized the inevitability of the existing situation. It is not these peasants who revolt, but those who "have gained enough to give them an appetite for more."[25]

The Rand Corporation's most notorious alternative to the strategy of good deeds was the work of economist Charles Wolf Jr. and Nathan Leites, the ubiquitous Rand Kremlinologist. In reports and articles spanning the period from 1966 to 1970, Wolf and Leites proposed a substitute for constructive counterinsurgency doctrine and its allegedly dismal results.[26] In accordance with the paradigm shift among Rand researchers, these two senior consultants found no connection between socioeconomic improvements and active resistance to insurgency. They acknowledged that improving the lot of the peasants could, theoretically, increase sympathy for the government. However, such support did not necessarily entail decreased material support for the enemy. In fact, they insisted that economic improvement increased the likelihood of insurgent successes.

As opposed to those who believed that a successful conduct of the war entailed political or social accomplishments rather than conventional military gains, the Vietcong in the Leites-Wolf model rejected the "myth" of hearts and minds. Vietnamese insurgents, they claimed, approached their mission as a straightforward military campaign. Its successful execution did not hinge upon the whims of the civilian population, but upon the aggressive acquisition of "supplies (food, recruits, small arms, information) at a reasonable cost, interpreting cost to include expenditure of coercion as well as money." The attainment of reasonable cost, they argued, had little to do with the rebels' popularity. In fact, they claimed that the rebels' most cost-effective procurement of such supplies occurred in affluent regions, where support for the government was high. As rational persons seeking safety in a volatile climate, the peasant-beneficiaries of constructive counterinsurgency tended to invest in their security by supporting the government as well as subsidizing insurgents. "Even if the villager's preference for the government is increased, the fact that he commands additional resources as a result of economic improvement will enable him to use more of these resources to buy his security or protection from the insurgent forces." The notion that "economic aid projects in Vietnam actually aid the Vietcong is as inevitable as it is unfortunate."[27] Constructive counterinsurgency was, therefore, an exercise in self-inflicted damage.

Having rejected constructive counterinsurgency, Wolf and Leites argued that effective control of the populace entailed "influencing behavior rather than attitudes" and applying coercion rather than persuasion. The peasants' actual conduct, in particular, the denial of material support for insurgents, was the only issue at stake. Such behavior was easily obtained by threats backed up by ruthless action against enemy collaborators. The war was not a popularity contest. Whether peasants sympathized with the central government or with insurgents was superfluous. Their behavior, not their sentiments, was the only factor of any military significance.

In this major challenge to contemporary counterinsurgency doctrine, Charles Wolf and Nathan Leites explained that variations of economic behavior, rather than psychological theory, were the key to victory. These senior Rand consultants argued that good deeds and skillful propaganda might produce favorable attitudes but would not induce significant changes in behavioral patterns. The "cost-effective" solution offered by the Wolf-Leites team was to raise the "price" of supporting insurgents rather than focus merely on economic aid and improvements. Peasants would cease and desist their support for insurgents if the price of such support—punitive measures by government forces—was sufficiently harsh and deterrent.

Relying on the patois of economics, Leites and Wolf argued that the incentive for collaboration with the enemy lay in the peasants' "damage limiting" and "profit maximizing" decisions. All men were first and foremost rationally motivated creatures. An individual's political decisions invariably resulted from predictable, cost-benefit calculations. Under these circumstances, they argued that the United States should raise the cost of supporting insurgency to intolerable levels, thereby assuring themselves of the peasants' loyal behavior. Coercive measures, rather than socioeconomic improvements, would diminish peasant support for insurgents. The two Rand consultants argued that the Vietnam War was fundamentally a "contest between R [insurgents—R.R.] and A [counterinsurgents—R.R.] . . . in the efficient management of coercion."[28] They explained that "if insurgent success derives from their use of coercion to gain the compliance of the populace, . . . counterinsurgents must utilize these tactics more efficiently."[29] The morality of such deeds, they implied, was not theirs to ponder; they were merely the technicians, suppliers of solutions.

Leites and Wolff could claim no empirical evidence to back their alternative strategy of coercive counterinsurgency. The correlation of affluence with support for insurgency was speculative at best, and their depiction of the Vietnamese peasant as a textbook rational-choicer was, by their own admission, a theoretical construct. Instead of empirical evidence, they drew support from the musings and theoretical innovation of colleagues at Rand and elsewhere. The Wolf–Leites model relied, presumably, on the findings of the M&M studies. Taking as point of departure the impotence of constructive measures, the second phase of the M&M project had focused mainly on force and fear. According to historian David Landau, M&M director Goure "held an unshakable belief that 'enemy' morale would deteriorate with increasing applications of force."[30] Goure and his colleagues consistently correlated increasing firepower with disintegration of the enemy's political resistance. Once faced with the alternative of certain and sudden death, the enemy would, according to this doctrine, seek evasive action, ranging from defection to capitulation.

An important source of inspiration for Wolf and Leites was the innovations in game theory offered by their illustrious Rand colleague, Thomas Schelling. In his magnum opus, *Arms and Influence* (1966), Schelling offered a deterrence theory based on the same logic of the coercive counterinsurgency model. Schelling explained that efficient warfare was a violent version of bargaining strategies in the marketplace. War "is always a bargaining process," in which "the bargaining power" comes from the "capacity to hurt" and inflict "sheer pain and damage." The power to hurt, he explained, was a value unto itself. The infliction of suffering "gains nothing and saves nothing directly; it can only make people behave to avoid it. Schelling argued that the potential to hurt . . . measured in the suffering it can cause and the victims' motivation to avoid it" was the United States's most important weapon in the arena of limited warfare. "Modern technology had drastically enhanced the United States's ability to employ "pure, unconstructive, unaquisitive pain and damage," thereby making all attempts at resistance "terrible beyond endurance." Given this qualitative advantage in the infliction of pain, the United States had the capability to intimidate enemies and avoid challenges to its power.[31]

While ostensibly aimed at planners of strategic, nuclear policy, Schelling argued that his theory applied to conventional war in general and the Vietnamese conflict in particular. The unleashing of exemplary "punitive attacks" in Vietnam constituted the only way of conveying to the enemy the price of continued resistance, and "the proffered avoidance or reward" that would follow a logical cost-benefit analysis on the part of the enemy. "Talk is cheap," Schelling reminded his readers. Therefore threats had to backed up by actual displays of coercive force; "it is often deeds and display that matter most."[32]

The Leites–Wolf reliance on coercion rather than persuasion received additional support from Harvard University's Samuel Huntington. The renowned defense analyst drew attention to the fact that the Vietnamese insurgents primarily claimed the loyalty of "backward" peasants, who were arrested at a premodern stage of development. In the cities, where dislocation prevailed, Huntington claimed that the Vietcong as a peasant movement had failed to garner support. The forced move from the rural Asian gemeinschaft to the leveling gesellschaft of the cities undermined support for the rural ideology of the Vietcong. Because of rapid urbanization, he argued that "the Vietcong are becoming increasingly dependent on North Vietnam for manpower as well as supplies." Consequently, Huntington urged a ruthless transfer of inhabitants from villages to cities as the most efficient manner for winning over the people.

> In an absent-minded way the United States in Vietnam may well have stumbled upon an answer to "wars of national liberation." The effective response lies neither in the quest for conventional military victory nor in the esoteric doctrines and gimmicks of counter-insurgency warfare. It is instead forced-draft urbanization and modernization which rapidly brings the country in question out of the phase in which a rural revolutionary movement can hope to generate sufficient strength to come to power.[33]

Huntington's forceful urbanization theory was by no means his own private opinion. George Carver, a senior CIA consultant, used the pages of *Foreign Affairs* to voice similar views. "In the cities, the Vietcong have an obvious terrorist capability but are politically weak," he observed. While never explicitly advocating forced urbanization, Carver emphasized that disruption of the rural-insurgent network demanded drastic measures. Even the most alienated of South Vietnam's urban population, he argued, had not "sought Vietcong support or entertained overtures of political alliance."[34]

Together with the work of Schelling, Huntington, and others, the Leites–Wolf strategy of repressive counterinsurgency gained rapid prominence during the Johnson administration. According to numerous accounts, this particular model served as the intellectual prop for the administration's 1965 escalation of the war.[35] Faced with the crumbling of the government of South Vietnam and its inability to achieve any significant political or military gains, the Johnson administration embraced a radical departure from previous strategies by escalating the war and Americanizing the actual fighting through the rapid and massive deployment of U.S. ground troops. As part of this general escalation of the war, U.S. forces initiated a ruthless "search and destroy" strategy aimed at undermining the NLF's logistical infrastructure. Strategies for ground warfare entailed an abandonment of political deeds and social improvement as a means of subverting the link between insurgents and the populace. Instead of good deeds, the JCS advocated destroying the insurgents' local lifeline by indiscriminate destruction of rural food supplies, the destruction of the protective cover of nature, and the indiscriminate destruction of villages in the insurgents' hinterland. The objective of these suppressive measures was very much along the lines of the Wolf–Leites model of repressive counterinsurgency. The ultimate objective of ruthless deployment of American fighting power was to raise the price of popular peasant support for the enemy to unacceptable levels.

Predictably, the Leites–Wolf study had its set of admiring disciples and kindred souls who sang the praises of "the rational peasant" and charted "the economics of insurgency."[36] Such enthusiasm for this revisionist approach did little to cover up its logical caveats. To begin with, the underlying logic of the coercive model did not reflect the actual transpiring of events. The social welfare approach to counterinsurgency had not failed; it had never been fully implemented. Due to mismanagement, occasional corruption, and the ambivalent attitude of military enforcers, the grandiose plans for pacification and economic improvements rarely moved beyond the squandering of large sums of money or half-hearted implementation. To state that the foundering program of the welfare approach to counterinsurgency had little chance of actually succeeding was, to say the least, unverified.[37]

The most scathing critique of this coercive strategy belonged to University of Colorado economist Kenneth Boulding, who labeled the concept of repressive counterinsurgency a "political profanity." In his contemporary critique of the theory, Boulding attacked the facile use of economic analogy to explain the imponderables of a committed people as an example of "economics imperialism." The very notion that ordinary individuals were motivated solely "by considerations of personal or perhaps familial advantage" struck him as misplaced plagiarism. "The weakness of this kind of economic analysis of essentially non-economic social systems is precisely that it neglects those aspects of human behavior which are not economic but which are 'heroic,' or more accurately, identity-originating." According to Boulding, Leites and Wolf appeared unwilling to entertain the idea that while people might, indeed, employ cost-benefit analysis as the main source of behavior, the actual definition of "price" was culturally derived.[38]

In another hostile review, sociologist J. F. Short expressed alarm over the model's anticipation of enemy behavior. Leites and Wolf had offered no empirical support for the premise that Western codes of rational behavior had universal attributes, Short complained. In assuming that force and coercion necessarily lead to obedience and acquiescence, they had simply brushed away—but did not disprove—conflicting sociological evidence. The leap of faith involved in accepting coercive counterinsurgency, Short feared, offered an intellectual excuse to avoid addressing the root causes of insurgency. "Those with political power—and particularly military power"—were liable to "accept the assumptions and concentrate entirely on strategic and coercive aspects of the struggle . . . to the neglect of the problems . . . underlying the conflict."[39]

Indeed, the Wolf–Leites model held a fatal attraction for policy makers. To begin with, the study was crisp, unambiguous, and readable. In contrast to previous assessments of enemy motives, beclouded by long-winded references to intellectually obscure psychological theories and sociological models, the doctrine of repressive counterinsurgency used the terse language of Econ. 101. This document, aimed at intellectual freshmen, contained no uncertainty; it was all summarized in forceful, unambiguous tones.

Rebellion and Authority's greatest asset was that it offered a little something for everyone. The frustrated policy maker, confronted by a manifest inability to sustain the central government of South Vietnam, presumably welcomed the document because it "privatized" the meaning of the war. The study moved the center of gravity away from the nature of the South Vietnamese regime to the individual level. According to Leites and Wolf, behavioral modification of individuals rather than structural reform of a corrupt political system would win the war. The nature of the regime, be it aspiring democrats or decadent elites, became superfluous under these circumstances.

The military establishment presumably welcomed repressive counterinsurgency as well, because it rejected all assessments of the Vietnam War as a political problem. All wars, including the fuzzy Vietnamese variation, were, first and foremost, contests in the efficient implementation of force. The document flatly stated that reform or any other political initiative to contain the enemy by means other than the use of threat and coercion had no place on the battlefield.

Perhaps the most salient element of *Rebellion and Authority* was its ability to advocate both expansion and restraint. No doubt both army and air force officials found in this document ample support for the massive expansion of their respective operations in Vietnam. Yet, even as it served as an intellectual rationale for aggressive escalation of American military operations, this revisionist model offered a clear restraining tone. The Leites–Wolf document advocated that forceful military moves could still be made without an irreversible territorial expansion of the war beyond Vietnam, and without inviting a Vietnamese version of the Chinese response to the Korean crisis. Coercive counterinsurgency could be read as an implementation of Korean lessons on the benefits of limited warfare. According to the Wolf–Leites model, the war could be won without aggravating the foreign supporters of insurgents, be they Russians, Chinese, or anyone else. The study urged applying pressure on native inhabitants, supporters of the insurgency, rather than on its external sources. The coercive model, however brutal and unrestrained, offered a powerful counterpoise to a territorial escalation of the war.

From Pacification to Coercion: The Intellectual Significance

The promotion of coercive counterinsurgency represented a major moral and intellectual watershed for the behavioral sciences community. Prior to the advocacy of coercive counterinsurgency, and in contrast to the dominant trends in strategic planning at Rand and elsewhere, behavioral scientists had consistently espoused social and psychological strategies however fantastic and unproven, for the military problems of the Cold War. As described in previous chapters, behavioral scientists had unfailingly offered psychological, nonlethal alternatives to conventional destructive weaponry. Through skillful psychological warfare, and by deciphering the inner psyches of adversaries, behavioral scientists had promised to pursue and subdue the enemy by means other than physical annihilation.

Such was not the case by the mid-1960s. The Leites–Wolf study represented a turn toward alternative, and harsher, theories for subduing the enemy. Fully aware of the moral dilemmas inherent in the infliction of indiscriminate suffering on civilians, Nathan Leites, formerly a prolific contributor to conventional behavioral strategies, argued that such issues were not his to ponder. In the introduction to *Rebellion and Authority*, the published, public version of the coercive counterinsurgency model, Leites was at pains to register his personal disavowal of American policy in Vietnam and his private, personal distaste with coercive counterinsurgency. As a concerned citizen, he rejected the very policy that he, as a scientist advocated; he doubted the "moral acceptability of these policies even if conducted efficiently."[40] However, as a scientist, he implied that he was bound to set his personal misgivings aside and pursue the task at hand.

Leites was not merely the dubious victim of torn loyalties between scientific rigor and personal values. His espousal of this economic model of coercion was a clear rejection of his own previous intellectual achievements. Leites had been the undisputed master of psychocultural explanations of human motivation; calculated decisions based on cost-benefit analysis contradicted his hitherto most cherished intellectual assumptions. The punitive approach to counterinsurgency did not necessarily deny imponderables such as culture, loyalty to a cause, and ideology as motivating factors. However, contrary to previous work, where Leites had argued that political loyalties were psychologically derived and impervious to change, the model of coercive counterinsurgency assumed that loyalties were neither static nor essentialist. In a crucial amendment to his previous assumptions, Leites now claimed that rational considerations overrode all behavioral codes and customs. "Fundamental to our analysis is the assumption that the population, as individuals or groups, behaves 'rationally': that it calculates costs and benefits." As for his previous psychological explanations, Leites explained that such "apparent irrationalities" resulted from faulty analysis, "misinformation; a shortage of information on the part of the population; or a misunderstanding on the observer's part."[41]

This disavowal of previous strategies of behavioralism was indicative of the epistemological importance of *Rebellion and Authority*. The Leites–Wolf study was one of the first major cooperative ventures at the trend-setting Rand Corporation between the poorly regarded social science division and the more august economics division. Collaborative studies with the physics division swiftly followed the removal of institutional and intellectual barriers that had kept behavioral scientists far from the center of prestige at Rand and elsewhere.

In part, the rising fortunes of behavioral scientists in particular and Rand's social science division in general had much to do with the political entanglements of the Vietnam War. During the early 1950s, futuristic nuclear scenarios had monopolized the collective agenda of policy makers and the upper caste of strategic academic advisors; they had paid scant attention to issues of conventional warfare. The growing embroilment on Asian battlefields, and its debilitating effect on the polity and economy of the United States, attracted the attention of elite defense intellectuals, many of whom had previously dismissed conventional warfare as an issue not worthy of their attention.[42]

The changing research interests of Herman Kahn, formerly one of Rand's most influential nuclear theorists, serves as a case in point. From the seminar rooms of his New York-based Hudson Institute, Kahn pondered, "Can we win in Vietnam?"[43] In typical style, Kahn inundated his readers with long lists of confusing and often conflicting suggestions, ranging from run-of-the-mill social reform to the expansion of free-fire zones in sensitive areas of South Vietnam. Yet, his most provocative suggestion had little to do with the likes of nuclear doomsday theories.

In 1968, with the publication of the Hudson Institute's recommendations on Vietnam, Kahn sketched out a political compromise, based on the "Balkanization" of Vietnam. He suggested dividing the country into 240 separate districts, each district to be governed by the most powerful political faction within its midst. The factional nature of politics in Vietnam, Kahn claimed, augured unfavorably for any future robust democratic system. The Vietnamese were "people of the past," and their ability to adapt to the abstract political mechanism of a large overarching democratic state merely played into the hands of the enemy. "Federalization," he argued, "might create a natural structure within which various anti-VC Vietnamese could in fact develop dedication and loyalty."[44]

Within the confines of Rand, the growing importance of Vietnam proved to be a boon for the hitherto marginal social science division and its preoccupation with conventional warfare. Rather than contesting the turf of conventional warfare with its current occupants, the members of Rand's more prestigious divisions offered their marginal colleagues in the social science division collaboration and access to the sweet realms of prestige and power.

Successful collaboration between behavioral scientists and their colleagues from physics and economics involved a crucial intellectual concession on the part of members of Rand's social science division. With few apparent signs of remorse, behavioral scientists at Rand and elsewhere abandoned their psychocultural models of human motivation and adopted, instead, the code of rational choice. The strategy of interdivisional collaboration and the theory of rational choice provided Rand's behavioral scientists with the opportunity to engage in the previously restricted area of global warfare, and even dabble in nuclear strategy as well. One of Rand's most significant documents on nuclear strategy in the 1960s was a collaborative effort of Andrew Marshall, a leading member of the economics division, Herbert Goldhamer, the Rand expert on psychocultural analysis of the enemy at the Korean armistice talks, and, of course, the omnipresent Nathan Leites. Entitled *The Deterrence and Strategy of Total War*, this document was lavishly praised as a "tour de force" for its innovative and mathematically rigorous use of game theory. It had little to do with any type of psychocultural model. In fact, it was a straightforward mathematical model.[45]

The Political Significance of Coercive Counterinsurgency

Aside from its epistemological importance, the Rand model of repressive counterinsurgency had a distinct and alarming political significance as well. The publication of *Rebellion and Authority* exemplified the aggressive intrusion of theories developed in a foreign, mostly military domain into the hitherto restricted territory of domestic American affairs.

While ostensibly an analysis of a foreign problem, Leites and Wolf stressed that their model applied to internal challenges to authority within the United States. At the very outset of their study they stated that "much of the analytical framework" derived from analysis of rebellion in foreign lands offered solutions for "contemporary urban disorders and campus rebellions." As far as they were concerned, there were no great analytical differences separating rebellion in Asia from internal American unrest. Just as they had refuted the supposedly false linkage between insurgency and poverty in Asia, the Rand investigators offered fairly explicit disapproval of much of the economic improvement underpinnings of the "Great Society." In analyzing the race riots of the late 1960s, they observed that, like the Asian setting, poverty explained little.

> From an economic standpoint, Watts in 1965 was probably among the most favorably situated of the black communities in the U.S. When one looks at the Detroit riots of 1967, it turns out that incomes of rioters were significantly higher than those of non-rioters. . . . Similarly, campus rebellions have often been most severe in those academic centers (for example, Berkeley, Columbia, Wisconsin, Cornell, Harvard, and Swarthmore) where living and learning conditions were among the best.[46]

In lumping together Vietnam and Watts, campus rebellions and peasant insurgencies, Wolf and Leites argued that much of America's political problems could be allayed by extracting a high price from those who either instigated or supported challenges to authority. "In discussions of campus rebellions, principal attention is often focussed on student demands and grievances, rather than on the actions (or inaction) of administrators and faculty that lower the costs and facilitate the organization and radicalization of student rebellion."[47]

Wolf and Leites were by no means alone in this intertwining of domestic and foreign, military and civilian. Nor for that matter, were they the first of America's academic warriors to cross the divide separating domestic and foreign issues. As early as 1953, Albert Biderman, who had earned his reputation as a senior analyst of enemy prisoners of war in Korea, produced a study for the air force's HRRI on the military applications of prison riot control in the United States. Based on an analysis of the January 1953 riots at the Rockview State Penitentiary in Pennsylvania, this study defined a universal code for efficient, cost-effective suppression of rebellious behavior, regardless of differing political or social causes. In line with his colleagues at Rand, Biderman explained that civilian "riots, domestic disturbances, protests, which constitute a challenge to established authority" were not significantly different from foreign military challenges to power. From a theoretical point of view, it was irrelevant whether such challenges to "established authority" occurred in Korea, Pennsylvania, or anywhere else. Urged on by the contracting air force agency, Biderman moved cautiously beyond prisoner-hostage situations, and offered observations of the use of airpower, in general, in the suppressions of all types "fundamental challenge[s] to the authority of government," civilian and military, domestic or foreign.[48]

Coming in the aftermath of the Koje Do riots in Korea, the Pennsylvania standoff offered an intriguing comparison. To begin with, the timing of Rockview riots, in January 1953, was distinctly political rather than an unforeseen eruption. The prisoners, according to Biderman, were intent on embarrassing the state's governor, who at the time was attending President Eisenhower's inaugural ceremonies. The American prisoner riots were permeated by crucial tensions between white and African American inmates, tensions which, at least superficially, were not unlike the divide separating communist and anti-communist inmates on Koje Do. Moreover, like the Korean rioters, the inmates at Rockview used hostages as bargaining chips; they had managed to kidnap some of the guards in the early stage of the riots.

The respective resolutions of the Koje and Rockview incidents were however, quite different. While Koje had ended in humiliating concessions in return for the release of General Dodd, the prisoners at Rockview had suddenly, and quite unexpectedly, capitulated. Moreover, the ensuing bloodbath that had followed the release of Brigadier General Dodd had not occurred at the Pennsylvania penitentiary. The Biderman study raised the possibility that these very different endings had transpired due to the discriminating use of airpower in the Rockview incident. Prisoners at Rockview had capitulated following the buzzing of the institute by National Guard aircrafts. Pennsylvania officials had claimed that the intimidating appearance of the planes had caused panic among prisoners. Alarmed at the very use of an aircraft to subdue the riots, the prisoners had supposedly capitulated rather than face the lethal use of airpower.

In his evaluation of the Pennsylvania incident, Biderman swiftly moved beyond the Koje Do parallel. He offered, instead, a series of conclusions on "challenges to authority," whether domestic or foreign, military or civilian. The basic rationale behind modern deterrence theory was that it attempted "by communication and demonstration" to avoid the actual "naked exercise of armed power." The display of planes over the penitentiary—"dramatic symbols of the violence potential of the State"—was a well-signed threat. Biderman argued that airpower was the ultimate and most clear-cut symbol of violence capability. The "sheer physical intensity" of a mock or symbolic bombing had a debilitating effect on the adversary. The conventional marshallng of ground troops as a means of signaling intentions had, according to Biderman, a certain quality of irrelevance. It assumed that the enemy could be scared into compliance by means of minor symbols of power. Airpower, by contrast, was much more unnerving. The physical shock of mock or symbolic bombing runs "may not result in serious" physical or structural damage. However, it invariably induced emotional disruption and "severe psychological shock."

While offering fairly explicit recommendations based on what he considered to be an irrefutable example of coercive rational choice, Biderman did, in all fairness, add a cautionary note. He explained that "we generally have difficulty in understanding the motivations of "powerless" people—prisoners, totalitarian subjects, school children, slaves, etc.,—who choose to resist total, official power." Such difficulties, resulted, in part "from attributing an overly rationalistic interpretation to their behavior. We ask 'what can they hope to gain?' without full realization of what might constitute 'gains' from the psychological standpoint of the subject[s]." The definition "of what constitutes a 'rational act' varies significantly from one situation to the other."[49]

Such caution and relativism had no apparent traces in the major models of rational choice, such as the Leites–Wolf presentation of *Rebellion and Authority*. In fact, the underlying premise of the Rand report on counterinsurgency was the universality of economically simulated rational choice. The suppressive model of counterinsurgency fit all forms of insurgency, regardless of location and irrespective of political context.

By the early 1960s most military-funded think tanks had adopted the format of mixing civilian and military case studies, as well as privileging the logic of violent rational choice. During the 1960s, the army-funded CRESS was the major center for the study of the cause and controls of rebellion. As part of the U.S. Army's attempt to emulate Rand's wide berth of research interests, CRESS associates, led by political scientist Ted Gurr, produced an ambitious multinational study of rebellion. Gurr offered a "general, explanatory theory of the conditions of violent civil conflict by applying complex and powerful statistical techniques to data from a large number of nations," including the United States.[50] Claiming that his theories were equally "applicable to riots and rural uprisings . . . *coups d'etat* and guerrilla wars," Gurr sought correlation among ten independent variables that affected "the likelihood and magnitude" of military rebellion and/or civil violence.

By his own account the correlations among his "predictive" variables, ranging from economic conditions to the political climate, produced poor results; the model failed, for example, to predict conflict in Vietnam. Gurr was, however, quite adamant that the employment of coercion was the only variable with satisfactory predictive power. Much like his Rand colleagues, Gurr found "no evidence that any particular level of economic performance is necessary . . . for civil peace." In fact, he claimed that "among less developed nations increasing levels of development are evidently associated with increasing strife."

By contrast, he found much positive evidence to support the Rand model of government-ordained coercion. "A high level of deterrent power, consistently applied, tends to inhibit civil strife."[51] Fear of retribution, measured by the number of military personnel per ten thousand adults, strikingly affected levels of civil strife. Such findings, he argued, were applicable to societies as far apart as the Congo and the United States, and were meaningful within the context of both civil war and mere civil disturbances.

Gurr would later use this study as the basis for a fledgling academic career, based on a recycling and extension of his theories on "Why Men Rebel."[52]

His indiscriminate mixture of different sociological contexts, and the cavalier blending of military conflicts and civilian standoffs, however, paled in comparison to a contemporaneous study by CRESS research associate Carl Rosenthal. Entitled "Phases of Civil Disturbances: Characteristics and Problems," Rosenthal's CRESS report was underwritten by a somewhat murky military agency, the U.S. Army Limited War Laboratory, stationed at the Aberdeen Proving Ground, Maryland. Ostensibly the Rosenthal study had nothing to do with limited war. It was a study of civilian riots in the United States. Nevertheless, the Limited War Laboratory's interest in the subject was an alarming sign of fusion between once clearly distinct domains.[53]

Like Gurr, Rosenthal produced a framework for identifying the variables leading to civil disorder. His report offered, as well, advice for the development of "sophisticated countermeasures." In one crucial element Rosenthal's report was particularly disturbing: it was based entirely on data derived from recent riots in American urban ghettos. Nowhere in the report did Rosenthal suggest that his study of domestic racial riots had any foreign applications. Rosenthal's ultimate objective was to inform the army on tools and tactics for riot control *within* the United States. Theoretically and, perhaps, politically, Rosenthal approached civilian unrest in the United States as a variation of limited warfare. His investigation made no mention of any universal significance of this specifically American dilemma. It would appear, then, that U.S. Army in the 1960s entertained the possibility, however distant and improbable, of engaging in guerrilla-like warfare within the United States. The always slim line separating domestic from foreign, military from civilian, appeared all the more faint and porous.[54]

The growing interest in rational choice and coercive methods, the dissipating borders separating civilian and military domains, and the fusion of foreign and domestic political concerns did not signify a mere technical adjustment in research interest and techniques. Instead, each and every one of these intellectual transformations were part and parcel of a major paradigm shift, an abandonment of an orthodoxy that had fallen into disfavor.

The demise of classic, psychocultural strategies was accompanied by a reexamination of other premises of behavioralism, ranging from the espousal of value-free science, predictability in human inquiry, and the very nature of the government-academic nexus. By the mid-1960s, the once unassailable assumption that only the presence of professional social and behavioral scientists could guide democratic governments through the dislocating periods of rapid technological advances was subverted by popular satire and learned treatises. The attack on behavioralism, by a combination of scientific critique and parody is the subject of the concluding chapters.

10.
Paradigm Lost
The Project Camelot Affair

In 1965, the military-academic enterprise became the focus of an intense public debate. The ostensible reason for such unwarranted scrutiny was the scandal-ridden Project Camelot. Established in 1963 by SORO, and funded by the Army Office of Research and Development, Project Camelot was the most conspicuous of several military-funded efforts to comprehend, contain, and combat political insurgency in the volatile new nations of the Cold War world.

The architects of Project Camelot contracted with an army of consultants for producing universal models of social unrest and designing strategies for obviating political strife in the "modernizing" countries of the post–World War II world. Camelot's main scientific objective was the formulation of a "general social systems model which would make it possible to predict and influence politically significant aspects of social change in the developing nations of the world."[1]

Despite the recruitment of academic advisors representing a wide spectrum of political and social persuasions, the type of change envisioned by Camelot's sponsors was unambiguously conservative. The tenor of Camelot documents left no doubt as to their antirevolutionary assumptions. "A 'stable society' is the considered norm no less than the desired outcome," a critic noted. By contrast "the 'breakdown of social order' is spoken of accusatively." As point of departure, the project accepted the "constructive" role of a foreign military force in promoting "steady growth and change in the less developed countries in the world."[2] The legitimacy of American military intervention in the civilian affairs of other countries was a given, never to be scrutinized under the project's guidelines.

Soon after its inception, the project suffered an untimely death when a junior associate attempted, on his own initiative, to recruit foreign collaborators. In his efforts to gain the cooperation of Chilean colleagues, University of Pittsburgh anthropologist Hugo Nuttini lied about the project's funding, claiming that the National Science Foundation, rather than the Defense Department, was Camelot's main sponsor. This clumsy misrepresentation was soon exposed, unleashing in its wake an embarrassing diplomatic scandal. Much to his chagrin, the secretary of state confronted charges of espionage and neo-imperialistic meddling in the affairs of others, even though his department had no ties with the project. Exposure of the project's international ambitions raised concerns that an aggressive military establishment was overly involved in the ostensibly civilian domain of international relations. The beginning of the Camelot scandal, at about the same time as the May 1965 American intervention in the Dominican Republic, merely added fuel to the public outcry.

In response to such criticism, Secretary of Defense Robert McNamara canceled Project Camelot on July 8, 1965. Soon thereafter President Johnson placed all future foreign area research under the jurisdiction of the State Department's newly formed Foreign Affairs Research Council, thereby, at least symbolically, restoring the preeminence of civilian authorities in American governmental activities in foreign lands.

The official end to Project Camelot did little to douse public interest. In fact, the significance of the project loomed particularly large after its nullification. The flurry of congressional testimonies, scholarly analysis, and investigative reporting reminded sociologist Robert Nisbett of the proverbial blind men and their disjointed descriptions of an elephant.[3] The mainstream media analyzed Project Camelot as an episode in the mutual poaching of the Departments of State and Defense. Congressional committees damned Camelot as a sorry illustration of the riotous, uncoordinated, and often hazily defined research agenda in major federal agencies. Critics of American foreign policy discovered in Camelot the ultimate instance of American neo-imperialism, academic mandarins having replaced businessmen as the ugly Americans.

As for the long roll call of academic commentators, they focused, predictably, on themselves. They provided the public with multiple and often contradictory definitions of behavioral scientists as priests, prophets, or merely technicians. This exercise in self-analysis revealed a crumbling of pivotal axiomatic assumptions. The relationship between scientific investigations and government funding and the meaning of value-free science in the social and behavioral sciences were all called into question during the course of the Camelot autopsy.

The Marketplace of Ideas

The Camelot debates were first and foremost a forum for airing concerns over intellectual creativity and government funding. Most participants in the public debate agreed with Stanford University's Gabriel Almond that Camelot exemplified the limits of intellectual independence in Cold War America. Referring, perhaps, to the clash between his own intellectual pretensions and his personal political worldview, Almond explained that scientists had certain cosmopolitan obligations that, theoretically, might curtail their affinity with the nation-state. The Camelot affair demonstrated that this pivotal prerequisite for competent scientific activity was difficult to achieve under the auspices of government funding. While conceding that there were many "excellent examples of research programs that have not been, in any way, influenced by" federal funding, Almond maintained that massive government support curtailed scientific creativity by its centralization of intellectual activities rather than through political censorship. Once support from one particular source crossed a critical "level of magnitude" a loss of creativity was imminent.

The problem, then, was not the nature of the client, but the monolithic source of funding and the threat that it posed to the "disintegrated nature of science." The autonomy of science hinged upon decentralization and the existence of multiple funders and sponsors. Almond maintained that intellectual enterprises, like economic activities, thrived best when guided by an invisible hand. Outstanding scientific achievements resulted from the spontaneous confluence of private, uncoordinated research activities. Almond explained:

> I am not arguing from a C. Wright Mills' position. I am not arguing that scholars who act as consultants to government agencies or who receive contracts for research from Government agencies thereby lose their independence of judgment. On the other hand, I cannot go along with those who feel that this kind of pattern of participation has no effect whatever on the independence of the social scientists.[4]

The loss of independence in government-funded research, such as Project Camelot, was not due to political or social pressures. It was, instead, more of a psychological constraint. Scientific creativity was generated by the extemporaneous interaction of free, self-serving researchers. In the past, he explained, private foundations and autonomous universities had created "a high-level market in ideas and regular opportunities for competitive discussion. . . . By contrast, the department of defense, the CIA and other government agencies had produced a 'clumsy' short-sighted and restrictive agenda." In other words, decentralization in funding and agenda setting was the indispensable key to "a high level market in ideas." "Disintegrated science" was not only beneficial; it was an indispensable element of the creative scientific process.

As was the case in the domain of economics, Almond argued that closed borders and high fences, generated by the predominance of defense-related research, was the antithesis of good science. Just as a thriving economy hinged upon open markets, science prospered within an open cosmopolitan academic milieu, where the concern for the expansion of knowledge without frontiers or military restrictions superseded national divisions and petty political priorities.

As for those who feared a loss of relevance in a free-enterprise scientific system, Almond argued that, in addition to creativity, freedom fostered order and relevance as well. Frequently falling back on market analogies, he stated that the scientific world, much like the marketplace, was governed by the rational choices of uncoordinated individuals. The scientific laws and regularities of the intellectual enterprise—the intellectual equivalent of market regularities—ensured that freedom and the lack of a central coordinating authority did not lead to chaos, but to an orderly accumulation of relevant knowledge.[5]

In response to his congressional interrogators, Almond conceded that nationalism, collective ideologies, and authoritarianism in other countries were partly to blame for restrictions in the academic domain. However, he identified a crucial American responsibility for the closing of intellectual frontiers. Most social science or behavioral research in the United States was "assimilated to American foreign and defense policy considerations" rather than the more abstract goal of furthering knowledge. Due to defense-related restrictions, the free exchange of information within the global marketplace of ideas faced severe limitations.

Almond conceded that existential crises, such as the Cold War, should and could impose restraining loyalties on the behavior of national scientists. However, despite the constraints of national security, the production of knowledge entailed the fostering of an epistemic community unrestrained by restrictive ideological, security, or political concerns. The locus of truth transcended national frontiers. Almond expressed belief in "a shared acceptance of the canons of science" among a transnational, epistemic community of scientists as the basis of cumulative knowledge. "Communication and colloquy" among scientists from all over the world sharing the same "pragmatic, impartial, orientation" was the essence of creativity. The very presence of massive, overt government funding affected such activities. National concerns, like every ideology, inevitably caused some sort of distortion of the truth, restricted the free flow of information, or introduced scientifically irrelevant bias into the academic agenda.[6]

Camelot's Academic Warriors

A brief glance at the list of Camelot participants suggests that many of the country's brightest minds had, indeed, diverted their research agenda to accommodate the concerns of the national security state. Prior to its public exposure and subsequent cancellation, Camelot attracted an impressive array of prominent academic collaborators with promises of lavish funding, exciting research, and, above all, the rewards associated with a significant contribution to the nation's security. Many of Camelot's associates had little prior experience in defense-related work. With no apparent hesitation they adapted themselves to the modes of thinking demanded by well-endowed defense projects such as Camelot.[7]

Among Camelot's three leading associates, only University of Michigan's Robert Hefner was first and foremost an expert on foreign affairs; his field of expertise was Indonesia. Camelot's other two senior consultants specialized in domestic areas. Johns Hopkins sociologist James Coleman was a leading expert on education and adolescence in the United States, as well as a renowned innovator in the field of mathematical models for sociology.[8] Perhaps sensing the shifting winds, Coleman formulated a secondary field of expertise in the late 1950s; he began publishing work on political trends in new African nations. Needless to say, Coleman could claim no background in the myriad of cultures, histories, and societies on the African continent.[9]

Camelot's other senior consultant, Pennsylvania State University sociologist Jessie Bernard, was an authority on American community life, the dynamics of the American family, and marriage patterns in the United States. As a woman in a profession dominated by men, and in a field that rarely accepted female contributors, Bernard was an extraordinary figure. An admiring biographer has noted that in both her personal life and professional activities, she emanated "defiance of family tradition, life styles, occupational trajectories, sociological paradigms, and popular myths, as well as age-related patterns."[10] The daughter of Jewish immigrants from Romania, the young Jessie Kanter challenged tradition and convention by marrying renowned sociologist Luther Lee Bernard, her mentor at the University of Minnesota, who was twenty-one years her senior and a Gentile to boot.

At the time of Project Camelot's establishment, Bernard had just completed her study on *Academic Women* (1964). This study was an analysis of academic women laboring under the "stag effect," the subtle, yet institutionalized exclusion of women from the "invisible college" that disseminated knowledge among, and offered employment opportunities for, a mostly male academic establishment. From this point and on Bernard moved into the field of what would later be known as women's studies, her only major respite being her brief association with Camelot. Bernard, like many of her male colleagues, was unable to withstand the lure of defense-related research; temporarily she abandoned her primary research interests in order to join the ranks of academic warriors.

In all fairness, Bernard did bring to Camelot some relevant intellectual property. During the early stages of her career she had co-authored with her spouse, L. L. Bernard, *Sociology and the Study of International Relations* (1934). In her work on American community life, Bernard offered some theoretical contributions that paved her way to Camelot. In *American Community Behavior* (1949), her modest contribution to the theoretical field of American community life, Bernard argued that conflict, rather than cooperation, undergirded American social life. Throughout this book as well as in a series of articles, Bernard claimed that elements of conflict that she had discovered within the American community were not peculiar to the United States, or to primary groups and small communal arrangements. The same features appeared, albeit in grand and elaborate form, in the arena of global conflict as well.[11] Bernard recognized no substantial difference between turf wars among street gangs in the United States and territorial conflict in the global arena. Both instances should and could be analyzed with the contours of the same theoretical framework.

Bernard argued that culture or the unique historical developments of any given society were not adequate explanations for conflict. As far as she was concerned, " 'culture' has become a facile explanation for almost anything, just as 'race' once was, or 'nature' or 'fate'." Much of what sociologists had dismissed as unique cultural phenomena were in actual fact generic instances of conflict, which could be contained, resolved, or even avoided by applying preemptive sociological tools. Bernard maintained that the analysis of conflict as a sociological rather than a cultural phenomenon had monumental political ramifications. "(W)hen the Communists turned their battery of conflict techniques on us, we had no theory to cover modern conflict situations." By avoiding theory, and falling back, instead, on the cultural explanations of anthropologists and humanists, sociologists were left with nothing "creative to offer in the cold war."[12]

Bernard's leap from the American family and community to the cutting edge of foreign policy was motivated by personal concerns as well. Professional frustration presumably played an important part in her decision to abandon her main research interests and join, at least temporarily, the ranks of academic warriors. Despite the awakening of interest in sex and gender in the 1960s, Bernard was discouraged by the condescending reception of academic investigations of women in general and her own work in particular; such work evoked "a great big yawn."[13] Defense sponsorship offered greater research opportunities than at a university, where a chauvinistic male establishment cramped her style. Defense-related work provided entry into a prestigious, male-dominated domain, and a comfortable bypass of the stag effect.

There were, of course, other motives for such career moves. In Bernard's case, at least, she remained convinced that a thorough theoretical analysis of seemingly intractable military problems might save the United States an unnecessary spilling of blood. In modern conflicts, she argued, "research may constitute as important an element of conflict as hardware."[14] According to Bernard and a host of other Camelot associates, "every example of violence in a conflict may be said to represent a failure in strategy. For when, or if, strategic solutions are available, strategy may supplant violence."[15]

While not all Camelot associates endorsed Bernard's belief in an intellectual antidote to violence, the presence of eminent scholars reflected a pervasive profession-wide identification with the political priorities of government and military benefactors. Opportunism existed, of course. However, sociologist Irving Louis Horowitz has argued that most Camelot participants joined the project because they sincerely believed that they were serving the best of the nation"s interests. Patriotism, rather than expedience, was the main motivating force. Camelot researchers who rallied to the flag "saw little difference between scholars engaged in the war on poverty and those directly concerned with the war" against those forms of worldwide insurgency threatening the United States.[16] Both types of research were aimed at saving the nation-state from existential threats.

Whatever their motivations, the defense-related brain drain of behavioral scientists was an issue of critical intellectual significance. Not only did such lavishly funded defense projects divert talent from other, modestly funded enterprises. The ideological attraction of Camelot was indicative of the limits of value-free science. Thus, the embattled concept of value-free science surfaced frequently during the course of Camelot's public deconstruction. These debates revealed a new and surprisingly painful recognition of the limits of objectivity and impartial research in Cold War academia.

Value-Free Science and Grand Theory

In one form or another most Camelot-related testimonies revised the core definition of "science" as a value-free intellectual enterprise associated with experimental, quantitative, objective inquiry. Contrary to previous self-definitions of their calling, Camelot's academic participants appeared resigned to the fact that value-free science was not a prerequisite for their scientific activity, but a utopian and, perhaps, unrealistic goal.

The binding power of a grand theory linking the disjointed members of the scientific enterprise seemed to most Camelot debaters an equally unrealistic goal. Testimonies ranged from tepid reaffirmations of the intellectual bonds between the sciences to other, more iconoclastic assessments. Some of Camelot's participants and commentators still claimed the ability to maintain an all-encompassing epistemological scientific community. However, the more prominent academic witnesses lacked such confidence. In a typical testimony, Alex Inkeles, professor of sociology at Harvard and senior member of Harvard's Russian Research Center, mustered only a wavering conviction on the unity of the scientific enterprise. While maintaining that the social, behavioral, and natural sciences shared "a common tradition," he acknowledged that "many will question how far one can soundly identify" the various branches of intellectual inquiry.[17]

Kalman Silvert, professor of government at Dartmouth, offered a compromise. While recognizing that there were unbridgeable gaps between the various formats of academic inquiry, he argued against the division of the academic world into the two separate domains of sciences and humanities. "A better differentiation might perhaps be between inquiries which study recurrent phenomena and those sciences which study historical, and thus, necessarily unique phenomena." While the natural sciences were mostly involved in the tracking of recurring phenomena, Silvert observed "that there are certain elements in biology" and other branches of the natural sciences that challenged the search for recurrent phenomena. It was, therefore, entirely conceivable that, as in the case of certain areas of the natural sciences, the scientific apparatus associated with the tracking of recurring phenomena was not always appropriate for the behavioral and social sciences either.[18]

Referring to the "Two Cultures" debate—C. P. Snow's division of the academic world into scientists, on the one hand, and humanistic craftsmen, on the other—Gabriel Almond hesitated, stumbled, and stuttered when called upon to define the position of the behavioral sciences. Contrary to the behavioralists of the 1950s, whose affinities with the natural sciences were quite explicit, Almond displayed indecision. "We have not paid sufficient attention to the consequences of our being isolated from the more traditional and humanistic, historical, and morally oriented" disciplines, Almond confessed. The confusing milieu of the 1960s had apparently taken its toll on previous confident definitions of behavioralism. In the aftermath of Camelot, a straightforward alignment with the intellectual methods and goals of physicists, chemists, and biologists appeared problematic, if not erroneous. At best, Gabriel Almond stated, "the boundary of the two cultures cuts right down the middle" of the behavioral and social sciences, "and we suffer as a consequence."[19]

Jessie Bernard expressed similar doubts, stating categorically that the social and behavioral sciences could never achieve the lofty status of the natural sciences. Bernard argued that the intellectual process associated with the social and behavioral sciences "is not in itself a science, nor even necessarily scientific. Like any other creative enterprise, it is an art. It involves hunches, insights, intuitive leaps, and the like." While acknowledging that creativity and hunches characterized the physical sciences as well, she explained that the difference lay in the life span of the "laws" and regularities extracted by behavioral and social scientists. Contrary to her colleagues of the 1950s, who believed in their ability to uncover immutable laws of human behavior, Bernard demurred. "The world to which much of past [physical] science pertained has not changed that rapidly; it is still possible to apply Newtonian physics, for example, to most earthly problems." In the behavioral and social sciences, by contrast, "not only does new science replace old, but the very world upon which the old was based also changes. It is difficult to formulate any scientific generalizations that are relevant in sociological phenomena" from the past, recent or distant.[20] The search for laws of human behavior— one of the primary objectives of Camelot—was, then, quite futile.

Bernard argued as well that the Camelot controversy revealed the flimsy underpinnings of objectivity in the behavioral and social sciences. "Project Camelot called forth a scrutiny not only of the ideological biases of others" but the politics of American academia as well. During the course of the Camelot autopsy Bernard made the then-startling declaration that all modes of representation in the behavioral and social sciences were bearers of ideology and, therefore, were not value-free. Citing a number of examples from Camelot research papers, Bernard declared that Camelot's consultants had more often than not engaged in the social construction of reality rather than discovering some objective truth; they were not discovering but, perhaps, inventing reality. Bernard acknowledged that in their attempt to define the dynamics of foreign societies, Camelot researchers had ethnocentrically applied the functionalist "social systems approach characteristic of American sociology in the last generation." The application of such theories to foreign surroundings was assumed rather than proven. Moreover, the emphasis on social systems was "ideological" rather than scientific.[21]

Bernard would find significant support for her position in the musings of Talcott Parsons, perhaps the most influential social scientist of his times. In his appraisal of the Camelot fallout, published in *The American Sociologist*, Parsons appropriated the "editor's prerogative" to describe the significance of the social and behavioral sciences in the post-Camelot era. They were, he claimed, latter-day equivalents of "the early Christians," a powerful body of believers who were able to change their surroundings through a well-managed dissemination of their gospel. Parsons, the son of a minister, did not, of course, mean that sociologists and their brethren in adjacent disciplines were bearers of some godly truth; that, he explained, "would be highly presumptuous." He approached social and behavioral scientists as forceful communicators of a belief system, rather than intrepid discoverers of divine reality. The social and behavioral sciences were similar to a comprehensive religious belief system, because they, like faithful bearers of a religious creed, offered "integrated bodies of knowledge, rather than aggregates of discrete items of particular problem solving." The central creed of this academic belief system was the dogma "formulated by Max Weber as 'value-neutrality' (Wertfreiheit)." It was, however, a belief rather than gospel truth.[22]

Parson's linking of behavioral and social sciences with belief systems rather than objective knowledge was indicative of erosion in the self-confidence of the previous decade. Daniel Lerner, one of the last of the Mohicans, would still, in 1959, claim that, despite the "carping" of humanists, the social and behavioral sciences had proven that "there are no more eternal mysteries" that scientific methodology could not decipher. Lerner declared that all human beings were "plastic, variable, and amenable to reshaping" when exposed to scientific and rigorously applied behavioral techniques.[23] However, by the mid-1960s most of Lerner's kindred spirits lacked this confidence in their scientific calling. Political scientist Samuel Huntington, formerly a partisan of behavioralism and its application in the Vietnam War, speculated in 1967 that perhaps much of the "shrillness and superficiality" of the academic contribution to the Vietnam conflict was due to a distinct lack of knowledge of Vietnamese history and culture. Behavioral codes, however incisive, were useless when removed from their cultural and historical context.[24]

Interdisciplinary Research

In addition to this critique of scientific pretensions, the Camelot debate revealed a marked disenchantment with interdisciplinary research. Once an axiomatic component of the behavioral creed, the fusion of methods from a wide range of social sciences did not withstand the test of political and intellectual pressures generated by Camelot.

Superficially, at least, the Camelot research agenda was an ambitious enterprise of integrated behavioral sciences. Anthropologists, psychologists, sociologists, and political scientists strove jointly to produce a heuristic model of a society susceptible to insurgency and dangerous political instability. In reality, however, Camelot researchers, all of whom espoused in principle the concept of a unified behavioral theory, had lost sight of this once-dominant paradigm.

In a retrospective paper written immediately after the termination of Camelot, Jessie Bernard acknowledged that the intellectual meeting of minds among the project's participants was uneasy at best. Once thrust together under the auspices of the project, they found little common ground. During the course of Camelot deliberations "specialists in specific approaches often became restless in the presentation of different approaches; there was a feeling of looseness," she recalled.[25] Dissension over fundamental theoretical issues left most researchers unable to bridge the gaps separating their own worlds from the domains of their colleagues. Contrary to previous practitioners of behavioral sciences, who agreed upon fundamental theoretical precepts, Camelot collaborators discovered that, in practice, they shared little in common.

Typically, Camelot teams were comprised of persons espousing opposing viewpoints. Such was the case in the critical area of rebellion and insurgency. Charles Wolf, the Rand expert on counterinsurgency, and University of California sociologist Neil Smelser, the author of the influential *Theory of Collective Behavior* (1962), were Camelot consultants in this field. Their respective theoretical approaches, were, however, irreconcilable.

Smelser, a prominent theorist of collective behavior, bunched together "craze, panics, riots, and revolutions."[26] The inclusion of revolution with other irrefutably emotional forms of crowd behavior was indicative of Smelser's point of departure: all manifestations of collective behavior were governed by fundamentally irrational instincts generated by conditions of stress. Moreover, in marked contrast to a central premise of the behavioral sciences, Smelser claimed distinct differences between the behavior of the individual and collective behavior. He defined collective behavior as "exaggerated," by which he meant, lacking the predictable elements of individual action. Collective behavior, usually the consequence of stressful situations, "short circuited" normal actions. Collective social or political challenges were, according to Smelser, rooted in "distorted" concepts of hostile forces, real or imaginary, as well as exaggerated assessments of the effectiveness of collective action.

Smelser, as some of his critics were quick to point out, characterized most challenges to authority, irrespective of the causes, as deviant or threatening and tended to discredit the beliefs and attitudes on "a priori grounds."[27] Mustering historical as well as contemporary illustrations, Smelser began by describing nineteenth-century industrial protest in Britain as episodes in "anxiety, hostility, and fantasy," that produced "extravagant claims concerning the effects of machinery and the factory on the health of the children, the morals of the factory population, and so on." In his analysis of the Chicago race riots of 1919, Smelser claimed that black participants, as a collective, developed an exaggerated, distorted depiction of the authorities. "The individual conduct of policemen was probably not so unfair as Negroes claimed," he asserted, albeit without providing supporting evidence.[28]

Smelser, of course, denied any linkage between his theories and the nineteenth-century European theorists of crowd behavior who dismissed collective action as fickle, emotional, and lacking in any meaningful social or political content. Yet, even an overtly friendly reading of his work suggests that, at the very best, he modified rather than rejected the irrationality of crowd behavior. While quite upset with those who compared his work to Gustave Le Bon's *The Crowd* (1895), the resemblance was striking. Like Le Bon, Smelser asserted that, when immersed in a crowd, individuals lost their personal identity, and assumed, instead, the primitive, mercurial, and highly imitative "crowd-mind."

Charles Wolf, by contrast, was very much a mainstream behavioralist. In his mind, collective action was a linear extension of individual behavior. An individual, a community, a country, all could be expected to behave in a rational manner aimed at maximizing personal benefits and minimizing loss, either physical, emotional, or material. Contrary to Smelser, Wolf dismissed the unanticipated impact of psychological motivation on the rational behavior of individuals or groups of any shape or form. A skillful behavioral scientist could elicit preplanned behavioral patterns in both individuals and groups by focusing on the most basic of human instincts—the avoidance of pain, discomfort, material loss, and existential threats.

On one important issue, Wolf and Smelser were quite united. Both endorsed a very negative approach to challenges to authority. Both researchers focused on what they considered to be the threatening disregard for "the law and for orderly means of expressing grievances." In describing the behavior of challengers, in all societies and circumstances, as socially destructive, Wolf and Smelser advocated invasive action to control, or contain, insurrection. Quoting philosopher Sidney Hook, Smelser argued that "the notion that repression cannot effectively crush revolutionary movements for long periods is a monstrous proposition."[29] When the decision falls to employ "sanctions against hostile outbursts, it is essential that authorities be both quick and decisive" as well as ruthless. Wolf, as noted in the previous chapter, held similar opinions.

This meeting of the minds did not gloss over the fundamental intellectual rift separating the two researchers. Wolf was a firm believer in rational choice; Smelser, by contrast, anticipated irrationality in collective behavior. Wolf assumed that collective behavior was the aggregate sum of individual actions. Smelser argued for fundamental differences between the emotional, exaggerated behavior of the crowd, and the normative behavior of individuals.

Of course, one may interpret the jostling of different approaches to such critical issues as stimulating rather than counterproductive. Intellectual clashes of this sort demanded the sharpening of concepts and the abandonment of intellectually weak theories. Perhaps the architects of Camelot assumed that the confrontation of researchers espousing conflicting strategies could yield some form of fusion or the creation of an entirely new theory upon which former sparring partners could agree.

The few working papers produced under the auspices of Camelot suggest the converse. Disagreement rather than integrative approaches characterized what little research was accomplished prior to the project's termination. In defining predictive tools for analyzing the rise of insurgencies, Camelot consultants were irreconcilably divided. Project documents promised "refinement of social conflict theory through the use of a research design which integrates data from analytical case studies, social system studies, and manual and machine simulation."[30] In actual fact, there was little convergence among different research methods. The goal of a predictive model remained within the realm of the fantastic. Divisions concerning the most fundamental of intellectual premises characterized Camelot research; collaborators could not agree on a binding theoretical framework. Fundamental intellectual conflict suggests that even without public exposure, Camelot's odds of longevity were slim at best.

Camelot's only published collection of research papers serves as a case in point. This conference held in late January 1965, on the eve of the indiscretions that led to the project's demise, proposed the lofty goal of producing a model for comprehending the process, direction, and significance of social change in the nation state. The collection of conference deliberations, published in 1967 as a posthumous recognition of Camelot's intellectual contributions, was, in actual fact, a confusing assembly of clashing models and disagreement on the motivating factors of social change.[31]

Disagreement began with James C. Coleman, the keynote speaker at the conference. Coleman, a member of Camelot's inner circle of senior consultants, argued that the trajectory of social change could be mathematically plotted. In accordance with prevailing behavioral orthodoxy, he assumed that rational considerations of self-interest were at the heart of all known organizational units. Therefore, one could produce a heuristic model of a nation-state by translating such rational interests into mathematical formulas.[32]

The underlying premise of such model building was modernization theory. Following in the footsteps of Daniel Lerner's classic analysis, Coleman approached "modernization as a process that has a distinctive quality of its own. The various elements in this process 'do not occur in haphazard and unrelated fashion,' they have gone together so regularly because 'in some historical sense they *had* to go together.' "[33] Coleman's measurements of choice were economic variables. The reason for plotting economic units was not, he argued, merely because they lent themselves to quantification. Modernization theorists believed that following the development of a competitive, modern economy, even the most truculent societies would eventually follow the path of political modernization. There appeared to be "a positive relationship between economic development"—the main indicator of a modernizing society—"and political competitiveness"—the backbone of democratic political systems.[34]

Sociologists Amitai Etzioni and Fredric Du Bow all but dismissed the value of such mathematical trajectories. They warned that the concept of "total societies" presented by their mathematically inclined peers at the Camelot conference were plagued by an "island approach." The simulations proposed by Coleman and others proceeded as if the society under study "was an island, a unit . . . that interacts only within its 'environment,' but is not related to any other units." In the interdependent reality of the modern world such constructs generated colossal misconceptions.[35]

Etzioni and Du Bow attacked, in particular, the underlying conservatism of the computer models. They accused their "island-oriented" colleagues of treating the very natural intrusion of external stimuli as pathological viruses, rather than natural phenomena in an interdependent, porous world. "(U)nlike change in the American society, few changes in other societies can be understood without accounting for the numerous and significant ways in which their parts are hooked into" foreign agents. In addition, they observed that mathematical models offered no mechanism for including unquantifiable data, ranging from the cultural influence of a neighboring country to the cultural idiosyncrasies of subcultures within the society under scrutiny. MIT political scientist Ithiel De Sola Pool, a partisan of computer simulations, countered that such attacks on mathematical models were specious and represented a return to antiquated forms of "verbal macro-theories," by which he presumably meant narrative or descriptive strategies.[36]

In addition to, or perhaps, because of, this fundamental methodological divide, conference participants squabbled over definitions of social change, the very heart of their research task. Duke University sociologist Edward Tiryakian chided his mathematically inclined colleagues for assuming that rational self-interest was the primary driving force for change. Such definitions, he argued, were scientifically imprecise, and poor material for model building. Tiryakian conceded that "social change," which he defined as slow and continuous evolutionary adjustments of existing mechanisms, might be quantifiable. However, fundamental, revolutionary "societal change"—the type of deep rifts that lay at the heart of the Camelot enterprise—were usually outbursts of unpredictable emotions and beliefs. In short, they were more like religious experiences than a rational development. As such, Tiryakian, Kenneth Boulding, and others argued that psychology, sociology, or perhaps biological models offered infinitely better predictive tools for tracking change.[37]

Anthropologist Marion Levy joined the attack on fundamental assumptions, claiming that behavioralists erroneously assumed that all societies were collections of unitary individuals. There was no such thing as a single self in a single world, Levy argued. In fact, his point of departure was not the individual, but kinship networks. He proposed that the family, rather than the individual, represented "the most general structural lead-in for the structural analysis of society, including highly modernized societies."[38]

Anatol Rapoport offered his own share of agnostic thoughts. The University of Michigan biologist and political sage argued that the search for a unified language of science, by quantification, psychology, or biological models, was counterproductive if not futile. As far as he was concerned, "the 'total' society is far too complex to be encompassed by a single set of concepts." In direct contradiction to the guiding theme of the conference, Rapoport advocated the development of "several paradigms at once in the hope that somewhere along the line, links can be established between conceptual systems and will reveal the underlying unity of something we call 'total society'."[39]

Rapoport's proposal for multiple strategies was presumably an effort to salvage some semblance of consensus from this abortive attempt to produce intellectual unity or at least compromise. Participants in this Camelot project had been chosen because they were interdisciplinarians. Yet, puzzled by the "complex nation-state," most fell back upon their narrow disciplinary specialties rather than on a unifying supertheory. The sociologists focused on social stratification; political scientists turned their attention to elites; the anthropologists and psychologists found comfort in familiar personality and national character studies. By 1967, when these studies were published, the interdependent links among these different analytical strategies remained as elusive as ever.[40]

Looking back on the tempestuous 1960s, MIT political scientist Lucien Pye explained that the diminishing hold of unifying paradigms resulted from the clash between political reality and academic theory. Pye, an expert on Asia who had been involved in Camelot and numerous other government-funded projects, singled out "the rising American frustration with Vietnam" and the manifest "decline in commitment to democratic institutions throughout the Third World" as the ostensible reason for disenchantment with behavioralism.[41] Unpredictable developments in Vietnam and the Third World challenged, in particular, modernization theory, the terse, discursive framework linking together the otherwise quite diversified body of academic experts who wore the badge of behavioral scientists. "What has happened to the theories of modernization and political development is precisely the swing from emphasizing essentials to detailing all the complexities," he explained.

Critiques of Modernization Theory

Throughout most of the 1950s, America's academic warriors espoused the belief of human progression from tradition-bound frameworks to a modernized end product. The entire Camelot enterprise was based on the assumption that modernization theory would contribute to "a general social systems model" for predicting and influencing politically significant aspects of social change in the developing nations of the world.[42] However, by the time of the Camelot debate, modernization theory was besieged by challenges to its theoretical assumptions and political implications.[43]

Doubtful scholars initiated the attack by questioning the dualistic division of the world into static traditional societies and "innovative" modernized states. Sociologist Joseph Gusfeld challenged the very definition of tradition, claiming that it was wrought with misconceptions. What struck uninformed American observers as unchanging static customs were, in actual fact, dynamic, ever-changing constructs, "shaped to present needs and aspirations in a given historical situation." Traditions, he argued, were invented; they were "justificatory" and dynamic narratives for grounding "present actions in some legitimating principle."[44]

Critics dismissed the modular mechanism of modernization theory as well. To begin with, they found nothing natural or beneficial in change itself. Based on the political experiences of developing nations, they challenged, as well, the assumption that changes in one sphere—industrialization, for example— would trigger eurythmic changes in social, political, and cultural spheres. Critics argued that the discipline of industrial life neither induced the automatic destruction of traditional social arrangements nor cultivated democracy. Modernization as a process had no cluster effect. In fact, political scientist Samuel Huntington argued, modernization occurred in a fragmented fashion and with unexpected, multidirectional political and social side effects. Each and all of the developing countries of the 1960s had adapted certain technological or organizational traits associated with modernity. However, attributes of modernization did not imply the inevitable acquisition of the entire 'package' of modernity. Selective modernization could conceivably strengthen traditional institutions and values, while social change in one sphere often served to inhibit change in others. Technological innovation, he explained, occasionally reinforced traditional values and even served the cause of the most reactionary of regimes.

> Modernization, in some degree, is a fact in Asia, Africa, Latin America: urbanization is rapid; literacy is slowly increasing; industrialization is being pushed; per capita gross national product is inching upward; mass media circulation is expanding; political participation is broadening. . . . In contrast, progress toward many of the other goals identified with political development—democracy, stability, structural differentiation, achievement patterns, national integration—often is dubious at best.[45]

The mustering of historical data served as the main device for undermining the integrity of modernization theory. Contrary to the reigning orthodoxy, the historically oriented scholars of the 1960s did not posit traditional societal arrangements as hostile to democracy and/or industrial growth.[46] Based on his historical analysis of industrial development in the West, sociologist Herbert Blumer argued that the process of "early industrialization" was "entirely neutral" in its social effect; it neither encouraged nor retarded social disorganization and political realignment.[47] Historical data undermined the notion of modernization as an evolutionary process as well. "One does not have to be a Marxist to accept the view that European development cannot be adequately described in evolutionary terms," sociologist Robert Rhodes observed. A cursory glance at history revealed that "development in the West was generally accompanied by revolution and civil war."[48]

Critical scholars invoked history to undermine the notion of underdevelopment as some sort of societal defect. Modernization theorists, they argued, denied the historical responsibility of the West for the underdevelopment of so-called traditional societies. Underdevelopment was not an evolutionary stage, and stagnation could not be blamed on psychological factors, child-rearing practices, motivations for achievement, or any other aspect of the individual or collective psyche. Underdevelopment was first and foremost the result of the stranglehold of colonialism, a situation in which indigenous trajectories of change and development were suppressed by the priorities of foreign colonial powers.[49] Modernization theory, critics stated, was, in actual fact, a political strategy masquerading as a scientific discovery.

As far as Camelot was concerned, such accusations were not far-fetched. Camelot's modernization partisans acknowledged their political preferences for existing political and social arrangements. During the course of his Camelot congressional testimony Harvard sociologist Alex Inkeles explained that his own work on modernization was aimed at bolstering the status quo rather than furthering the romantic quest for objective knowledge. His comparative study of modernization and the working class in six developing countries offered the ruling establishment in each of these countries a series of tools for avoiding any meaningful restructuring of society. His research was aimed primarily at providing "management or government" with the tools and knowledge for a materialistic pacification of the working class.

> What we are trying to do is to understand . . . the process whereby men have their attitudes and values changed in a direction that we call more modern. . . . For example, in order to distinguish between a man who is more open to experience and one who is much more backward and traditional, not an innovator, we ask the kind of question which can be reanalyzed for purposes of determining what may be the incentives important to the labor force. On that basis, if management or the government were considering making an investment in higher wages, on the one hand, or investing the same amount of capital in social services, on the other, they would be guided by the results of our research as to whether the workers would be more responsive to an increase in wages or would be more responsive to an increase in the social welfare benefits.[50]

The work of Inkeles and others, according to Robert Nisbett, illustrated that modernization theory was not only a politically conservative theory. The language and semantics employed by its academic partisans suggested that its scientific basis was flimsy, at best. The concepts of "growth," "development," and "progress"—the buzzwords of modernization theory—were hollow metaphors rather than scientific concepts. "No one has ever seen a civilization die, and it is unimaginable, short of cosmic disaster or thermonuclear holocaust, that anyone ever will. . . . We have seen none of these in culture: death, degeneration, development, birth." The use of such metaphors for describing societies, Nisbett explained, revealed much about the political and cultural biases of those who used such terms, and very little about the societies described by the metaphors.[51]

The metaphors of growth and development—the underpinnings of modernization theory—were scientifically invalid. "Metaphor," as an "iconic, encapsulating," yet often illusionary device for conveying ideas, was not the exclusive province of poets, writers, or the devout. Science, too, was affected by such unscientific discourse. Underneath the hard analysis that rigorous thought requires lay an illusory and dangerous reliance on romantic concepts of growth and decay. Referring to Westernization as growth or progress was, Nisbett reminded his colleagues, the very antithesis of value-free science. It assigned subjective value to change.

In addition to its flimsy scientific basis, Nisbett argued that modernization theory, as exemplified in Project Camelot, was inherently racist as well. He recalled the testimony of Theodore Vallence, the director of SORO (the Camelot funding agency) who, for the benefit of congressional committee members, reduced the meaning of modernization to a metaphor laden with thick cultural bias. Vallence related the anecdote of an American who, during the course of a visit to an African nation, had observed the seemingly pathetic demeanor of a group of Africans staring helplessly at an automobile with a flat tire; they had no idea how to handle this breakdown in technology. According to Vallence, only Americans who had moved beyond the stage of the "flat tire" could supply African nations with the necessary knowledge for dealing with political, cultural, and social equivalents of a deflated wheel.[52]

Such metaphors of Eurocentric progress led Third World academic critics—those who supposedly belonged to the same epistemic community as their American counterparts—to condemn modernization theory as a variation of Social Darwinism, as racially tainted as all previous explanations of Western superiority. Nigerian social scientist Ali Mazrui declared that differences between Social Darwinism and modernization theory—supposedly a theory with no racist connotations—were semantic rather than intrinsic. He argued that "Darwinian evolution . . . is evolution toward western ways," not much different from modernization theory as a developmental process bearing "the stamp of ethnocentric preference for a 'regime of representative institutions' of the Western kind." Marzui singled out for criticism the leading proponents of value-free science, including Talcott Parsons, Gabriel Almond, and James Coleman. According to Marzui, these major proponents of modernization theory were anything but practitioners of objective research; their work bore the stamp of deeply embedded ethnocentricity and an ultimate belief in the superiority of Western ways.

Stopping short of branding these eminent researchers as racists, Marzui acknowledged that the significant difference between modernization theory and Social Darwinism was that "in the modern theories of modernization, Darwinianism had been 'debiologized.'" Cultural determinism replaced biological determinism. "It is no longer racial bigotry that is being invoked to explain stages of political growth. What is now invoked is at the most ethnocentric pride." Nevertheless, the optimism that the world, through a process of modernization, would adapt the ways of the West had deep "ancestral roots in Darwinism, both biological and social."[53] Modernization theory, according to its critics, created a rigid political discourse in which all other divisions, other than the traditional-modern trajectory, could only be seen as dangerous and subverting some natural development.

Extensive disenchantment with modernization as dominant theory and the demise of Project Camelot as exemplary praxis were symptoms of a phenomenon far greater than this localized tempest suggests. Such shifting fortunes were indicative of radical changes in the role of science and scientist in America of the 1960s. The many subversive themes of the Camelot debate suggest that the behavioral sciences had reached the end of their journey from periphery to center with impeccably bad timing. By the time that the behavioral sciences had been accepted by their military sponsors as an "an indispensable tool," science—whether soft or hard, natural or behavioral—no longer enjoyed the privileged status of an intrinsically valuable cultural activity. Science in general and the behavioral sciences in particular appeared in the Camelot hearings as merely one other resource in the competitive ventures of American society, be they military, economic, or political.

In the Camelot hearings the supernarrative of behavioralism as an extension of the natural sciences appeared to self-destruct. The mixing of metaphors, at times mundane and political, at times grand and universal, signaled the type of existential confusion often associated with the end of an era. At best, Project Camelot was a collage of diverse worlds, rather than a formidable unitary vision. Sensing no inherent contradiction, the behavioral sciences offered both value-free "basic" science and immediate development of practical tools for the nation-state. Behavioral scientists endorsed skepticism as their guide, but, in the same breath, agreed not to challenge the status quo. Behavioral scientists claimed autonomy and adherence to an epistemic universal community of scientists, but accepted their role as academic warriors in the battle with the nation's Cold War adversaries.

In 1949, Bernard Brodie, one of America's most prominent academic warriors, had claimed that modern warfare without the imput of social and behavioral scientists was a doomed prospect. The captains of military affairs, he declared, lacked the intellectual tools to assess the changing nature of modern warfare. Only the academic warrior equipped with theory and insight could ensure victory in the wars of the future.[54]

By 1968, that bold vision of the academic expert as part and parcel of the management of modern warfare had lost much of its luster. The prime movers of the behavioral sciences lacked the convictions of scientific certainty and disciplinary cohesiveness that had characterized their guild in the previous decade. Fundamental assumptions concerning the nature of the scientific enterprise, the distinct divisions separating the humanities from the social and behavioral sciences, were, for the first time since the "founding" of the behavioral sciences, open to debate.

11.
Epilogue

Report from Iron Mountain

and Beyond

Sociologist Jessie Bernard's revelations on her role in the Iron Mountain Project dismayed her sympathetic biographer, Robert Bannister. Bernard's participation in this notorious analysis of the political dangers of world peace was, according to Bannister, an unfortunate blemish on her career. Nonetheless, Bannister added, Bernard had not succumbed to the project's sinister agenda; she had stood her high moral ground. When confronted by a reluctance to address the exclusionary implications of war and peace for women, she abruptly resigned, well before her chauvinistic collaborators had produced their disturbing assessment of the contribution of war to robust democratic societies.[1]

Bernard's confession was particularly intriguing because she had not participated in the Iron Mountain Project; in fact the study had never taken place. *Report from Iron Mountain* (1968), the alleged bootlegged copy of a government-sponsored seminar on the dangers of world peace, was the figment of the mischievous imagination of journalist Leonard Lewin. Written most prob-

ably in collaboration with John Kenneth Galbraith, and enjoying the cooperation of E. L. Doctorow, at the time editor-in-chief at Dial Press, Lewin used
the guise of a factual report to produce a parody of the culture of think tanks.
The unfortunate Robert Bannister had merely misread Jessie Bernard's
tongue-in-cheek review of the report.[2]

Bannister's gift of life to this fictitious event was not a unique occurrence.
Over the years, the Iron Mountain report has been quoted as if it had actually
transpired. Much to the discomfort of Lewin and his collaborators, *Report
from Iron Mountain* became a cult favorite among right wing militias, supposedly because it illustrated government duplicity.[3] But its longevity has not
been restricted to the fringes of American society. Well aware of its imaginative
origins, scholarly articles on the costs of national defense and the economic
ramifications of peace have accepted the report as a substantive source.[4]

The Iron Mountain Report

Report from Iron Mountain was supposedly the final paper of a clandestine
government-sponsored task force charged with identifying the domestic implications of a possible superpower reconciliation. Following two and a half years
of monthly meetings at the secret underground shelter of Iron Mountain "located near the town of Hudson," New York, the group issued the report that
was allegedly leaked to Lewin by an anonymous participant.

The central premise of the document, and the main reason for its public
prominence, was its description of war as a vital component of democratic
nations in general and the United States in particular. War, commonly held
as a temporary, pathological state of affairs, appeared in the report as a
lynchpin of the Western way of life. By contrast, the report asserted that peace
was socially destabilizing, economically unsettling, and politically dangerous.

Contrary to the "incorrect assumption that war, as an institution, is subordinate to the social system it is believed to serve," the Iron Mountain document
argued that "war itself is the basic social system." Using the affected jargon of
think-tankese, the document dismissed definitions of war as temporary, pathological, or serving some greater cause. War was the most stable and natural
state of affairs. "All other modes of social organization conflict or conspire"
with the maintaining of stability by war. Western democracies, such as the
United States, functioned under the guiding light of a "war system," without
which its basic institutions would collapse.

Among the many constructive functions of war, the report emphasized in
particular its crucial economic role. Defense spending was "an essential economic stabilizer" and neutralizer of the often harsh, invisible hand of the
marketplace. Removed from the erratic and destabilizing cycles of supply and
demand, military expenditures allowed governments to keep the economy on

an even keel. War production represented the "only critically large segment of the total economy that is subject to complete and arbitrary central control." Being "entirely outside the framework of supply and demand," socially responsible government could and had used defense expenditures to maintain prosperity and full employment in periods of economic slump, thereby maintaining the peace among its citizens. Thus, in the event of a peace process and the subsequent reduction of military funding, Western societies would have to find surrogates for economically wasteful but politically beneficial war expenditures.[5]

In addition to its economic functions, the report argued that the perpetual cloud of war provided crucial social ballast for unstable times. By gathering "the hostile, nihilistic, and potentially unsettling elements of society into its ranks, the national security state's martial institutions provided "antisocial elements with an acceptable role in the social structure." Military inductment and other forms of national service served as a "generational stabilizer" by allowing the "older generation to maintain control" over the volatile young. The military establishment as "the custodian of the "economically or culturally deprived" was, as well, "the forerunner of most contemporary civilian social-welfare programs, from the W.P.A. to various forms of 'socialized medicine' and social security."[6]

In an apparent jab at the work of prominent conflict theorist Lewis Coser, the report argued that conflict in general and war in particular fostered creativity. This fictitious document offered a correlation between "war-making potential" and the "cultural explosion" in the United States. Moreover, the most significant scientific advances were "at least indirectly initiated by an implicit requirement of weaponry." Among the milestones mentioned in the report were the assembly line (an outgrowth of the Civil War) the transistor radio, and advancements in medical technology.

By far the most important function of war was its provision of political stability. According to the functionalist logic of Iron Mountain's imaginary participants, war served as "the foundation for stable government;" and "the basis for general acceptance of the political process." War generated patriotism, fostered allegiance to the nation, and muffled domestic political strife. In sum, it provided essential mechanisms for maintaining the Western version of the nation-state. In lieu of a real and immediate enemy, "threats against the 'national interest' are usually created" in order to perpetuate the stabilizing effect of a war-oriented society. Without the threatening presence of enemies a centralized government could claim only temporary and tenuous legitimacy. With the disappearance of a common and formidable adversary, the report envisioned an American society of chaotic, fragmented, and mutually incompatible loyalties superseding a broad, all-encompassing national identity. "The historical record reveals one instance after another where the failure of a regime to maintain the credibility of a war threat led to its dissolution, by forces of private interest, of reactions to social injustice, or other disintegrative elements." Allegiance to the nation-state hinged upon "a cause" and "a cause requires an enemy."[7]

In the unlikely and apparently undesirable event of world peace, the report urged, therefore, the creation of surrogates for the cohesive bonds of war. The absence of actual enemies entailed the invention of alternative "external menaces," human or otherwise. Domestic stability hinged upon the semblance of existential threats. In assessing how best to prepare, at least hypothetically, for peace, the report noted, "we must first reply, as strongly as we can, that the war system cannot responsibly be allowed to disappear until 1) We know exactly what it is we plan to put in its place, and 2) We are certain, beyond reasonable doubt, that these substitute institutions will serve their purposes in terms of the survival and stability of society."[8]

The main substitutes for an external threat, according to the report, would most likely be "fictitious alternate enemies," such as extraterrestrials or large-scale environmental threats. These surrogate threats raised little enthusiasm among Iron Mountain's imaginary participants, as they lacked the social and political resonance of an authentic war. The war on poverty or environmental campaigns—the possible alternatives for war expenditures—would always suffer from politically motivated fiscal constraints. Even imaginary space invaders could never compete with an immediate, human enemy.

The Iron Mountain Debate

Report from Iron Mountain elicited a contentious exchange between sympathetic reviewers and ruffled detractors. Critical reviewers, most often members of think tanks smarting from their portrayal as intellectual and moral cretins, used literary criticism and personal insults in their defense. A chagrined Herman Kahn dismissed the report as "very bad satire," while Henry Kissinger diagnosed the author as "an idiot."[9] Henry Rowen, president of the Rand Corporation declared that the report's assessments of the social benefits of a war economy, and the political necessity for subterfuges for an external enemy were not "ludicrous versions of serious views; they are merely ludicrous." Perhaps forgetting that he was critiquing a farce, Rowan faulted the report for ignoring Thomas Schelling's work on disarmament and other genuine products of Rand and its clones.

Other critics focused upon the document's claims of authenticity, scouring the report in search of inconsistencies, mistakes, and logical caveats. University of St. Louis economist Murray Weidenbaum painstakingly enumerated factual errors, calling attention to "real" sources of information, namely, government publications that belied most of Iron Mountain's assumptions. In discrediting the report's claim that the Johnson administration had escalated

American involvement in Vietnam to curb rising unemployment, Weidenbaum offered data from "authentic" sources. Government reports and statistics, he stated, proved that unemployment rates were falling prior to the massive American buildup in Vietnam.

It was, however, the report's masquerading of fantasy as an authentic document that angered Weidenbaum in particular. "Until now the debates have
centered on different interpretations of a common factual basis." *Report from
Iron Mountain* had altered this state of affairs. "We are now reduced to the
lower-level chore of cleaning up Lewin's literary litter before it pollutes the
intellectual environment," Weidenbaum complained. The fictional, yet con-
vincingly conspirational tone of the report defamed think tank practitioners.
Its rhetorical strategy reminded a melodramatic Weidenbaum of *The Protocols
of the Elders of Zion* in its maligning of innocents "by distortion, innuendo,
and half-truths."[10] A somewhat less hyperbolic Herbert Gans agreed that
"the report has created its own external menace; by attacking the social scientists who carry out war research, it diverts attention from the war system that
hires them."[11]

Sympathetic reviewers responded that critical tests of authenticity were beside the point. "Whether this book is a hoax or not is irrelevant," a typical
review noted. "What is important is the fact . . . that it reflects a particular
style of thinking."[12] The significance of the report, sociologist Irving Louis
Horowitz argued, "hinges not on its authenticity, but rather on how far the
blueprints outlined have already been, or are in the process of being, opera-
tionalized."[13] The insistence on a clear distinction between reality and fantasy
was trivial. The contribution of *Report from Iron Mountain* resided in its exposure of the metanarrative of government-funded science. the report had managed to reproduce the aura of the think tank, and expose how logic, when
unchecked by morals, might lead to maniacal options.[14]

Citing the work of nuclear strategist Herman Kahn, where reality and fantasy coalesced into a computerized morass of doomsday scenarios, favorable
reviewers of the report argued that its surrealistic tone was a facsimile of such
logic. Anatol Rapoport reminded his readers that when Herman Kahn's notorious *On Thermonuclear War* was first published, "the late James R. Newman
refused to believe in its authenticity. Now we know better."[15] In other words,
the report was what Jean Baudrillad has called in another context, a "simulacrum," an identical copy without an original. It contained very little that
stretched credulity and it was saturated with authentic intellectual trappings
of think tank culture.

As a simulacrum of the behavioral tradition, the report reproduced pseudo-
authentic psychocultural statements. Violence, for example, appeared as a
constant, unchangeable component of human nature; it could only be "displaced," not eradicated. Citing a series of studies supposedly demonstrating

the existence of warlike instincts among all animals, including human beings, Iron Mountain could claim that consistent recourse to violence was not an aberration but an essential component of routine human conduct.[16] The inventors of Iron Mountain had perhaps erred in choosing studies dismissed by most behavioral scientists as popular and unscientific.[17] Yet, models claiming biologically based aggressive behavior were very much part of the contemporary behavioral discourse.[18] Much like the Neo-Freudian founders of the behavioral sciences, the report's authors stressed the perpetual struggle between biological impulses—in this case, violence prone behavior—and the limited ability of human beings to control these instincts. In accordance with contemporary behavioral discourse the report dismissed futile attempts to change the violent nature of human beings and advocated, instead, the channeling of warlike violent behavior into constructive areas.

Much like their real-life colleagues, the virtual authors of the report affected the role of guardians of the existing social order. There was nothing original or even satirical in the assertion that the survival of the state legitimized an unscrupulous conduct that would be considered immoral among mortals. Duplicity, coercion, and predatory policies were all acceptable weapons of defense intellectuals. *Iron Mountain*'s advocacy of the stabilizing and essential role of war was, as well, far from original. The nation's academic warriors routinely analyzed the "function" of violence—internal or external—as "necessary and useful in preserving national societies."[19] As early as 1959, and upon the unlikely stage of the *Journal of Conflict Resolution*, a prominent behavioralist observed nonchalantly that "war is not a social problem!" Instead, he argued that war was "*a social institution* . . . compatible with the prevailing theory of social order in the West."[20]

The report's assessment of the political benefits of war expenditures in democracies was not imaginative farce, either. Hans Speier, the founding father of Rand's social science division, appears to have been the source of inspiration. In his well-received *Social Order and the Risks of War* (1952), Speier had depicted a scenario in which the economic conditions of a hypothetical state deteriorate, ensuing unemployment causes mass unrest, scapegoats are found in some external enemy, real or imagined, and workers accept or even demand war in order to get back to work. "Since armament creates employment," Speier theorized, "it can be presented and popularized . . . as an effective measure against unemployment."[21]

Central to the report's production of a simulacrum was its reliance on mainstream functionalism as a diviner of human development. Much like their real academic colleagues, the report's virtual authors assumed that the main contribution of social and behavioral theory was maintaining order and stability; social justice was not theirs to ponder. The central axis of the study was to devise strategies for containing primitive instincts, and diverting them toward the ultimate goal of maintaining the existing social order. The very existence of violent norms implied that they were indispensable. Their removal, according to the report, would lead to social unrest and upheaval.

The Dissenting Academy

By the mid-1960s, this netherworld of the national security state confronted formidable questioning of its origins, motives, and theories. For growing numbers of critics, the warfare state appeared to be an aberration, an erroneous and dangerous response to a poorly defined external threat. The conflation of the internal and external roots of national security suggested that America's wars would cease only if that society would undergo fundamental changes. "There are two governments in the United States today," journalists David Wise and Thomas Ross argued in their popular deconstruction of the national security state. "The first is the government that citizens read about in their newspapers and children study about in their civics books. The second is the interlocking, hidden machinery that carries out the policies of the United States in the Cold War."[22] Behind such conspirational accusations lay an ironic subversion of an enduring and powerful myth. Originally, in the early 1950s, "the invisible government" had "referred to a small group of highly placed traitors . . . secreted within the government to assist a future Communist takeover." By contrast, the late 1960s version of the invisible government referred to the republic's patriotic leaders rather than the enemy, "and it held out the frightening prospect of turning the government into something akin to an enemy entity."[23]

The blurring of distinctions between good and evil, foreign and domestic, enemy and ally, reflected acute instability in the nation's collective concepts of self. Such fusionist gestures produced harsh and widespread criticism of the nation's opinion leaders—including the intellectuals and academic agents who had aided and abetted the invisible government's spread of rumors of an enemy.

The nation's academic warriors were lambasted for their pernicious conservatism, their distrust of popular democracy, and their avoidance of vital political reform. Critics found the dominant academic discourse all the more threatening because its conservatism was implicit and, therefore, deliberately difficult to decipher. Rather than overtly condemning change or popular sovereignty, the nation's mobilized academics argued that change "must come gradually, through established institutions and in a manner acceptable to the political elite."[24] The academic establishment, according to its detractors, held a partisan belief in a "national interest" which rises above "politics." In other words, they accepted existing political and social arrangements as natural. As for the universalistic tendencies of the behavioral and social sciences, critics argued that these practitioners of knowledge merely assumed and hoped, rather than proved, that their questionable findings on American behavioral patterns were universally applicable. "We simply regard foreign nationals as 'underdeveloped Americans'," anthropologist Edward Hall complained.[25]

Frontal attacks on the behavioral sciences as a particularly harsh instance of collaboration with the military-intellectual complex commenced with the deconstruction of its methodology. Critics accused behavioralists of selecting topics according to criteria determined by quantitative strategies rather than intellectual significance. Whether the subject matter could be examined by quantification appeared to override all other criteria for selection. Writing in the discipline's flagship, *Public Opinion Quarterly*, a repentant behavioralist acknowledged that "a considerable proportion of the literature commonly classified under the heading of 'political behavior' has no real bearing on politics." Much of the subject matter, he confessed, was chosen because it was "amenable to quantification."[26] The obsession with quantification was derived, in part, from a fatal attraction to the physical sciences, in particular, the simplistic belief that the key to deciphering the human condition lay in imitating "the models, postulates, and methods of physical science."[27] As prisoners of this reductionist concept of science, behavioralists disregarded topics that could not be reduced to mathematical equations. Failing to address many of the complex, nonquantifiable issues of contemporary society, the behavioralist creed "often seems trivial, narrow," and disingenuously apolitical.

The ostensibly apolitical nature of behavioralism was, skeptical observers claimed, a thinly disguised sign of a harsh political vision. Behind the claims of value-free science and the focus on methodology rather than normative values lay an intellectually rigid acceptance of the political order. The behavioralist assumption that the social world shared many of the properties of the physical world was, according to critics, first and foremost a political statement. Much like natural and physical scientists, who sought to uncover regularities within a well−defined natural microcosm, behavioralists espoused "the fixity" of political, social, and behavioral arrangements and limited themselves to the study of "behavior within the limits fixed by these structures."[28] Behavioralists described deviances from balanced political arrangements—by which they invariably meant the contemporary American system—as temporary "imbalances" or pathologies rather than social or political correctives to existing inequities. Thus, the behavioral sciences were reduced to offering advice on the social control of deviance. The development of new social arrangements or modifications of existing social relations were not part of their agenda. "What is good is what is static."

What accounted for such intellectual partisanship? Political scientist Maure Goldschmidt speculated that academia's acceptance of the values of contemporary power wielders was linked to the declining alienation of American intellectuals, the result of increased employment opportunities in university and government-funded research institutes. Goldschmidt claimed that the prestige of academics "as consultants and advisors has confirmed their sense of well-being" and the demand for their services "has satisfied a very human craving for influence and power."[29]

With typical rhetorical flourish, political scientist Samuel Huntington acknowledged that behavioral and social scientists were the ideological soulmates rather than the mercenary agents of their clients; they were the articulators and agents of a new national ethic rather than the complicit collaborators with a partisan political agenda. The traditional capitalist-liberal creed of the United States, Huntington stated, was an inadequate and obsolete solution for contemporary domestic and foreign challenges. In fact, he argued that the classic individualism of the American political tradition represented the "greatest domestic threat to American military security." Consequently, Huntington stated, the nation's academic establishment had a civic duty to create a new political order in which national concerns would eclipse, control, and domesticate the former excesses of democracy, American style. As an illustration of the new political ethic that he and other defense intellectuals supported, Huntington contrasted the garishness of Main Street—the reflection of outmoded political values—with the purpose and order of a modern military base.

> Just south of the United States military academy at West Point is the village of Highland Falls. Main street at Highland Falls is [the] familiar . . . tiresome monotony of and the incredible variety and discordancy of small-town commercialism. The buildings form no part of a whole; they are simply a motley, disconnected collection of frames coincidently adjoining each other, lacking common unity or purpose. On the military reservation the other side of South Gate, however, exists a different world. There is ordered serenity. The parts do not exist on their own, but accept their subordination to the whole. . . . The post is suffused with the rhythm and harmony which comes when collective will supplants individual whim. . . . West Point is a community of structured purpose, one in which the behavior of men is governed by a code.[30]

This search for order was part of an ethic that was only partly the result of external threats. Political mobilization and employment in government-funded military-intellectual enterprises exposed the domestic political underpinnings of America's preeminent knowledge seekers. Behind the stance of methodological objectivity lurked what Philip Green described as "another persona of the scientist—the would-be policy maker who . . . manipulates his esoteric knowledge" to foist his partisan views upon the general public. Professions of value-free inquiry had the illusory effect of suggesting that the sciences were concerned with refining tools for objective research rather than establishing a particular political vision. In actual fact, Green argued, the facade of objectivity was a tool for fitting essentially political questions into "the strait jacket of so-called scientific analysis." The "separation of 'analytical' components of a policy problem from political and moral ones" was at, best, misleading.[31] Moreover, Green complained, the attribution of expertise to an intellectual elite whose main credentials were ideological rather than scientific effectively blocked their adversaries from gaining access to prestigious journals, academic appointments, and positions of power within the government-academic nexus. A supposedly scientific set of criteria was in effect a test of political acceptability.

Closure

The probing of behavioralism and its intellectual kin had spilled over into the public arena due to the exposure of political priorities in the production of knowledge. The subversion of behavioralism was not simply the result of new theoretical advances or evidence that had rendered existing scientific knowledge obsolete. It was, rather, that fundamental definitions of the academic persuasion were being called into question. The broad dimensions of this debate were the result of what Bill Readings has described in another context as the decline of the national cultural mission that was once the "raison d'être" of American academia.

By the mid-1960s academic culture had parted ways with its traditional role "as producer, protector, and inculcator of an idea of national culture."[32] The very notion of academia as legitimizing the nation-state had reached a turning point. No longer were the virtues of the nation's political establishment uncontestable ground. Hence, the academic establishment, as a primary prop of existing political arrangements, was open to attack.

Disenchantment with the nation-state voided the prestige of its primary academic agents. The demolishing of their transparent ideology, methodological pretensions, and political undertones became possible because of what Jean-François Lyotard described as a growing "incredulity toward metanarratives." By the mid-1960s academia reacted with skepticism toward hitherto cherished narratives that had so effectively excluded other voices in the name of illusory shared principles, unified methodology, and homogenizing goals.[33] There was little patience for a discourse on value-free science of any sort, physical, natural, or behavioral.[34]

Looking back on the halcyon days of a privileged academia, a chastened Margaret Mead explained that the road to this now-tarnished academic-intellectual confluence had been paved with honorable intentions. Appearing before a congressional hearing on the "Psychological Aspects of Foreign Policy," Mead offered a series of historical explanations for the once promising relationship between government and the behavioral and social sciences. In the anti-intellectual climate of the post–World War II years, the performance of controversial and politically sensitive social inquiry had elicited unwarranted political scrutiny, she explained. Fearing harassment by petty politicians, an overzealous FBI, and a paranoid public, the nation's social and behavioral scientists had cowered under the "umbrella of military protection." Protected by the secrecy of defense-related think tanks, behavioralists and their academic allies were able to produce substantive and critical investigations of American society.[35]

Mead acknowledged that protection from political censorship was not the only reason for maintaining ties with the military establishment. She confided that there had been ideological reasons for such institutional commitments. The nation's knowledge producers and the country's political elite had espoused the same value system. Focusing in particular on the behavioralist creed, Mead acknowledged that this paradigm had been governed by an implicit belief in a pluralistic, yet unified and stable American body politic. Under the auspices of what appeared to be an uncontestable national creed, behavioralists had been "deeply committed to putting their skills at the disposal of the federal government."[36] In the United States of the 1950s, she claimed, the values of the American polity and academia were indistinguishable.

In 1969, as she struggled to come to terms with increasing criticism of the government-academic nexus, Mead admitted that the symbiotic relationship with government had tarnished the nation's knowledge seekers. Government sponsorship had, indeed, allowed researchers great freedom to deal with the delicate issues of race and the attractions of competing social systems. However, accepting the role of academic custodians of the nation had led to a crippling self-censorship. As guardians of the status quo, the nation's mobilized academics had imposed voluntary restrictions on the type of questions that they could or were able to pose. When faced with the fragmentation of the 1960s, a politically and intellectually besieged academia lacked both the public approval and the appropriate conceptual tools for addressing the national crisis.

By 1969, when Mead delivered her testimony, the extent of these limitations was painfully obvious. "The association of the behavioral scientist with military sponsorship in a period of national disgruntlement with the Vietnam War" and a host of other public grievances had undermined the image of the scientist as an honest broker and dispassionate seeker of knowledge. Given their bonds with a much-maligned military establishment, the nation's academics could no longer rely on public perceptions that their actions were without personal or partisan considerations.

From the vantage point of hindsight Mead mused that, perhaps, the nation's mobilized scholars should have returned to their university campuses in the aftermath of World War II and established themselves as self-sufficient, critical intellectuals. Referring to the restrictive horizons of the sciences during the Cold War years, Mead acknowledged that "our quiver was empty. We had shot all the arrows we had and the few we had not."[37] It was time, she declared in 1969, to make up for lost time, sever the dependency on government-related projects, and return to the ivory tower. Seeking closure, Mead anticipated the immanent resurrection of academic authority based on the formation of clear boundaries separating the domains of theoretical knowledge from the world of politics and policy. Some thirty years later, we still wait for that moment.

Notes

Introduction

1. My understanding of rumor is derived from the classic study by Tamotsu Shibutani, *Improvised News: A Sociological Study of Rumor* (Indianapolis, 1966).

2. H. Bruce Franklin, *War Stars: The Superweapon and the American Imagination* (New York, 1988).

3. Shibutani, *Improvised News*, 108.

4. Ibid., 155.

5. Ibid., 499.

6. Rebecca Lowen, *Creating the Cold War University: The Transformation of Stanford* (Berkeley, Calif., 1997), 1.

7. Eva Etzioni-Halevy, *The Knowledge Elite and the Failure of Prophecy* (London, 1985), provides a succinct description of this fatal conflation of theory and policy.

8. Ellen Herman, *The Romance of American Psychology: Political Culture in the Age of Experts* (Berkeley, Calif., 1995). Herman defines the behavioral sciences in two footnotes: p. 319 n.5; p. 349, n.29.

9. Anatol Rapoport, "Critique of Strategic Thinking," in Roger Fisher (ed.), *International Conflict and Behavioral Science* (New York, 1964), 234.

10. Gabriel Weimann, "The Theater of Terror: Effects of Press Coverage," *Journal of Communication* 33 (1983): 33–45. Weimann accords authorship of the term to Brian Jenkins of the Rand Corporation.

11. For some recent examples, see Fred Kaplan, *The Wizards of Armageddon* (Stanford, Calif., 1991); John Baylis and John Garnett (eds.), *Makers of Nuclear Strategy* (London, 1991); Stuart Leslie, *The Cold War and American Science: The Military-Industrial-Academic Complex at MIT and Stanford* (New York, 1993).

12. This felicitous phrase belongs to Richard Barnet, *Roots of War* (New York, 1972).

13. For a historiographical introduction to this often forgotten war, see Rosemary Foot, "Making Known the Unknown War: Policy Analysis of the Korean Conflict Since the Early 1980s," in Michael Hogan (ed.), *America in the World: The Historiography of American Foreign Relations Since 1941* (Cambridge, Mass., 1995), 270–99.

14. Thomas Kuhn, *The Structure of Scientific Revolutions* (Chicago, 1962).

15. See Gary Gutting (ed.), *Paradigms and Revolutions; Appraisals and Applications of Thomas Kuhn's Philosophy of Science* (Notre Dame, Ind., 1980), for a comprehensive survey of the application of paradigms in a wide array of academic fields.

16. Kuhn, *Structure*, x.

17. Ibid., 19.

Chapter 1

1. For comprehensive, retrospective reflections on TAS, see Robin Williams, "The American Soldier, an Assessment, Several Wars Later," *Public Opinion Quarterly* 53 (1989): 155–74, as well as the collection of articles entitled "The American Soldier and Social Psychology," *Social Psychology Quarterly* 47 (June 1984): 184–13.

2. Ethel Shanas, "Review of TAS," *American Journal of Sociology* 55 (November 1949): 590–94.

3. Nathan Glazer, " 'The American Soldier' as Science: Can Sociology Fulfil its Ambitions?" *Commentary* 8 (1949): 491.

4. Arthur Schlesinger Jr., "The Statistical Soldier," *Partisan Review* 16 (1949): 852–56.

5. John Riley, "Review of 'TAS'," *American Sociological Review* 14 (1949): 557–59; Paul Lazarsfeld, "The American Soldier: An Expository Review," *Public Opinion Quarterly* 13 (Fall 1949): 377–404.

6. Hana Selvin, "Methods of Survey Analysis," in David Shils (ed.), *International Encyclopedia of the Social Sciences*, vol. 15 (New York, 1968), 411–18; Robin Williams, "Sociology in America: The Experiences of Two Centuries," *Social Science Quarterly* 57 (June 1976): 77–111.

7. Riley, "Review"; Lazarsfeld, " 'The American Soldier.' "

8. Daniel Lerner, "The 'American Soldier' and the Public," in Robert Merton and Paul Lazarsfeld (eds.), *Continuities in Social Research: Studies in the Scope of and Method of the American Soldier* (Glencoe, Ill., 1950), 212–47.

9. Robin Williams, "The American Soldier: An Assessment, Several Wars Later," *Public Opinion Quarterly* 53 (1989): 155–73.

10. TAS, vol. 1, 250–58, 550–66; Glazer, "The American Soldier as Science," 493; Robert Merton and Alice Kitt, "Contributions to the Theory of Reference Group Behavior," in Merton and Lazarsfeld, *Continuities in Social Research*; Robin Williams, "Relative Deprivation," in Lewis Coser (ed.), *The Idea of Social Structure: Papers in Honor of Robert K. Merton* (New York, 1975), 355–73.

11. Williams, " 'The American Soldier,' " 167.

12. For an analysis of the generational-intellectual nexus in American social sciences, see Henrika Kuklick, "A 'Scientific Revolution': Sociological Theory in the United States, 1930–1945," *Sociological Inquiry* 43 (1973): 3–22; William Sewell, "Some Reflections on the Golden Age of Interdisciplinary Social Psychology," *Annual Review of Sociology* 15 (1989): 1–16.

13. Robert Dahl, "The Behavioral Approach in Political Science: Epitaph for a Monument to a Successful Protest," in Heinz Eulau (ed.), *Behavioralism in Political Science* (New York, 1969), 71.

14. M. Brewster Smith, "The American Soldier and Its Critics: What Survives the Attack on Positivism?" *Social Psychology Quarterly* 47 (June 1984): 192–97.

15. For an excellent discussion of general trends in the social and behavioral sciences during World War II and the Cold War, see Ellen Herman, *The Romance of American Psychology: Political Culture in the Age of Experts* (Berkeley, Calif., 1995), chapters 4–6.

16. Robert Bannister, *Sociology and Scientism: The American Quest for Objectivity, 1880–1940* (Chapel Hill, N.C., 1987), 6.

17. On the formation of epistemic communities, see the excellent special edition of *International Organization* 46 (Winter 1992).

18. David Hollinger, "Science as a Weapon in Kulturkampfe in the United States During World War II," *ISIS* 86 (1995): 440–54.

19. My definition of the behavioral sciences is derived in large part from congressional hearings. It was during the course of such hearings that the field's major practitioners provided patient and elaborate definitions of their calling. See in particular U.S. House of Representatives, Committee on Foreign Affairs, Subcommittee on International Organizations and Movements, "Behavioral Sciences and the National Security," Report No. 4, Together with Part IX of the Hearings on "Winning the Cold War: The U.S. Ideological Offensive," July–August 1965, 89th Cong., 2nd sess., H.R. Report 1224; U.S. Senate, Committee on Government Operations, Subcommittee on Government Research, Hearings on "Federal Support of International Social Science and Behavioral Research," June–July 1966, 89th Cong., 2nd sess.

20. Testimony of Carl Pfaffmann in "Hearings on Federal Support of International Social Science and Behavioral Research," 120.

21. For early forays into universalist social and behavioral theory, see the classic study by Talcott Parsons, *The Structure of Social Action* (Glencoe, Ill., 1949).

22. See the various disciplinary treatises in Bernard Berelson (ed.), *The Behavioral Sciences Today* (New York, 1963).

23. Ibid., 3.

24. James Charlesworth, "Foreword," in James Charlesworth (ed.), *The Limits of Behavioralism in Political Science* (Philadelphia, 1965), iv.

25. Harvard University, *The Behavioral Sciences at Harvard* (Cambridge, Mass., 1954); University of Chicago Behavioral Sciences Self-Study Committee, *Report on the Behavioral Sciences at the University of Chicago* (Chicago, 1954).

26. Edward Wilson, *Consilience: The Unity of Knowledge* (New York, 1998).

27. Such fusionist gestures were not limited to behavioralists. The postwar years saw numerous unification initiatives aimed at purging " 'superfluous' metaphysics and replacing it with a clarity, precision, and empiricism for which science provided the template." Peter Galison's history of the Unity of Science Movement documents the attempts by Harvard and MIT physicists to unify the scientific enterprise not by creating a "pyramid of knowledge" with physics on the top, but instead, by producing a "coordinated encyclopedia," a heterogeneous enterprise associated with as many branches of science as possible. See Peter Galison, "The Americanization of Unity," *Daedalus* 127 (Winter 1998): 45.

28. Robert Merton and Daniel Lerner, "Social Scientists and Research Policy," in Daniel Lerner and Harold Lasswell (eds.), *The Policy Sciences: Recent Developments in Scope and Method* (Stanford, Calif., 1951), 284.

29. James Miller, "Toward a General Theory of the Behavioral Sciences," in Leonard White (ed.), *The State of the Social Sciences* (Chicago, 1956), 29–65.

30. An almost identical description of the founding of the behavioral sciences appears in all historical descriptions of the field. See, for example, Bernard Berelson, "Introduction to the Behavioral Sciences," in Berelson, *The Behavioral Sciences Today*, 1–11; David Easton, *A Framework for Political Analysis* (Englewood Cliffs, N.J., 1965), 12–13.

31. David Thelen, "Memory and American History," *Journal of American History* 75 (March 1989): 1117–29.

32. Miller, "Toward a General Theory."

33. John Dewey and Arthur Bentley, *Knowing and the Known* (Boston, 1949), 65.

34. Ford Foundation, *Annual Report for 1953* (New York, 1953), 64.

35. Sam Bass Warner, *The Private City: Philadelphia in Three Periods of Its Growth* (Philadelphia, 1968).

36. Michael Latham, "Ideology, Social Science, and Destiny: Modernization and the Kennedy-Era Alliance for Progress," *Diplomatic History* 22 (Spring 1998): 203.

37. Dean Tipps, "Modernization Theory and the Comparative Study of Societies: A Critical Perspective," *Comparative Studies in Society and History* 15 (March, 1973): 199–226.

38. For concise explanations of modernization theory, see Daniel Lerner, "Modernization: Social Aspects," in *International Encyclopedia of the Social Sciences*, vol. 9 (New York, 1968), 386–94; James Coleman, "Modernization: Political Aspects," ibid., 395–402; Ronald Dore, "The Bourgeoisie in Modernizing Societies," ibid., 402–9; Michael Haas, *Polity and Society: Philosophical Underpinnings of Social Science Paradigms* (New York, 1992), 13–57.

39. Seymour Martin Lipset, *The First New Nation: The United States in Historical and Comparative Perspective* (New York, 1963).

40. Edward Shils, *Political Development in the New States* (The Hague, 1965), 10.

41. For an elaboration on the theme of modernization and diffusion, see the important study: Everett Rogers, *Diffusion of Innovations* (Glencoe, Ill., 1962).

42. David McClelland, "The Impulse to Modernization," in Myron Weiner (ed.), *Modernization: The Dynamics of Growth* (New York, 1961), 17; idem, "The Achievement Motive in Economic Growth," in Bert Hoselitz and Wilbert Moore (eds.), *Industrialization and Society* (The Hague, 1963), 74–96.

43. McClelland, "The Achievement Motive."

44. Alex Inkeles and David Smith, *Becoming Modern: Individual Change in Six Developing Countries* (Cambridge, Mass., 1974). See also Leonard Doob, *Becoming More Civilized* (New Haven, 1960).

45. On the political reception of modernization theory, see Latham, "Ideology, Social Science, and Destiny."

46. Robert Rhodes, "The Disguised Conservatism in Evolutionary Development Theory," *Science and Society* 32 (Fall 1968): 385.

47. Carl Pletsch, "The Three Worlds, or the Division of Social Scientific

Labor, circa 1950–1975," *Comparative Studies in Society and History* 23(October, 1981): 577.

48. See, for example, Pitirim Sorokin, "Mutual Convergence of the United States and the U.S.S.R. to the Mixed Sociocultural Type," *International Journal of Comparative Sociology* 1 (1960): 143–76; Marion Levy, *Modernization and the Structure of Societies* vol. 2 (Princeton, 1966), 709.

49. Ruml cited in Franz Samelson, "Organizing for the Kingdom of Behavior: Academic Battles and Organizational Policies in the Twenties," *Journal of the History of the Behavioral Sciences* 21 (January 1985): 39.

50. Among the many works on the social sciences at the University of Chicago, see Dennis Smith, *The Chicago School: A Liberal Critique of Capitalism* (London, 1988); Martin Bulmer, *The Chicago School of Sociology: Institutionalization, Diversity, and the Rise of Sociological Research* (Chicago, 1984).

51. Roger Geiger, *Research and Relevant Knowledge: American Research Universities Since World War II* (New York, 1993), 93.

52. Gene Lyons, *The Uneasy Partnership: Social Science and the Federal Government in the Twentieth Century* (New York, 1969); Samuel Klausner and Victor Lidz (eds.), *The Nationalization of the Social Sciences* (Philadelphia, 1986).

53. See, for example, Edward H. Berman, *The Ideology of Philanthropy: The Influence of the Carnegie, Ford, and Rockefeller Foundations on American Foreign Policy* (New York, 1983); Roger Geiger, "American Foundations and Academic Social Science, 1945–1960," *Minerva* 26:3 (Autumn 1988): 315–41; Donald Fisher, "The Role of Philanthropic Foundations in the Reproduction and Production of Hegemony: Rockefeller Foundations and the Social Sciences," *Sociology* 17 (May 1983): 206–33. For a dissenting opinion, see Martin Bulmer, "Philanthropic Foundations and the Development of the Social Sciences in the Early Twentieth Century," *Sociology* 18 (November 1984): 572–79.

54. Alvin Gouldner, *The Coming Crisis of Western Sociology* (New York, 1971), 188–96.

55. Dorothy Ross, *The Origins of American Social Science* (New York, 1991), 400.

56. Bulmer, "Philanthropic Foundations."

57. Geiger, *Research and Relevant Knowledge*, 101.

58. This explanation is partly belied by Ford's continuing financial support for behavioral sciences projects. Even after the division's expiration, the behavioral sciences continued to enjoy funding issued under different headings and through grants to individual researchers who supported the behavioralist persuasion. See Ford Foundation *Annual Report, October 1, 1956 to September 30, 1957* (New York, 1957) 15, 78–87.

59. Congressional hearings cited in Lyons, *The Uneasy Partnership*, 278. The memoirs of the division's director, Bernard Berelson, do, indeed, acknowledge that the division was terminated in partial response to political pressures. Berelson recalled that many of the trustees of the Ford Foundation were wary of the political credentials of behavioralists. He offered as an example the scuttling of funding for a new edition of the *Encyclopedia of the Behavioral Sciences*. The foundation's trustees feared that some of the prospective contributors might have supported communist causes in the past, thereby jeopardizing the reputation of the foundations.

60. Geiger, "American Foundations and Academic Social Science," 318.

Chapter 2

1. Thomas Schelling, "Models of Segregation," *American Economic Review* 59 (1969): 488–93; "Dynamic Models of Segregation," *Journal of Mathematical Sociology* 1 (1971): 143–86; "What is the Business of Organized Crime?" *American Scholar* 40 (1971): 643–52; *Micromotives and Macrobehavior* (New York, 1978).

2. Morris Janowitz, "Remarks," in William Lybrand (ed.), "Symposium Proceedings: The U.S. Army's Limited-War Mission and Social Science Research"(Washington, D.C., SORO, 1962), 147.

3. Schelling, "What is the Business of Organized Crime?"

4. Schelling, "Models of Segregation"; "Dynamic Models of Segregation."

5. Philip Green, "Science, Government and the Case of Rand: A Singular Pluralism," *World Politics* 2 (January 1968): 321.

6. Bruce L. Smith, *The Rand Corporation: Case Study of a Nonprofit Advisory Corporation* (Cambridge, Mass., 1966), 315.

7. Green, "Science, Government, and the Case of Rand," 317.

8. JCS, "Review of the Current World Situation and Ability of the Forces Being Maintained to Meet United States Commitments," *Foreign Relations of the United States, 1951* (hereafter: *FRUS*), vol. 1 (Washington, D.C., 1979), 61–75.

9. Ibid., 62, 70.

10. For the Cold War as a crisis in historical reasoning, see Frank Ninkovich, *Modernity and Power: A History of the Domino Theory in the Twentieth Century* (Chicago, 1994), in particular, 186–202.

11. On this issue, see Samuel Klausner and Victor Lidz (eds.), *The Nationalization of the Social Sciences* (Philadelphia, 1986).

12. Henry Loomis/Psychological Strategy Board (hereafter: PSB), "Report on Social Science Research in Cold War Operations" (April 1952), Harry S. Truman Papers (hereafter: HST), PSB files, box 1.

13. Presidential Directive in *FRUS, 1951*, vol. 1, 58–59. For a historical analysis of PSB, see Scott Lucas, "The Psychological Strategy Board and American Ideology, 1951–1953," *International History Review* 18 (February 1996): 279–302.

14. Edward P. Lilly, "The Psychological Strategy Board and its Predecessors: Foreign Policy Coordination, 1938–1953," in Gaetano Vincitorio (ed.), *Studies in Modern History* (New York, 1968), 369.

15. See, for example, PSB, "Doctrinal Warfare" (September 16, 1952), 14, Dwight D. Eisenhower Library (hereafter: DDE), Operations Coordination Board Secretariat Files (hereafter: OCB), box 2.

16. See exchange of letters between Edward Lilly and William Dix (March 6, 1953), DDE, OCB, box 2. Dix was the chief librarian at Princeton University, and chairman of the American Library Association

17. On the OCB, see Blanche Wiesen Cook, "First Comes the Lie: C. D. Jackson and Political Warfare," *Radical History Review* 31 (1984): 42–70; Lilly, "The Psychological Strategy Board and its Predecessors."

18. Don K. Price, *The Scientific Estate* (Harvard, 1965).

19. Allan Needell, " 'Truth is Our Weapon': Project TROY, Political Warfare, and

Government-Academic Relations in the National Security State," *Diplomatic History* 17:3 (Summer 1993): 400.

20. Ibid.

21. Ibid.

22. On the unwillingness of different services and government agencies to co-ordinate activities, see PSB, "Inter-Agency Coordination of Social Science Research; Memorandum of Conversation" (August 4, 1952) and PSB, "Memorandum of Conversation with Wilbur Schramm, Dean School of Communications, University of Illinois" (July 18, 1952), HST, PSB, box 1. See also Gene Lyons, *The Uneasy Partnership: Social Science and the Federal Government in the Twentieth Century* (New York, 1969), 138–39.

23. Smith, *The Rand Corporation*, 64.

24. Stephen Waring, "Cold Calculus: The Cold War and Operations Research," *Radical History Review* 63 (Fall 1995): 39. See also Fred Kaplan, *The Wizards of Armageddon* (Stanford, Calif., 1983), 74–84.

25. Michael Bernstein, "American Economics and the National Security State, 1941–1953," *Radical History Review* 63 (Fall 1995): 8–27.

26. Kaplan, *The Wizards of Armageddon*, 76.

27. On simulation games in Rand's social science division, see Herbert Goldhamer and Hans Speier, "Some Observations on Political Gaming," *World Politics* 12 (October 1959): 71–83.

28. For some of the reigning differences concerning the causes of war among behavioral scientists, see Hadley Cantril (ed.), *Tensions that Cause War* (Urbana, Ill., 1950).

29. For contemporary criticism of behavioral analysis of war, see Kenneth Waltz, *Man, the State, and War: Theoretical Analyses* (New York, 1954), 16–79.

30. Herbert Goldhamer, "The Psychological Analysis of War," *Sociological Review* 26 (July 1934): 249–67. Goldhamer, at the time a graduate student at the University of Chicago, would later become a central figure in Rand's social science division. See chapter 6 on the armistice negotiations in Korea.

31. Paul Kecskemeti, *Strategic Surrender: The Politics of Victory and Defeat* (Stanford, Calif., 1958).

32. On the debate surrounding the book, see James E. King, "*Strategic Surrender*: The Senate Debate and the Book," *World Politics* 11 (April 1959): 418–29.

33. U.S. House of Representatives, "Report of the Special Committee to Investigate Tax Exempt Foundations and Comparable Organizations," Report No. 2681, December 16, 1954, 83rd Cong., 2nd sess., 60.

34. See two of Kahn's most provocative publications: *On Thermonuclear War* (Princeton, 1960), and *Thinking about the Unthinkable* (New York, 1962).

35. Hans Speier and Margaret Otis, "German Radio Propaganda to France During the Battle of France," in Daniel Lerner (ed.), *Propaganda in War and Crisis* (New York, 1951), 210. The article appeared originally in Paul Lazarsfeld and Frank Stanton (eds.), *Radio Research, 1942–1943* (New York, 1944).

36. The other two centers were The Human Resources Research Center (HRRC) of the Air Training Command, Lackand Air Force Base, Texas, and the Human Resources Research Laboratory (HRRL) of the Headquarters Command, Bolling Air Force Base, Washington, D.C.

37. The final product of this study was published in Raymond Bauer, Alex Inkeles, and Clyde Kluckhohn, *How the Soviet System Works* (Cambridge, Mass., 1956) and Alex Inkeles and Raymond Bauer, *The Soviet Citizen: Daily Life in a Totalitarian State* (Cambridge, Mass., 1959).

38. Raymond Bowers, "The Military Establishment," in Paul Lazarsfeld, William Sewell, and Harold Wilensky (eds.), *The Uses of Sociology* (New York, 1967), 239–40.

39. On HRRI, see Lyons, *The Uneasy Partnership*, 144–45.

40. Harvey Sapolsky, *Science and the Navy: The History of the Office of Naval Research* (Princeton, 1990), 63–64.

41. On deterrence theory, see Larson, "Deterrence Theory and the Cold War," 86–109.

42. For a brief description of various service activities in the behavioral and social sciences, see Carroll Shartle, "Selected Department of Defense Programs in the Social Sciences," in "Symposium Proceedings: The U.S. Army's Limited-War Mission," 322–43.

43. On operations research in the Cold War, see Stephen Waring, "Cold Calculus, The Cold War and Operations Research," *Radical History Review* 63 (Fall 1995): 28–51.

44. Cited in Leo Bogart (ed.), *Social Research and the Desegregation of the U.S. Army* (Chicago, 1969), 20.

45. Ibid., 23.

46. Smith, *The Rand Corporation*, 271–72; Paul Dickson, *Think Tanks* (New York, 1972), 149–72.

47. Project Camelot will be discussed in detail in subsequent chapters.

48. Dickson, *Think Tanks*, 135.

49. Ibid., 148.

50. IDA, *Annual Report, 1966* (Arlington, Va., 1966), 15.

51. Needell, " 'Truth is our Weapon'," 418–19.

52. Dorothy Nelkin, *The University and Military Research: Moral Politics at M.I.T.* (Ithaca, N.Y., 1972).

53. See, for example, Barry Katz, *Foreign Intelligence: Research and Analysis in the Office of Strategic Studies* (Cambridge, Mass., 1989); Ron Robin, *The Barbed Wire College: Reeducating German POWS in the United States During World War II* (Princeton, 1995).

54. Henry Loomis, "Report on Social Science Research in Cold War Operations," 19–20.

55. The results of this study were published a few years after its completion. See:Ira DeA. Read and Emily L. Ehle, "Leadership Selection in Urban Locality Areas," *Public Opinion Quarterly* 14 (Summer 1950): 262–84.

56. Bernard Brodie, "Strategy as a Science," *World Politics* 1 (July 1949): 467–88.

Chapter 3

1. See, for example, Karl Erik Rosengren, Peter Arvidson, and Dahn Sturesson, "The Barseback 'Panic': A Radio Programme as a Negative Summary Event," *Acta Sociologica* 18:4 (1975): 303–21.

2. "The Invasion from Mars," in Shearon Lowery and Melvin DeFleur, *Milestones*

in Mass Communication Research (New York, 1988), 31–54, provides a succinct summary of the broadcast, subsequent inquiries, and its social context.

3. Hadley Cantril, Hazel Gaudet, and Herta Herzog, *The Invasion from Mars: A Study in the Psychology of Panic* (Princeton, 1940).

4. Gordon Allport, "The Trend in Motivational Theory," *American Journal of Orthopsychiatry* 23 (January 1953): 107.

5. See, for example, the entire edition of the *American Journal of Sociology* 45 (November 1939), dedicated to the impact of Freud on American sociology in particular and American social thought in general.

6. Samuel Stouffer et al., TAS, vol. 1 (Princeton, 1949), 431.

7. Frederic Thrasher, *The Gang: A Study of 1,313 Gangs in Chicago* (Chicago, 1927). For other important studies of the primary group and gang life, see John Landesco, *Organized Crime in Chicago* (Chicago, 1929); Clifford Shaw, *The Natural History of a Delinquent Career* (Chicago, 1931).

8. For a recent analysis of the Hawthorne experiments and the work of Elton Mayo, see Richard Gillespie, *Manufacturing Knowledge: A History of the Hawthorne Experiments* (Cambridge, U.K., 1991). See also Eugene Cass and Frederick Zimmer, *Man and Work in Society: A Report on the Symposium Held on the Occasion of the 50th Anniversary of the Original Hawthorne Studies* (New York, 1975).

9. TAS, vol. 2, 149.

10. Ibid., vol. 1, 431.

11. Ibid., vol. 2, 130–49.

12. See, for example, Edward Shils and Morris Janowitz, "Cohesion and Disintegration of the Wehrmacht in World War II," *Public Opinion Quarterly* 12 (1948): 280–315.

13. Shils and Janowitz, "Cohesion and Disintegration."

14. Paul Lazarsfeld, Bernard Berelson, and Hazel Gaudet, *The People's Choice: How the Voter Makes Up His Mind in a Presidential Campaign* (New York, 1948).

15. Bernard Berelson, Paul Lazarsfeld, and William McPhee, *Voting: A Study of Opinion Formation in a Presidential Election* (Chicago, 1954), 309.

16. Ibid., 315.

17. Edward Shils, "Some Academics, Mainly in Chicago," *American Scholar* 50 (1980–81): 193.

18. Walter Lincoln Whittlesey's review of *World Politics and Personal Insecurity* in *American Political Science Review* 29 (June 19, 1935): 500–501.

19. Everett C. Hughes review of *World Politics and Personal Insecurity* in *American Journal of Sociology* 41 (November 1935): 400–401.

20. Mark C. Smith, *Social Science in the Crucible: The American Debate Over Objectivity and Purpose, 1918–1941* (Durham, N.C., 1994), 243. Smith's survey of the life and times of Harold Lasswell is the definitive study of Lasswell's intellectual contribution.

21. This biographical account of Lasswell is based on ibid., 212–52; Gabriel Almond, "Harold D. Lasswell: A Biographical Memoir," in Almond, *A Discipline Divided: Schools and Sects in Political Science* (Newbury Park, Calif., 1990), 290–308; Daniel Lerner, "Harold D. Lasswell," in *International Encyclopedia of the Social Sciences*, vol. 18 (New York, 1979), 405–10.

22. A comprehensive if somewhat hagiographic collection of Lasswell's work appears in Rodney Muth, Mary Finley, and Marcia Muth, *Harold D. Lasswell: An Annotated Bibliography* (New Haven, Conn., 1989).

23. Harold Lasswell, "The Psychology of Hitlerism," *Political Quarterly* 4(July–September 1933): 373–78.

24. Harold Lasswell, *Psychopathology and Politics* (Chicago, 1930, 1977), 177.

25. Ibid., 184.

26. Ibid., 261–63.

27. Ibid., 173–75.

28. Ibid., 255.

29. Arnold Rogow, "Towards a Psychiatry of Politics," in Arnold Rogow (ed.), *Politics, Personality, and Social Science in the Twentieth Century: Essays in Honor of Harold D. Lasswell* (Chicago, 1969), 128.

30. Harold Lasswell, "The Study of the Ill as a Method of Research into Political Personalities," *American Political Science Review* 23 (1929): 996–1001.

31. Harold Lasswell, *Politics: Who Gets What, When, and How* (New York, 1936, 1950), 235.

32. Harold Lasswell, *World Politics and Personal Insecurity* (New York, 1965), 3.

33. Harold Lasswell, "Propaganda," in *Encyclopedia of the Social Sciences* (New York, 1933), 521.

34. Harold Lasswell and Dorothy Blumenstock, *World Revolutionary Propaganda: A Chicago Study* (New York, 1939).

35. Smith, *Social Science in the Crucible*, 246.

36. Harold Lasswell, Nathan Leites, and associates, *Language of Politics: Studies in Quantitative Semantics* (New York, 1949), v.

37. Theodore Porter, *Trust in Numbers: The Pursuit of Objectivity in Science and Public Life* (Princeton, 1995).

38. Arjun Appadurai, "Number in the Colonial Imagination," in Carol Breckenridge and Peter van der Veer (eds.), *Orientalism and the Postcolonial Predicament: Perspectives on South Asia* (Philadelphia, 1993), 315–39.

39. Shawn Parry-Giles, "Propaganda, Effect, and the Cold War: Gauging the Status of America's 'War of Words'," *Political Communication* 11 (1994): 203–13.

40. For an assessment of content analysis in its early stages, see Morris Janowitz, "Content Analysis and the Study of the 'Symbolic Environment'," in Rogow, *Politics, Personality, and Social Science*, 155–70.

41. Deborah Welch Larson, "Deterrence Theory and the Cold War," *Radical History Review* 63 (Fall 1995): 98–99.

42. James A. Smith, *The Idea Brokers: Think Tanks and the Rise of the New Policy Elite* (New York, 1991), 138.

43. Porter, *Trust in Numbers*, 8. Emphasis is my own.

Chapter 4

1. On Wilbur Schramm's stature as founding father of mass communication research, see Everett M. Rogers, *A History of Communication Study: A Biographical Study* (New York, 1994), 1–32, 445–95; Emile McAnany, "Wilbur Schramm, 1907–

1987: Roots of the Past, Seeds of the Present," *Journal of Communication* 38 (Autumn 1988): 109–22.

2. HRRI, "A Preliminary Study of the Impact of Communism on Korea" (Air University, Maxwell Air Force Base, 1951), iii (hereafter: PSICK).

3. Ibid.

4. Ibid., 126–27.

5. John Riley, Wilbur Schramm, and Frederick Williams, "Flight from Communism: A Report on Korean Refugees," *Public Opinion Quarterly* 15 (Summer 1951): 276.

6. Bruce Cumings, *The Origins of the Korean War*, vol. 2: *The Roaring of the Cataract, 1947–1950* (Princeton, 1990), 628.

7. PSICK, 7.

8. Ibid., 88.

9. Ibid., 246–50.

10. Alex Inkeles, "Understanding a Foreign Society: A Sociologist's View," *World Politics* 3 (January 1951): 251.

11. Wilbur Schramm and John Riley, "Communication in the Sovietized State as Demonstrated in Korea," *American Sociological Review* 16 (December 1951): 758.

12. For an informative summary of current communication theory in the 1940s and 1950s, see Joseph Klapper, "What We Know About the Effects of Mass Communication," *Public Opinion Quarterly* 21 (Winter 1957–58): 453–74. See also Steven Chaffee and John Hochheimer, "The Beginnings of Political Communication Research in the United States: Origins of the 'Limited Effects' Model," in Everett Rogers and Francis Balle (eds.), *The Media Revolution in America and Western Europe* (Norwood, N.J., 1985), 267–96; Todd Gitlin, "Media Sociology: The Dominant Paradigm," *Theory and Society* 6 (1978): 205–53.

13. PSICK, 65.

14. Ibid., 121.

15. The source of information on opinion leaders was Paul Lazarsfeld, Bernard Berelson, and Hazel Gaudet, *The People's Choice* (New York, 1948); Bernard Berelson, Paul Lazarsfeld, and William McPhee, *Voting: A Study of Opinion Formation in a Presidential Campaign* (Chicago, 1954). See as well Elihu Katz and Paul Lazarsfeld, *Personal Influence: The Part Played by People in the Flow of Mass Communication*: (Glencoe, Ill., 1955); Elihu Katz, "The Two Step Flow of Communication; An Up-to-Date Report on an Hypothesis," *Public Opinion Quarterly* 21 (1957): 61–78.

16. Paul Lazarsfeld and Herbert Menzel, "Mass Media and Personal Influence," in Wilbur Schramm (ed.), *The Science of Human Communication* (New York, 1963), 97. See Gabriel Weimann *The Influentials: People Who Influence People* (New York, 1994) for an analysis of the origins and developments of the concept of opinion leaders.

17. Schramm and Riley, "Communication in the Sovietized State," 758.

18. PSICK, 67.

19. Schramm and Riley, "Communication in the Sovietized State," 758; PSICK, 11, 59–60.

20. Carl Hovland et al., *Experiments on Mass Communication* (Princeton, 1949).

21. PSICK, 79.

22. Ibid., 21–22.

23. Ibid., 80.

24. For the rationale behind the study, see Theodore H. E. Chen, "Preface: The Chinese Documents Project," in Henry Wei, "State and Government in Communist China: Their Ideological Basis and Statutory Pattern in the Spring of 1953" (HRRI, Maxwell Air Force Base, Ala., 1955), viii.

25. Ibid.; Frederick T. C. Yu, "The Propaganda Machine in Communist China, With Special Reference to Ideology, Policy, and Regulations as of 1952" (HRRI, Maxwell Air Force Base, Ala., 1955); idem, "The Strategy and Tactics of Chinese Communist Propaganda as of 1952" (HRRI, Maxwell Air Force Base, Ala., 1955), xi; Wen-Hui C. Chen, "Chinese Communist Anti-Americanism and the Resist-America Aid-Korea Campaign" (HRRI, Maxwell Air Force Base, 1955); Wen-Hui Chen, "Wartime 'Mass' Campaigns in Communist China; Official Country-wide 'Mass Movements' in Professed Support of the Korean War" (HRRI, Maxwell Air Force Base, Ala., 1955).

26. Raymond Bauer and David Gleicher, "Word-of-Mouth Communication in the Soviet Union" (HRRI, Maxwell Air Force Base, Ala., 1953), v.

27. The articles distilled from this report were Riley, Schramm, and Williams, "Flight from Communism," 274–86; Schramm and Riley, "Communication in the Sovietized State," 757–66.

28. On the Russian Research Center, see Charles T. O'Connell, "Social Structure and Science: Soviet Studies at Harvard" (Ph.D. diss., UCLA, 1990).

29. Clyde Kluckhohn, "Foreword," in Alex Inkeles, Public Opinion in Soviet Russia: A Study in Mass Persuasion (Cambridge, Mass., 1962), vii.

30. Ibid., 89–90.

31. John Riley, Frank Cantwell, and Katherine Ruttiger, "Some Observations on the Social Effects of Television," Public Opinion Quarterly 13 (Summer 1949): 223–34; Matilda White Riley and John W. Riley, "A Sociological Approach to Communication Research," Public Opinion Quarterly 15 (Fall 1951): 445–55.

32. On Riley's continuing association with the behavioral military complex following his move to the private sector, see William Lybrand (ed.), "Symposium Proceedings: The U.S. Army's Limited-War Mission and Social Science Research" (Washington, D.C., Special Operations Research Office, 1962), 151–59.

33. See, for example, Wilbur Schramm, Jack Lyle, and Edwin Parker, Television in the Lives of Our Children (Stanford, Calif., 1961).

34. Daniel Lerner, The Passing of Traditional Society: Modernizing the Middle East (Glencoe, Ill., 1958).

35. Interview with Schramm cited in Everett Rogers, A History of Communication Study: A Biographical Approach (New York, 1994), 471.

36. Ibid., 471.

37. Emile McAnany, "Wilbur Schramm," 109.

38. Christopher Simpson, Science of Coercion: Communication Research and Psychological Warfare, 1945–1960 (New York, 1994), 107–17.

39. Steven Chaffee (ed.), "The Contributions of Wilbur Schramm to Mass Communication Research," Journalism Monographs 36 (October 1974): 1–8.

40. Jack McLeod and Jay Blumler, "The Macrosocial Level of Communication Science," in Charles Berger and Steven Chaffee (eds.), Handbook of Communication Science (Newbury Park, Calif., 1987), 286.

41. See the now classic article by Todd Gitlin, "Media Sociology: The Dominant Paradigm," Theory and Society 6 (1978): 205–53.

42. See Schramm's introduction to *The Process and Effects*, in particular pp. 17–18.

43. See, for example, Eunice Cooper and Marie Jahoda, "The Evasion of Propaganda: How Prejudiced People Respond to Anti-Prejudice Propaganda," originally published in *Journal of Psychology* 23 (1947): 15–25. The theories and assumptions of this study of racial and ethnic prejudice among civilians in the United States were derived from the wartime research published in TAS, and had obvious military implications for nascent Cold War psychological warfare programs. Another important article in the Katz compilation was Irving Janis and Seymour Feshbach, "Effects of Fear Arousing Communications," originally published in the *Journal of Abnormal and Social Psychology* 48 (1953): 78–92. This experiment on a "standard communication of dental hygiene for high school students" sought to identify the most productive level of anxiety for eliciting changes in beliefs, practices, and attitudes by means of a fear-arousing propaganda campaign. The study recognized no significant differences between military and civilian contexts.

Chapter 5

1. Harry S. Truman, *Memoirs*, vol. 2: *Years of Trial and Hope* (New York, 1956), 377–95; Dean Acheson, *Present at the Creation: My Years at the State Department* (London, 1969), 402–13. See also Deborah Welch Larson, *Origins of Containment: A Psychological Explanation* (Princeton, 1985).

2. Acheson, *Present at the Creation*, 405.

3. Truman, *Memoirs*, 379.

4. Edward Shils, "The End of Ideology?" *Encounter* 5 (November 1955): 52–58. For contemporary expositions of the "end of ideology" debate, see Ralf Dahrendorf, *Class and Class Conflict in Industrial Society* (Stanford, Calif., 1959); Daniel Bell, *The End of Ideology: On the Exhaustion of Political Ideas in the Fifties* (Glencoe, Ill. 1960); Chaim Waxman (ed.), *The End of Ideology Debate* (New York, 1968).

5. David Riesman, "Some Observations on the Limits of Totalitarian Power," *Antioch Review* 12 (June 1952): 155–68.

6. Harold Lasswell, "Political and Psychological Warfare," in Daniel Lerner (ed.), *Propaganda in War and Crisis: Materials for American Policy* (New York, 1951), 264.

7. Gisela J. Hinkle, "Sociology and Psychoanalysis," in Howard Becker (ed.), *Modern Sociological Theory in Continuity and Change* (New York, 1957), 574–606.

8. Martin Herz, "Some Psychological Lessons from Leaflet Propaganda in World War II," *Public Opinion Quarterly* 13:3 (1949): 471–86.

9. Paul Linebarger, *Psychological Warfare* (Washington, D.C., 1954), 7.

10. Hans Speier, "Psychological Warfare Reconsidered," in Daniel Lerner and Harold Lasswell (eds.), *The Policy Sciences* (Stanford, Calif., 1951), 259.

11. Ibid.

12. Edward Shils and Morris Janowitz, "Cohesion and Disintegration in the Wehrmacht in World War II," *Public Opinion Quarterly* 12 (Summer 1948): 280–315. See also related research in Murray Gurfein and Morris Janowitz, "Trends in Wehrmacht Morale," *Public Opinion Quarterly* 10 (Spring 1946): 78–84; Donald McGranahan and Morris Janowitz, "Studies of German Youth," *Journal of Abnormal and Social Psychology* 41 (January 1946): 3–14.

13. W. Victor Madej, "Effectiveness and Cohesion of the German Ground Forces in World War II," *Journal of Political and Military Sociology* 6 (Fall 1978): 242.

14. Shils and Janowitz, "Cohesion and Disintegration," 280.

15. Omer Bartov, *Hitler's Army: Soldiers, Nazis, and War in the Third Reich* (New York, 1991), 32.

16. See, for example, Roger Little, "Buddy Relations and Combat Performance," in Morris Janowitz (ed.), *The New Military* (New York, 1964); Charles Moskos, *The American Enlisted Man* (New York, 1970); Paul Savage and Richard Gabriel, "Cohesion and Disintegration in the American Army," *Armed Forces and Society* 2 (May 1976): 340–76; Stanford Gregory, "Toward a Situated Description of Cohesion and Disintegration in the American Army," ibid., 3 (May 1977): 463–69; John Faris, "An Alternative Perspective to Savage and Gabriel," ibid., 457–62; Anthony Wermuth, "A Critique of Savage and Gabriel," ibid., 481–90.

17. Savage and Gabriel, "Cohesion and Disintegration in the American Army," 345. See also William Henderson, *Why the Vietcong Fought: A Study of Motivation and Control in a Modern Army in Combat* (Westport, Conn., 1979), xv–xxix.

18. Most of the reports of Project Revere appear in Melvin DeFleur and Otto Larsen, *The Flow of Information: An Experiment in Mass Communication* (1948). A summary of Revere appears in Shearon Lowery and Melvin DeFleur, "Project Revere: The Quality and Pathways of Message Diffusion," in *Milestones in Communication Research* (New York, 1983), 204–32.

19. "Psychological Warfare in Korea," *Public Opinion Quarterly* 15 (Spring 1951): 65–75.

20. Wilbur Schramm, "FEC Psychological Warfare Operations: Radio; ORO Technical Report T-20 (FEC)" (Washington, D.C., 1952).

21. General Headquarters, FEC, Military Intelligence Section, Psychological Warfare Branch, "Plans for Psychological Warfare Against Chinese Target Groups" (December 8, 1950), Douglas MacArthur Archives, Norfolk, Va. (hereafter: MAC), RG 6, box 4.

22. Donald McGranahan, "U.S. Psychological Warfare Policy," *Public Opinion Quarterly* 10 (Fall 1946): 446–50.

23. "Interview with Brigadier General Robert A. McClure," *U.S. News and World Report* (January 2, 1953), 60–69.

24. Gurfein and Janowitz, "Trends in Wehrmacht Morale."

25. ORO, "Testing Procedures, Psychological Warfare, Printed Media; Phase 1: Group Interview Method, ORO-T-19 (FEC)" (April 17, 1952), 53. See also William Daugherty, "Organization and Activities of Psywar Personnel in Lower Echelons of Eighth Army, 24 January–5 April, 1951; ORO Technical Memorandum, ORO-T-10 (FEC) (July 10, 1951)"; John Ponturo and Willmoore Kendall, "FEC Psychological Operations: Intelligence; ORO Technical Memorandum ORO-T-28 (FEC) (April 28, 1952)"; Willmoore Kendall and John Ponturo, "FEC Psychological Warfare Operations: Theater Staff Organization; ORO Technical Memorandum ORO-T-27 (FEC) (1 January, 1952)."

26. OCPW to Psychological Warfare Center, Fort Bragg, "Psychological Warfare Operational Deficiencies in the Korean Campaign" (November 10, 1953), Korean Psychological Warfare Files, Army Historical Center, Carlisle Barracks.

27. Ibid.

28. HumRRO, "Psychological Warfare Research: A Long-Range Program; Part One: Essential Background Information, HumRRO-SR-2 (March 1953)," 29.

29. Paul Linebarger, "Immediate Improvement of Theater-level Psychological Warfare in the Far East; ORO Technical Memorandum ORO-T-11 (June 7, 1951)," 6.

30. Carl Berger, "An Introduction to Wartime Leaflets" (SORO, Washington, D.C., 1959); John Riley and Leonard Cottrell, "Research for Psychological Warfare," *Public Opinion Quarterly* 21 (Spring 1957): 147–58.

31. The centerpiece of Gulf War psychological warfare was the surrender leaflet, disguised as paper currency so as to enhance its worth. Leaflet operations in Desert Storm/Desert Shield were limited to four fundamental themes only: "(1) The futility of resistance, (2) safety and fair treatment as a result of fair treatment, (3) separation of enemy soldiers from their equipment, and (4) peace, unity and family." Politics and ideological themes were conspicuously absent. See Jay Parker and Jerold Hale, "Psychological Operations in the Gulf War: Analyzing Key Themes in Battlefield Leaflets," in Thomas McCain and Leonard Shyles (eds.), *The 1,000 Hour War: Communication in the Gulf* (Westport, Conn., 1994), 89–109.

Chapter 6

Herbert Goldhamer, *The Korean Armistice Conference* (Santa Monica, Calif., 1994), 2 (hereafter: KAC).

2. For a summary of these studies, see Alexander George, "Psychological Aspects of Tactical Operations (Korea), Rand Corporation Memorandum RM-3110-PR" (Santa Monica, April 1962).

3. KAC, 3.

4. Walter Hermes, *Truce Tent and Fighting Front* (Washington, D.C., 1966), 19–20.

5. For examples of this project, see material in Rand Corporation, "Western Elite Studies" (December 1948), National Archives, Record Group 319, Korean Armistice Negotiations (hereafter: RG 319), box 698.

6. Morris Janowitz, "The Systematic Analysis of Political Biography," *World Politics* 6 (April 1954): 405.

7. In the early 1950s, and aided by generous foundation grants, Lasswell and a group of associates produced the series of publications known as The Hoover Institute Elite Studies. These studies ranged from an ambitious, almost cosmic comparison of elites in a large international perspective, to the more focused investigations of the Soviet Politburo, Kuomintang and Chinese communist elites, and, of course, the Nazi elite. See Harold Lasswell, Daniel Lerner, and C. Easton Rothwell, *The Comparative Study of Elites: An Introduction and Bibliography* (Stanford, Calif., 1952); George Schueller, *The Politburo* (Stanford, Calif., 1952); Maxwell Knight, *The German Executive; 1890–1933* (Stanford, Calif., 1952); Robert North, *Kuomintang and Chinese Communist Elites* (Stanford, Calif., 1952).

8. Harold Lasswell, *Psychopathology and Politics* (Chicago, 1930). See also Lasswell's "The Study of the Ill as a Method of Research into Political Personalities," *American Political Science Review* 23 (November 1929): 996–1001.

9. Lasswell, "The Study of the Ill," 1001.

10. Clyde and Florence Kluckhohn, "American Culture: Generalized Orientations and Class Patterns," in Lymon Bryson (ed.), *Seventh Conference of Philosophy, Science and Religion and Their Relation to the Democratic Way of Life: Conflicts of Power in Modern Culture* (New York, 1946), 106–28.

11. Margaret Mead, *And Keep Your Powder Dry* (New York, 1943) 101–7.

12. Ruth Benedict, *Rumanian Culture and Behavior* (New York, 1943), 54.

13. Geoffrey Gorer, "Themes in Japanese Culture," *Transactions of the New York Academy of Sciences* 5 (1943): 106–24; Ruth Benedict, *The Chrysanthemum and the Sword: Patterns of Japanese Culture* (Boston, 1946).

14. Roger Money-Kyrle, *Psychoanalysis and Politics: A Contribution to the Psychology of Politics and Morals* (New York, 1951). See also Richard Brickner, *Is Germany Incurable?* (Philadelphia, 1943); and "What shall We Do With Germany? A Panel Discussion of *Is Germany Incurable?*" *Saturday Review of Literature* 24 (May 29, 1943), 4–10.

15. Henry Dicks, "Personality Traits and National Socialist Ideology: A War-time Study of German Prisoners of War," *Human Relations* 3 (1950): 111–54.

16. Henry Dicks, "Observations on Contemporary Russian Behavior," *Human Relations* 5 (1952): 137.

17. Dinko Tomasic, *The Impact of Russian Culture on Soviet Communism* (Glencoe, Ill., 1953).

18. Geoffrey Gorer, "Some Aspects of the Psychology of the People of Great Russia," *The American Slavic and East European Review* 8 (October 1949): 155–66. See also a rebuttal of Gorer's theory in Irving Goldman, "Psychiatric Interpretation of Russian History: A Reply to Geoffrey Gorer," ibid. 9 (October 1950): 151–62. Gorer wrote this article during the course of his association with Columbia University's Research in Contemporary Cultures Project, which was inaugurated by Ruth Benedict in 1947 under a grant from the Office of Naval Research. Following Benedict's death, work continued under the tutelage of Margaret Mead. Gorer's work, along with the work of other psychoculturalists, was reproduced in abbreviated form in the interdisciplanary collection of essays entitled *Soviet Attitudes Toward Authority* (1951).

19. Edward Shils, "Authoritarianism: 'Right and Left'," in Richard Christie and Marie Jahoda (eds.), *Studies in the Scope and Methods of 'The Authoritarian Personality'* (Glencoe, Ill., 1954), 28.

20. Edward Shils, "The End of Ideology?" *Encounters* 5 (1955): 52–58.

21. Raymond Bauer, "The Psycho-Cultural Approach to Soviet Studies," *World Politics* 7 (October 1954): 123.

22. Mead, *Soviet Attitudes Toward Authority*, 11–12.

23. For an annotated collection of Leites's work, see Elizabeth Wirth Marvick (ed.), *Psychopolitical Analysis: Selected Writings of Nathan Leites* (New York, 1977).

24. Hans Speier, "Appeasement: The Last Hopkins Mission to Moscow (May–June 1945); Western Elite Studies, case no. 1 (December 1, 1948).

25. Ibid.

26. Paul Kecskemeti and Nathan Leites, "Some Psychological Hypotheses on Nazi Germany" (Library of Congress, Experimental Division for the Study of Wartime Communication, Doc. No. 60, July 30, 1945). This study was later published piecemeal in the *Journal of Social Psychology* 26 (1947): 141–83; 27 (1948): 91–117, 241–70; 28 (1948): 141–64.

27. Nathan Leites, *A Study of Bolshevism* (Glencoe, Ill., 1953), 21.

28. Nathan Leites, *The Operational Code of the Politburo* (New York, 1951), xii.

29. Ibid., xiv.

30. Ibid., xv.

31. Ibid., 78.

32. Nathan Leites, "Panic and Defenses Against Panic in the Bolshevik View of Politics," in Geza Roheim (ed.), *Psychoanalysis and the Social Sciences*, vol. 4 (New York, 1955), 138. The coupling of homosexuality with communism in particular and authoritarian cultures in general was by no means a Leites invention. See, for example, Dicks, "Observations on Contemporary Russian Culture," 146, as well as references to homosexuality in the classic "Berkeley studies," Theodore Adorno et al. , *The Authoritarian Personality* (New York, 1949).

33. Leites, *Study of Bolshevism*, 403.

34. Nathan Leites and David Nelson Rowe, "Choice in China," *World Politics* 1 (1948–49): 277–307.

35. On the distribution of copies of the *Operational Code* among the delegates, see *KAC*, 20–21.

36. Daniel Bell, "The Study of Man: Bolshevik Man, His Motivations; a Psychoanalytic Key to Communist Behavior," *Commentary* 19 (1955): 180.

37. Ibid., 179.

38. Leites, *The Operational Code*, xii.

39. See, for example, ibid., 58.

40. This interpretation is from Alexander George, "The 'Operational Code': A Neglected Approach to the Study of Political Leaders and Decision-Making," *International Studies Quarterly* 13 (June 1969): 196.

41. *KAC*, 61.

42. Ibid., 8.

43. Ibid., 66.

44. Ibid., 66, 72.

45. Ibid., 133.

46. This description of Joy belongs to Ernest R. May in his introduction to *KAC*, xxiv.

47. Ibid., 45–45.

48. Ibid., 71.

49. Ibid., 65–66.

50. Ibid., 142.

51. On Goldhamer's admiration for Machiavelli, and his concept of the academic advisor, see his *The Advisor* (New York, 1978).

52. *KAC*, 136.

53. Ibid., 92.

54. Ibid., 149.

55. Ibid., 103.

56. Joy, *Negotiating While Fighting*, 64.

57. See, for example, ibid., 35–37.

58. Leites, *The Operational Code*, 13.

59. Ibid., 88–90.

60. Joy, *How Communists Negotiate*, 170–71.

61. Ibid., 172.

62. A detailed description of the POW predicament appears in subsequent chapters.

63. Hermes, *Truce Tent and Fighting Front*, 500–501. During the same period, the enemy lost about 250,000 men, killed, wounded, or captured.

Chapter 7

1. This reconstruction of life on Koje Do is derived in part from Edwin Thompson, "Koje-Do" (n.d.), National Archives, Record Group 389, Records of the Provost Marshal General, 22nd Army, POW-Civilian Information Center, (hereafter: RG 389), box 19; Major General Haydon Boatner to General Harold Johnson, Chief of Staff, United States Army (January 1966), RG 389, box 18; Haydon Boatner, "Our Sons— Future Prisoners of War)" (1960), Haydon Boatner Papers, Hoover Institution of War, Revolution and Peace, Stanford University, box 7 (hereafter: HBP); "Proceedings of Board of Officers Appointed to Investigate the Circumstances Surrounding the Seizure of Brigadier General Francis T. Dodd" (May 1952), National Archives, Record Group 319, Records of the Army Staff, G-3, (hereafter: RG 319), box 229.

2. "Memorandum by P. W. Manhard of the Political Section of the Embassy to the Ambassador in Korea (Muccio)" (March 14, 1952), *Foreign Relations of the United States* (hereafter: FRUS), 1951, vol. vii, *Korea and China*, part 1 (Washington, D.C., 1983), 98–99.

3. Thompson, "Koje-Do."

4. Discussions of the various divisions affecting Korean society following World War II may be found in Bruce Cumings, *The Origins of the Korean War*, vol. 1: *Liberation and the Emergence of Separate Regimes, 1945–1947* (Princeton, 1981); Carter Eckert, "Total War, Industrialization, and Social Change in Late Colonial Korea," in Peter Duus, Ramon Myers, and Mark Peattie (eds.), *The Japanese Wartime Empire, 1931– 1945* (Princeton, 1996), 3–39; Dae-Hong Chang and John C. Oh, "The Changing Status of the Paekchong in the Traditional Class System of Korea," *International Review of History and Political Science* 8 (May 1971): 56–74.

5. See, for example, CIE, "Report on the Evaluation Phase of the program of Orientation and Education for Korean and Chinese Prisoners of War and Civilian Internees" (December 1952), National Archives, Record Group 338, Records of US Army Commands Headquarters, 22nd US Army, POW-Internee Information Center (hereafter: RG 338), confidential files, box 32.

6. Chief Field Operations Division, CIE, UN COM, "Results of Chinese General Survey (Census)" (March 29, 1952), National Archives, Record Group 333, Records of Headquarters, UN COM, Korea (hereafter: RG 333), box 2.

7. Ibid.

8. The HumRRO studies were published in their original form in William Bradbury, Samuel Meyers, and Albert Biderman, *Mass Behavior in Battle and Captivity* (Chicago, 1968). See in particular the major study produced by HumRRO included in this study: "The Political Behavior of Korean and Chinese Prisoners of War in the Korean War: A Historical Analysis," 209–366.

9. Ibid., 266.

10. Interview with inmate in ibid., 260–61.

11. Ibid., 64.

12. Ibid., 281.

13. ORO, "Beliefs of Enemy Soldiers About the Korean War" (May 24, 1952), 3, RG 338, box 15. This survey, subcontracted by ORO to the private consultant firm of International Public Opinion Research, Inc., was conducted from January to March 1951.

14. Ibid., 4.

15. Ibid.

16. Ibid., 26.

17. Ibid., 40.

18. Ibid., 42.

19. Meyers and Bradbury, "The Political Behavior of Korean and Chinese Prisoners of War," 282.

20. The report, with minor adjustments, was published as Alexander L. George, *The Chinese Communist Army in Action: The Korean War and its Aftermath* (New York, 1967).

21. Ibid., 27–28.

22. Ibid., 164.

23. Ibid., 230.

24. Ibid., 229.

25. Ibid., 32.

26. Ibid., 158–62.

27. Ibid., 192.

28. Ibid., 28.

29. CIE, UNC, "First Interim Report on Progress of Educational Program for Prisoners of War" (January 10, 1952), RG 319, Army Operations, Decimal Files, 1952, 383.6, box 309.

30. On the World War roots of the Korean reeducation program, see memorandum by Colonel Fehr, Office of the Chief of Psychological Warfare, "Exploitation and Reorientation of Prisoners of War" (July 9, 1951), RG 319, box 21.

31. Toshio Nishi, *Unconditional Democracy: Education and Politics in Occupied Japan, 1945–1952* (Stanford, Calif., 1992), 2.

32. Ibid.

33. This description of American school educators appears in Paula Fass, *Outside In: Minorities and the Transformation of American Education* (New York, 1989), 26.

34. Ibid., 5.

35. CIE, FOD, "Report on Results of Achievement Testing, Korean Instructional Unit 17" (March 28, 1952), RG 333, box 1. CIE, FOD, "Report on Administration of Quotation Test in Chinese Compounds," RG 333, box 1.

36. CIE, FOD, "Preliminary Report on Results on Achievement Test on Instructional Units 1–16" (January 18, 1952) RG 333, box 1.

37. Hunter cited in Fass, *Outside In*, 25.

38. CIE, "Interim Report on Progress of Educational Program for POWs," 13; RG 319, Army Operations, Decimal files 1952, 383.6.

39. "Pilot Plant Reorientation Program," attached to letter from Colonel R. Conner, Acting Adjunct General, G-1, Far East Command, to Department of Army, Subject: Reorientation Program for North Korean Prisoners (February 28, 1951), RG 319, Records of Chief of Special Warfare, box 19.

40. Bruce Cumings, *The Origins of the Korean War: The Roaring of the Cataract* (Princeton, 1990), 104–5.

41. See, for example, General Headquarters, FEC, "Leftist Infiltration into SCAP" (February 27, 1947), Douglas MacArthur Archives (hereafter: MAC), Record Group 23, Charles A. Willoughby Papers, box 18.

42. Ibid., 242.

43. MacArthur cited in Nishi, *Unconditional Democracy*, 43.

44. Jones, *The Years of MacArthur*, 288.

45. Kenneth Hansen, *Heroes Behind Barbed Wire* (Princeton, 1957), 47.

46. Ibid., 76–78, 110–11.

47. Lieutenant Colonel Robert E. O'Brien to Lieutenant Colonel Donald R. Nugent (March 2, 1952), RG 333, CIE, Field Operations Division, box 1.

48. Lieutenant Colonel Donald Nugent to Lieutenant Colonel Robert E. O'Brien (March 12, 1952), RG 333, Correspondence of the CIE, Field Operations Division, box 1.

49. See references to Christianity and CIE in US Army, FEC, Psychological Warfare Section, Research, Analysis and Evaluation Section, "Interviews With 24 Korean POW Leaders: APO 500" (May 1954).

50. The most comprehensive survey of the armistice talks in general and the POW issue in particular appears in Rosemary Foot, A *Substitute for Victory: The Politics of Peacemaking at the Korean Armistice Talks* (Ithaca, N.Y., 1990). See as well Barton Bernstein, "The Struggle over the Korean Armistice: Prisoners of Repatriation?" in Bruce Cumings (ed.), *Child of Conflict: The Korean-American Relationship, 1943–1953* (Seattle, 1983), 261–307.

51. Hickey cited in Walter Hermes, *Truce Tent and Fighting Front* (Washington, D.C., 1966), 169.

52. "Memorandum of Conversation by the Deputy Assistant, Secretary of State for Far Eastern Affairs (Johnson)" (February 25, 1952), *FRUS, 1952–1954, part 1, Korea*, vol. xv, 58–59.

53. On CIE agitation against repatriation, see Hansen, *Heroes Behind Barbed Wire* (Princeton, 1957), 1–22.

54. For analyses of the reasons for the communist acceptance of the American position on repatriation, ranging from fears of instability following the death of Stalin to American threats to break the stalemate by employing nuclear weapons, see Roger Dingman, "Atomic Diplomacy During the Korean War," *International Security* 13 (Winter 1988–89): 50–91; Rosemary Foot, "Nuclear Coercion and the Ending of the Korean Conflict," ibid., 92–112; Daniel Calingaert, "Nuclear Weapons and the Korean War," *Journal of Strategic Studies* 11 (June, 1988): 177–202; Edward Keefer, "President Dwight D. Eisenhower and the End of the Korean War," *Diplomatic History* 10 (Summer 1986): 267–89; William Stueck, *The Korean War: An International History* (Princeton, 1995), 308–47.

55. A concise, accurate summary of the Dodd incident appears in Hermes, *Truce Tent and Fighting Front*, 243–54.

56. Monta Osborne to Lieutenant Colonel Robert O'Brien (June 6, 1952).

57. CIE UN COM, "Report of the Evaluation Phase of the Program of Orientation and Education for Korean and Chinese Prisoners of War and Civilian Internees" (December 1952), 27, 30, RG 338, box 32.

58. Ibid., 12, 17

59. Ibid., 19.

60. Ibid., 51–56.

61. Ibid., 51.

Chapter 8

1. Eugene Kinkead, *Why They Collaborated?* (New York, 1959), 18. See also Kinkead, "A Reporter at Large: A Study of Something New in History," *The New Yorker* (October 26, 1957), 102–53. For some recent analyses of the brainwashing crisis, see Adam Zweiback, "The 21 'Turncoat GIs': Nonrepatriations and the Political Culture of the Korean War," *The Historian* 60 (Winter 1998): 345–62; Catherine Lutz, "Epistemology of the Brainwashed and other New Subjects of the Cold War," in Joel Pfister and Nancy Schnog (eds.), *Inventing the Psychological: Toward a Cultural History of Emotional Life in Cold War America* (New Haven, Conn., 1997), 245–67.

2. See, for example, Robert Alden, "X-Ray of the Communist Mind," *New York Times Magazine* (December 20, 1953), 12, 34–37.

3. H. H. Hubben, "American Prisoners of War in Korea: A Second Look at the 'Something New in History' Theme," *American Quarterly* 22 (Spring 1970): 3–19; Albert Biderman, *March to Calumny: The Story of American POWs in the Korean War* (New York, 1963).

4. Kinkead, *Why They Collaborated?* 15.

5. William E. Mayer, "Why Did So Many GI Captives Cave In?" *U.S. News and World Report* (February 24, 1956), 65–72. See also William Ulman, "The GIs Who Fell for the Reds," *Saturday Evening Post* 226 (March 6, 1954), 17–19, 64–67.

6. Ibid.

7. Ralf Dahrendorf, "Democracy Without Liberty: An Essay on the Politics of Other-Directed Man," in Seymour Martin Lipset and Leo Lowenthal (eds.), *Culture and Social Character: The Work of David Riesman Reviewed* (Glencoe, Ill., 1962), 192–95.

8. Mayer, "Why Did So Many GI Captives Cave In?" Mayer was referring to Philip Wyllie's best-seller *Generation of Vipers* (1942). Wylie described how, following the waning of traditional domestic roles for women, American society had become "a matriarchy in fact, if not in declaration," in which women dominated their spouses and encouraged the dependency of their male offspring to the detriment of a once healthy society.

9. Betty Friedan, *The Feminine Mystique* (New York, 1963, 1983), 274–76. Catherine Lutz, "The Psychological Ethic and the Spirit of Containment," *Public Culture* 9 (1997): 135–59 offers a jaundiced assessment of the role of psychology in the national security state in general and the Korean War in particular.

10. On the changing image of the American POW, see Robert Doyle, *Voices from Captivity: Interpreting the American POW Narratives* (Lawrence, 1994).

11. On draft deferment for college youth during the Korean War, see Thomas Mahoney, "Lessons from Korea," *Annals of the American Academy of Political and Social Science* 276 (July 1951): 45–46.

12. Julius Segal, "Factors Related to the Collaboration and Resistance Behavior of U.S. Army PWs in Korea" (HumRRO Technical Report 33, December 1956), 45–47.

13. Leo Bogart (ed.), *Social Research and Desegregation of the U.S. Army* (Chicago, 1967), 50–52.

14. See exchange of correspondence between families of POWs and the White House in Official File, Harry S. Truman Presidential Library (hereafter: HST), box 1351.

15. Letter from Ben H. Brown, acting assistant secretary of state, to Senator George Smathers (July 11, 1952) in ibid.

16. Edward Hunter, *Brainwashing in Red China* (New York, 1951).

17. Henry P. Laughlin, "Brainwashing; a Supplemental Report" (June 10, 1953), 3, Psychological Strategy Board Files, HST, box 32.

18. Joost Meerloo, *The Rape of the Mind: The Psychology of Thought Control, Menticide, and Brainwashing* (Cleveland, 1956), 49.

19. George Winokur, " 'Brainwashing'—A Social Phenomenon of Our Time," *Human Organization* 13:4 (Winter 1965): 17.

20. Edgar Schein, "Brainwashing and Totalitarianization in Modern Society," *World Politics* 11 (April 1959): 430–41. See also Albert Biderman, "The Image of 'Brainwashing,' " *Public Opinion Quarterly* 26 (Winter 1962): 547–63.

21. The movie, directed by John Frankenheimer, was based on a novel written by Richard Condon (1959). For an analysis of this and other Korean War POW movies, see Charles Young, "Missing Action: POW films, Brainwashing, and the Korean War, 1954–1968," *Historical Journal of Film, Radio, and Television* 18 (March 1988): 49–74.

22. Michael Rogin, *Ronald Reagan; the Movie* (Berkeley, Calif., 1987), 267.

23. Other, sometime conflicting interpretations of the movie appear in Susan Carruthers, "The Manchurian Candidate (1962) and the Cold War Brainwashing Scare," *Historical Journal of Film, Radio, and Television* 18 (March 1998): 75–94. See also the analysis of the movie within a large cultural context offered by Margot Henriksen, *Dr. Strangelove's America: Society and Culture in the Atomic Age* (Berkeley, 1997), 264–69.

24. Raymond Bauer, "Brainwashing: Psychology or Demonology?" *Journal of Social Issues* 13:3 (1957): 41. The entire edition of the journal is devoted to the debunking of brainwashing.

25. "Statement: To Set Straight the Korean POW Episode," *Harvard Business Review* 40 (November–December, 1962): 94–95.

26. The Walter Reed–ORO material appears in Robert Lifton, "Home by Ship: Reaction Patterns of American Prisoners of War Repatriated from North Korea," *American Journal of Psychiatry* 110 (1954): 732–39; Henry Segal, "Initial Psychiatric Findings of Recently Repatriated Prisoners of War," *American Journal of Psychiatry* 111 (November 1954): 358–63; Edgar Schein, "The Chinese Indoctrination Program for Prisoners of War," *Psychiatry* 29 (May 1956): 149–72; Harvey Strassman, Margaret Thaler, and Edgar Schien, "A Prisoner of War Syndrome: Apathy as a Reaction to Severe Stress," *American Journal of Psychiatry* 112 (June 1956): 998–1003; Edgar Schein, Winfried Hill, and Harold Williams, "Distinguishing Characteristics of Collaborators and Resisters Among American Prisoners of War," *Journal of Abnormal and Social Psychology* 55 (September 1957): 197–201; Edgar Schein, "Reaction Patterns to Severe, Chronic Stress in American Army Prisoners of War of the Chinese," *Journal of Social Issues* 13:3 (1957): 21–30.

27. Segal, "Factors Related to the Collaboration and Resistance Behavior," 17. For additional HumRRO material, see Julius Segal, "Correlates of Collaboration and Resistance Behavior Among U.S. Army POWs in Korea," *Journal of Social Issues* 13:3 (1957): 31–47.

28. Albert Biderman, "Effects of Communist Indoctrination Attempts: Some Comments Based on an Air Force Prisoner-of-War Study," *Social Problems* 6 (Spring 1956): 304–13. See also other published reports of associates in the air force project—in particular, I. E. Farber, Harry Harlow, and Louis Joslyn West, "Brainwashing, Conditioning, and DDD (Debility, Dependency, and Dread)," *Sociometry* 20 (1957): 271–285; Louis Joslyn West, "Psychiatry, 'Brainwashing,' and the American Character," *American Journal of Psychiatry* 120 (March 1964): 842–50; Albert Biderman, "Communist Techniques of Coercive Interrogation," (Air Force Personnel and Training Research Center, Project No. 7733, December 1954).

29. Schein, "The Chinese Indoctrination Program for Prisoners of War," 149–72; Schein, "Distinguishing Characteristics of Collaborators," 197–201.

30. Segal, "Factors Related to the Collaboration and Resistance," 66.

31. Ibid., 96.

32. Biderman, *March to Calumny*, 25.

33. HumRRO, "Analysis of Interrogation Data from 'Little Switch' " (July 1953), RG 319, box 407.

34. Letter from Edgar Schein to Faith Gleicher-Boninger and Ron Robin (December 1, 1997).

35. Edgar Schein, "The Chinese Indoctrination Program for Prisoners of War: A Study of Attempted 'Brainwashing,' " *Psychiatry* 29 (May 1956): 167–68.

36. Bogart, *Social Research*, 50–52; Albert Mayer and Thomas Hoult, "Social Stratification and Combat Survival," *Social Forces* 34 (1955): 155–59.

37. Fred Wacker, "Culture, Prejudice, and an American Dilemma," *Phylon* 42:3 (1981): 255–61.

38. Letter from Schein.

39. Schein, "Distinguishing Characteristics of Collaborators and Resisters," 197–201.

40. Segal, "Correlates of Collaboration and Resistance."

41. Schein, "The Chinese Indoctrination Program for Prisoners of War"; Schein, "Reaction Patterns to Severe, Chronic Stress," 28.

42. Biderman, "Effects of Communist Indoctrination Attempts," 310.

43. Ibid., 310–11.

44. Ibid., 308.

45. David Hollinger, "Science as a Weapon in Kulturkaempfe in the United States During and After World War II," *Isis* 86 (1995): 442.

46. David Hollinger, *Science, Jews, and Secular Culture: Studies in Mid-Twentieth-Century American Intellectual History* (Princeton, 1996), ix.

47. On the high percentage of Jews in fields such as psychology and sociology and, by contrast, their underrepresentation in the arts and humanities, see Stephen Steinberg, *The Academic Melting Pot* (New York, 1974), 117–30.

48. Hollinger, *Science, Jews, and Secular Culture*, x.

49. Bernard Berleson, Paul Lazarsfeld, and William McPhee, *Voting* (Chicago, 1954), 311–23.

50. Seymour Martin Lipset, "Three Decades of the Radical Right," in Daniel Bell (ed.), *The Radical Right* (New York, 1955), 391–407.

51. Will Herberg, "McCarthy and Hitler: A Delusive Parallel," *New Republic* 131 (August 23, 1954), 13–15.

52. George H. Nash, *The Conservative Intellectual Movement in America Since 1945* (New York, 1945), 42.

53. Bernard Iddings Bell, *Crisis in Education* (New York, 1949), 124.

54. Howard Mumford Jones, *One Great Society: Humane Learning in the United States* (New York, 1959), 44–55.

55. United States Department of Defense, *POW: The Fight Continues After the Battle; the Report of the Secretary of Defense's Advisory Committee on Prisoners of War* (Washington, D.C., 1955), 20–21.

56. Ibid., 14.

Chapter 9

1. Joint Chiefs of Staff, *A Dictionary of United States Military Terms* (Washington, D.C., 1963), 58. See also U.S. Marine Corps, *Counterinsurgency Operations; FMFM 8-2* (Washington, D.C., 1967), 2. Michael Shafer, *Deadly Paradigms: The Failure of U.S. Counterinsurgency Policy* (Princeton, N.J., 1988), and Yuen Foong Khong, *Analogies at War: Korea, Munich, Dien Bien Phu, and the Vietnamese Decisions of 1965* (Princeton, 1992) are indispensable background reading for understanding counterinsurgency policy in Vietnam and its historical roots.

2. William Lybrand, "Foreword," in idem (ed.), "Symposium Proceedings: The U.S. Army's Limited War Mission and Social Science Research" (Washington, D.C., SORO, June 1962), ix.

3. Elvis Stahr, "The U.S. Army's Limited-War Mission and Social Science Research," in ibid., 7.

4. Roger Hilsman, "Recent Trends in Department of State Research," in ibid., 308. Hilsman, who had been an OSS guerrilla coordinator in Japanese-occupied Burma during World War II, described his thoughts on constructive counterinsurgency and its misapplication in Vietnam in his autobiographical *To Move a Nation: The Politics of Foreign Policy in the Administration of John F. Kennedy* (New York, 1967), 424–39.

5. General Clyde D. Eddleman, "Limited-War and International Conflict," in "Symposium Proceedings: The U.S. Army's Limited War Mission," 25–47.

6. Testimony of Seymour Deitchman, Special Assistant for Counterinsurgency in the Department of Defense, in U.S. House of Representatives, Committee on Foreign Affairs, Subcommittee on International Organizations and Movements, "Behavioral Sciences and the National Security," Report No. 4, Together with Part ix of the Hearings on "Winning the Cold War: The U.S. Ideological Offensive," July–August 1965, 89th Cong., 2nd sess., H.R. Report 1224, 5R.

7. Brigadier General Richard W. Stilwell, "Invited Address," in "Symposium Proceedings: The U.S. Army's Limited War Mission," 104–14.

8. Larry Cable, *Conflict of Myths: The Development of American Counterinsurgency Doctrine and Vietnam War* (New York, 1986), 115.

9. Roger Hilsman, "Internal War: The New Communist Threat," in Lieutenant Colonel T. N. Greene (ed.), *The Guerrilla and How to Fight Him* (New York, 1966), 22–36.

10. Klaus Knorr, Opening Remarks to Session on "Aspects of Warfare in Developing Nations," in "Symposium Proceedings: The U.S. Army's Limited War Mission," 250.

11. William Lybrand, "Foreword," in ibid., i–viii.

12. Guy Pauker, "Sources of Turbulence in the New Nations," in ibid., 170–79. In later years, Pauker changed his mind and became an enthusiatic supporter of constructive counterinsurgency and economic aid. See Guy Pauker, "An Essay on Vietnamization: R-604-ARPA" (Santa Monica, Calif., March 1971).

13. Hans Speier, "Revolutionary War: P-3445" (Santa Monica, Calif., 1962), 28; Edward Banfield, "American Foreign Aid Doctrines," in Carl Friedrich and Seymour Harris (eds.), *Public Policy: A Yearbook of the Graduate School of Public Policy* (Cambridge, Mass., 1961), 44–95.

14. An early assessment of the M&M studies appears in David Landau, "The Rand Papers," *Ramparts* 11 (November 1972): 25–37, 60–61. See also Anthony Russo, "Looking Backward; Rand and Vietnam in Perspective," ibid., 40–42, 52–60. Russo was a participant in the second stage of the M&M project.

15. For a concise summary of the first stage of the M&M project, see John Donnell, Guy Pauker, and Joseph Zasloff, "Vietcong Motivation and Morale in 1964; A Preliminary Account, RM-4507/3-ISA" (Santa Monica, Calif., 1965). See also the study by Zasloff's student, William Henderson, *Why the Vietcong Fought: A Study of Motivation and Control in a Modern Army in Combat* (Westport, Conn., 1979).

16. Nathan Leites, "The Vietcong Style of Politics RM-5487-1-ISA/ARPA" (Santa Monica, Calif., 1969).

17. Ibid., xvi.

18. John Donnell, "Vietcong Recruitment: Why and How Men Join, RM-5486-1-ISA/ARPA" (Santa Monica, Calif., 1967), 31.

19. "Comments," in ibid., xxv. A full list of the Rand studies on Vietcong morale, motivation, and organization appears in this publication.

20. Landau, "The Rand Papers," 36. Landau has described Goure's tenure as aimed primarily at undoing the work of Zasloff. I, by contrast, see the endorsement of force under Goure as a natural continuation of previous studies on the enemy's psychological advantages and the GVN's political weaknesses.

21. R. Michael Pearce, "The Insurgent Environment: RM-5533-1-ARPA" (Santa Monica, Calif., 1969).

22. Ibid., 13.

23. Leon Goure, "Inducements and Deterrents to Defection: An Analysis of the Motives of 125 Defectors: RM-5522-1-ISA/ARPA" (Santa Monica, Calif., 1968).

24. Edward Mitchell, "Land Tenure and Rebellion: A Statistical Analysis of Factors Affecting Government Control in South Vietnam RM-5181-ARPA" (Santa Monica, Calif., 1967). This study was summarized and published in Edward Mitchell, "Inequality and Insurgency: A Statistical Study of South Vietnam," *World Politics* 4 (April 1968): 421–38; Edward Mitchell, "The Significance of Land Tenure in the Vietnamese Insurgency," *Asian Survey* 7 (August 1967): 577–80.

25. Mitchell, "Inequality and Insurgency," 437.

26. Charles Wolf, "Insurgency and Counterinsurgency: New Myths and Old Realities," *Yale Review* 56 (December 1966): 225–41; Nathan Leites and Charles Wolf Jr., *Rebellion and Authority: Myths and Realities Reconsidered* (Rand Corporation, 1966); Nathan Leites and Charles Wolf Jr., *Rebellion and Authority: An Analytical Essay on Insurgent Conflicts* (Chicago, 1970).

27. Wolf, "Insurgency and Counterinsurgency," 229.

28. Wolf and Leites, *Rebellion and Authority*, 56.

29. Richard Shultz, "Breaking the Will of the Enemy During the Vietnam War: The Operalization of the Cost-Benefit Model," *Journal of Peace Research* 15 (1978): 110.

30. Landau, "The Rand Papers," 36.

31. Thomas Schelling, *Arms and Influence* (New Haven, 1966), v, 2–3.

32. Ibid., 75, 136, 171.

33. Samuel Huntington, "The Bases of Accommodation," *Foreign Affairs* 46 (July 1968): 642–56.

34. George Carver, "The Faceless Vietcong," *Foreign Affairs* 44 (April 1966): 371.

35. Richard Shultz, "Coercive Force and Military Strategy: Deterrence Logic and the Cost-Benefit Model of Counterinsurgency Warfare," *Western Political Quarterly* 32 (December 1979): 444–46; Robert Sansom, *The Economics of Insurgency in the Mekong Delta of Vietnam* (Cambridge, Mass., 1970), 241; David Halberstam, "Voices of the Vietcong," *Harper's Magazine* (January 1968), 47.

36. See, for example, Douglas Pike, *Viet Cong: The Organization and Techniques of the National Liberation Front of South Vietnam* (Cambridge, Mass., 1966); Eric Wolf, *Peasant Wars of the Twentieth Century* (New York, 1979); Samuel Popkin, *The Rational Peasant: The Political Economy of Rural Society in Vietnam* (Berkeley, Calif., 1979).

37. Richard Hunt, *Pacification: The American Struggle for Vietnam's Hearts and Minds* (Boulder, Colo., 1995). See also Richard Hunt and Richard Shultz (eds.), *Lessons from an Unconventional War: Reassessing U.S. Strategies for Future Conflicts* (New York, 1982), in particular the articles by Richard Shultz, "The Vietnamization-Pacification Strategy of 1969–1972: A Quantitative and Qualitative Reassessment," 48–117; and Lawrence Grinter, "Requirements of Strategy in Vietnam," 118–42.

38. Kenneth Boulding, review of *Rebellion and Authority* in *The Annals of the American Academy of Political and Social Sciences*, 392 (November 1970): 184–85.

39. J. F. Short, review of *Rebellion and Authority* in *American Journal of Sociology* 76 (January 1971): 768. For contemporary views regarding the efficacy of government-sponsored violence as a coercive measure, see David Snyder, "Theoretical and Methodological Problems in the Analysis of Governmental Coercion and Collective Violence," *Journal of Political and Military Sociology* 44 (Fall 1976): 277–294. See also Rod Aya, "Theories of Revolution Reconsidered: Contrasting Models of Collective Violence," *Theory and Society* 8 (1979): 40–99.

40. Leites and Wolf, *Rebellion and Authority*, vi.

41. Ibid., 30.

42. For an early assessment of this trend, see Colin Gray, "What Rand Hath Wrought," *Military Review* 52 (May 1972): 22–33; Bernard Brodie, "Why Were We So Strategically Wrong?" ibid., (June 1972): 40–46.

43. Frank Armbruster, Raymond Gastil, Herman Kahn, William Pfaff, and Edward Stillman, *Can We Win in Vietnam?* (New York, 1968).

44. Kahn in ibid., 340–41. A contemporary variation of this theme appears in Ithiel de Sola Pool, "Political Alternatives to the Viet Cong," *Asian Survey* 7 (August 1967): 555–67.

45. Herbert Goldhamer, Andrew Marshall, and Nathan Leites, "The Deterrence and Strategy of Total War, 1959–1961: A Method of Analysis; RM-2301" (Santa Monica, Calif., April 1959).

46. Leites and Wolf, *Rebellion and Authority*, 17–18.

47. Ibid., 29.

48. Albert Biderman and Fred Davis, "A Use of Aircraft as a Counter-Riot Measure: HRRI Research Memorandum No. 17" (Maxwell Airforce Base, 1953).

49. Ibid., 19–20.

50. Ted Gurr with Charles Ruttenberg, *Cross-National Studies of Civil Violence* (CRESS, Washington, D.C., 1969). For a very different reading of Gurr's, work see Shultz, "Limits of Terrorism," and his "Coercive Force and Military Strategy."

51. Gurr and Ruttenberg, *Cross-National Studies*, 6, 17, 78.

52. Tedd Gurr, *Why Men Rebel?* (Princeton, 1970).

53. Carl Rosenthal, "Phases of Civilian Disturbances: Characteristics and Problems" (CRESS, Washington, D.C., June 1969). See also Guy Pauker, "Black Nationalism and Prospects for Violence in the Ghetto" (Rand, June 1969); Brian Jenkins, "The Five Stages of Urban Guerrilla Warfare: Challenges in the 1970s; RP-4670" (Santa Monica, Calif., 1971).

54. See Tracy Tullis, "A Vietnam at Home: Policing the Ghettos in the Counterinsurgency Era" (Ph.D. diss., University of New York, 1999) for a fascinating analysis of the crumbling of boundaries between foreign and domestic security issues.

Chapter 10

1. Guidelines for Project Camelot, December 4, 1964, reprinted in Irving Louis Horowitz (ed.), *The Rise and Fall of Project Camelot: Studies in the Relationship Between Social Science and Practical Politics* (Cambridge, Mass., 1967), 47. In addition to this comprehensive collection of essays on Project Camelot, see Seymour J. Deitchman, *The Best-Laid Schemes: A Tale of Social Research and Bureaucracy* (Cambridge, Mass., 1976); Ellen Herman, *The Romance of American Psychology: Political Culture in the Age of Experts* (Berkeley, Calif., 1995), chap. 6.

2. Irving Louis Horowitz, "The Rise and Fall of Project Camelot," in Horowitz, *The Rise and Fall*, 30–31.

3. Robert Nisbet, "Project Camelot," in Philip Rieff, *On Intellectuals: Theoretical Studies, Case Studies* (New York, 1969), 283–313.

4. Testimony by Gabriel Almond in U.S. Senate, Committee on Government Operations, Subcommittee on Government Research, "Hearings on Federal Support of International Social Science and Behavioral Research," June–July 1966, 89th Cong., 2nd sess., 110.

5. According to political scientist Yaron Ezrahi, "the notion that competing egotists can, involuntarily, advance a collective goal," and the very idea that "freedom can generate order" lay at the heart of the liberal-democratic tradition that informed sci-

ence in America of the 1960s. See his *The Descent of Icarus: Science and the Transformation of Contemporary Democracy* (Cambridge, Mass., 1990).

6. Testimony by Gabriel Almond, 115.

7. For a list of Camelot's most prominent consultants, see U.S. House of Representatives, Committee on Foreign Affairs, Subcommittee on International Organizations and Movements, "Behavioral Sciences and the National Security," Report No. 4, together with Part ix of the Hearings on 'Winning the Cold War: The U.S. Ideological Offensive,' " July–August 1965, 89th Cong., 2nd sess., H.R. Report 1224, 62.

8. See, for example, Coleman's most prominent publications: *Adolescent Society* (Glencoe, Ill., 1961), and *Introduction to Mathematical Sociology* (New York, 1964).

9. Coleman's earliest publication in this new field was "Current Political Movement in Africa," *Annals of the American Academy of Political and Social Science* 298 (March 1955): 95–105. His most significant contributions appear in Gabriel Almond and James Coleman (eds.), *The Politics of Developing Areas* (Princeton, 1966).

10. Jean Lipman-Blumen, "Jessie Bernard," *International Encyclopedia of the Social Sciences*, vol. 15 (New York, 1973), 49.

11. Jessie Bernard, *American Community Behavior* (New York, 1949, 1962). See also Jessie Bernard, "Some Current Conceptualizations in the Field of Conflict," *American Journal of Sociology* 70 (June 1965): 442–54. The most comprehensive biography of Bernard is Robert Bannister, *Jessie Bernard: The Making of a Feminist* (New Brunswick, 1998).

12. Jessie Bernard, "Where is the Modern Sociology of Conflict?" *American Journal of Sociology* 51 (July 1950): 11–16.

13. Preface, *Academic Women* (New York, rev. ed., 1974), 27.

14. Jessie Bernard, "Conflict as Research and Research as Conflict," in Horowitz, *The Rise and Fall*, 135.

15. Ibid., 136.

16. Horowitz, "The Rise and Fall of Project Camelot," 8.

17. Testimony of Alex Inkeles in "Federal Support of International Social Science and Behavioral Research," 181.

18. Testimony of Kalman Silvert in ibid., 228.

19. Testimony of Gabriel Almond in ibid., 111–12.

20. Bernard, "Conflict as Research and Research as Conflict," 131, 138.

21. Ibid., 145–46.

22. Talcott Parsons, "Editor's Column," *The American Sociologist* 12 (February 1967): 62–64.

23. Daniel Lerner, "Introduction," in Lerner (ed.), *The Human Meaning of the Social Sciences* (New York, 1959).

24. Samuel Huntington, "Social Science and Vietnam," *Asian Survey* 7 (August 1967): 503–4.

25. Bernard, "Conflict as Research and Research as Conflict," 146.

26. Neil Smelser, *Theory of Collective Behavior* (New York, 1962).

27. Elliot Currie and Jerome Skolnick, "A Critical Note on Conceptions of Collective Behavior," *Annals of the American Academy of Political and Social Science* 391 (September, 1970): 34–45. See also Smelser's rely to his critics: "Two Critics in Search of a Bias," in ibid., 46–55.

28. Smelser, *Theory of Collective Behavior*, 79–85, 268.

29. Sidney Hook, "Violence," in *Encyclopedia of the Social Sciences*, vol. 15, 264–67, cited in Smelser, *Theory of Collective Behavior*, 261.

30. Brief Description of Project Camelot (June 15, 1965), in Horowitz, *The Rise and Fall*, 60.

31. Conference papers were published in Samuel Klausner (ed.), *The Study of Total Societies* (New York, 1967).

32. James Coleman, "Game Models of Economic and Political Systems," in ibid., 30–44.

33. James S. Coleman, "The Political Systems of the Developing Areas," in Gabriel Almond and James Coleman, *The Politics of the Developing Areas* (Princeton, 1960), 536. Coleman's quotes are from Daniel Lerner, *The Passing of Traditional Society* (Glencoe, Ill., 1958), 438.

34. Coleman, "Political Systems," 538.

35. Amitai Etzioni and Fredric Du Bow, "Some Workpoints for a Macrosociology," in Klausner, *The Study of Total Societies*, 147–62.

36. Ithiel De Sola Pool, "Computer Simulations of Total Societies," in ibid., 45–68.

37. Edward Tiryakian, "A Model for Social Change and its Leading Indicators," in ibid., 69–97, Kenneth Boulding, "The Learning Process in the Dynamics of Total Societies," in ibid., 98–113.

38. Marion Levy, "Family Structure and the Holistic Analysis of Societies," in ibid., 171.

39. Anatol Rapoport, "Mathematical, Evolutionary, and Psychological Approaches to the Study of Total Societies," in ibid., 141.

40. A similar sense of frustration and multiple disagreement appears in Harry Eckstein (ed.), *Internal War: Problems and Approaches* (New York, 1964). Most of the participants in this conference on insurgency were, at one time or another, Camelot consultants.

41. Lucien Pye, "Political Modernization: Gaps Between Theory and Reality," *Annals of the American Academy of Political and Social Sciences* 442 (March 1979): 34.

42. Description of Project Camelot, December 4, 1964, in Horowitz, *The Rise and Fall*, 47.

43. For a survey of the most important challenges to modernization theory published in the early 1960s, see Ian Weinberg, "The Problem of the Convergence of Industrial Societies: A Critical Look at the State of a Theory," *Comparative Studies in Society and History* 11 (1969): 1–15. See also Dean Tipps, "Modernization and the Comparative Study of Societies: A Critical Perspective," *Comparative Studies in Society and History* 15 (1973): 215.

44. Joseph Gusfeld, "Tradition and Modernity: Misplaced Polarities in the Study of Social Change," *American Journal of Sociology* 72 (January, 1967): 358.

45. Samuel Huntington, "Political Development and Political Decay," *World Politics* 17 (April 1965): 386–91. See also Samuel Huntington, "Political Modernization: America Vs. Europe," *World Politics* 18 (April 1966): 378–414.

46. See, for example, Karl de Schweinitz, *Industrialization and Democracy* (New York, 1964) and Manning Nash, *Primitive and Peasant Economic Systems* (San Francisco, 1966).

47. Herbert Blumer, "Early Industrialization and the Laboring Class," *Sociological Quarterly* 1 (January 1960): 5–14.

48. Robert Rhodes, "The Disguised Conservatism in Evolutionary Development Theory," *Science and Society* 32 (Fall 1968): 385.

49. Andre Gunder Frank, *Capitalism and Underdevelopment in Latin America* (New York, 1967); Walter Rodney, *How Europe Underdeveloped Africa* (Washington, D.C., 1972).

50. Testimony of Alex Inkeles in "Federal Support of International Social Science and Behavioral Research," 192.

51. Robert Nisbet, *Social Change and History: Aspects of the Western Theory of Development* (New York, 1969), 3–11.

52. Robert Nisbet, "Project Camelot and the Science of Man," in Horowitz, *The Rise and Fall*, 316.

53. Ali Marzui, "From Social Darwinism to Current Theories of Modernization: A Tradition of Analysis," *World Politics* 21 (1968): 69–83.

54. Bernard Brodie, "Strategy as a Science," *World Politics* 1 (July 1949): 467–87.

Chapter 11

1. Robert Bannister, *Jessie Bernard: The Making of a Feminist* (New Brunswick, 1998), 136–41.

2. Bernard's review and the source of Bannister's error appears in *Trans-Action* 5 (January–February, 1968): 10–12.

3. See, for example, the conspiracy-driven website: http://www.beyond-the-illusion.com/lists/iufo/1998/Aug/0191.html

4. Bruce Russett, "Who Pays for Defense?" *American Political Science Review* 63 (June 1969): 415; Emile Benoit, "Economics of Arms Control and Disarmament: The Monetary and Real Costs of National Defense," *American Economic Review* 58 (May 1968): 412.

5. Leonard Lewin, *Report from Iron Mountain on the Possibility and Desirability of Peace* (London, 1967), 66–70.

6. Ibid., 75.

7. Ibid., 76.

8. Ibid., 120.

9. Kahan and Kissinger quoted in Leonard Lewin, "The Guest Word," *New York Times* (November 19, 1972).

10. Comments of Murray Weidenbaum, in *Trans-Action* 5 (January–February 1968): 16–17.

11. Herbert Gans, "War and Peace," *Commentary* 45 (February, 1968): 84.

12. Comments of Leonard J. Duhl, *Trans-Action* 5 (January–February 1968): 18.

13. Irving Louis Horowitz, "The Americanization of Conflict: Social Science 'Fiction' in Action," *Bulletin of the Atomic Scientists* 24 (March 1968): 24.

14. On the rhetorical devices employed in the report, see Ray Anderson, "The Rhetoric of the Report from Iron Mountain," *Speech Monographs* 37 (November 1970): 221–31.

15. Comments of Anatol Rapoport in *Trans-Action* 5 (January–February 1968): 10.

16. The studies mentioned in the report were Robert Ardrey, *Territorial Imperative* (New York, 1966) as well as the German-language original of Konrad Lorenz, *On Aggression* (New York, 1966).

17. An example of the condescending approach to the work of Lorenz and Audrey appears in the review article by Marion Levy, "Our Ever and Future Jungles," *World Politics* 22 (January 1970): 301–27.

18. See, for example, the survey by Peter Corning, "The Biological Bases of Behavior and Some Implications for Political Science," *World Politics* 23 (April 1971): 321–70, and *Journal of Conflict Resolution* 3 (1959), a special issue dedicated to "Psychology and Aggression."

19. H. L. Nieburg, "Uses of Violence," *Journal of Conflict Resolution* 7 (March 1963): 43–54.

20. Joseph Schneider, "Is War Necessary?" *Journal of Conflict Resolution* 4 (December 1959): 353–60. See also the classic work of Lewis Coser, *The Functions of Social Conflict* (Glencoe, Ill., 1956) and "Social Conflict and the Theory of Social Change," *British Journal of Sociology* 8 (1957): 197–207.

21. Hans Speier, *Social Order and the Risks of War: Papers in Political Sociology* (New York, 1952), 258.

22. David Wise and Thomas Ross, *The Invisible Government* (New York, 1964), 4.

23. Tom Engelhardt, *The End of Victory Culture: Cold War America and the Disillusioning of a Generation* (New York, 1995), 23.

24. "Introduction," in Charles McCoy and John Playford (eds.), *Apolitical Politics: A Critique of Behavioralism* (New York, 1967), 3.

25. Edward Hall, *The Silent Language* (New York, 1959), 13.

26. V. O. Key, "The Politically Relevant in Surveys," *Public Opinion Quarterly* 24 (1960): 54.

27. Francis Wormuth, "Matched-Dependent Behavioralism: The Cargo-Cult in Political Science," *Western Political Quarterly* 20 (December 1967): 809–40.

28. Maure Goldschmidt, "Democratic Theory and Contemporary Political Science," *Western Political Quarterly* 19, supplement (1966): 5–12.

29. Ibid.

30. Samuel Huntington, *The Soldier and the State: The Theory and Politics of Civil-Military Relations* (New York, 1957), 464–65.

31. Philip Green, *Deadly Logic: The Theory of Nuclear Deterrence* (Columbus, Ohio, 1966), 259.

32. Bill Readings, *The University in Ruins* (Cambridge, Mass., 1996), 3.

33. Jean-François Lyotard, *The Postmodern Condition: A Report on Knowledge* (Manchester, U.K., 1984).

34. Robert Proctor, *Value-Free Science? Purity and Power in Modern Knowledge* (Cambridge, Mass., 1991), 163–272.

35. Testimony of Margaret Mead in U.S. Senate, Committee on Foreign Relations, "Psychological Aspects of Foreign Policy," June 1969, 91st Cong., 1st sess. On political pressures and contemporary American science, see Jessica Wang, *American Science in an Age of Anxiety: Scientists, Anticommunism, and the Cold War* (Chapel Hill, N.C., 1999).

36. Testimony of Margaret Mead, 96.

37. Ibid., 100.